DICTIONARY OF CHINESE HISTORY

A SIMPLE MAP OF CHINA

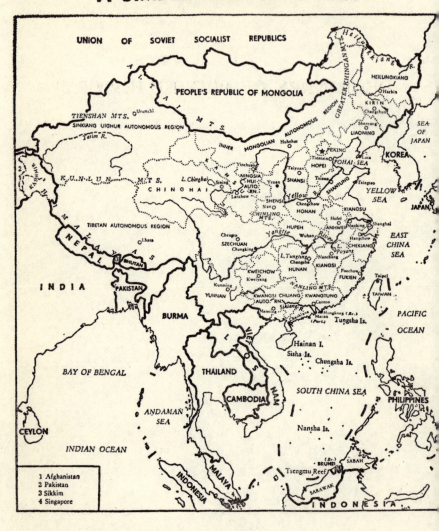

Dictionary
of
Chinese History

Michael Dillon

FRANK CASS

First published 1979 in Great Britain by
FRANK CASS AND COMPANY LIMITED
Gainsborough House, Gainsborough Road,
London, E11 1RS, England

and in the United States of America by
FRANK CASS AND COMPANY LIMITED
c/o Biblio Distribution Centre
81 Adams Drive, P.O. Box 327, Totowa, N.J. 07511

British Library Cataloguing in Publication Data

Dillon, Michael
   Dictionary of Chinese history.
   1. China — History — Dictionaries
   I. Title
   951'.003   DS733

ISBN 0–7146–3107–8

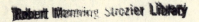
Printed in Great Britain by
The Bourne Press, 3 – 11 Spring Road, Bournemouth

Preface

This Dictionary has been compiled as a handbook for those who are interested in some aspect of Chinese civilisation and would like a guide to the multiplicity of historical events and personalities that are constantly referred to. It is not encyclopaedic, as that would be impossible in a work of this size and probably beyond the competence of any single author. Rather it is an attempt to provide a quick and easy reference to the names and terms which occur most frequently in English-language works on China and which can be usefully explained in a few hundred words.

In time, entries range from pre-history to the end of 1977. They cover the classical pre-imperial period, the whole of the empire from 221 BC until its collapse in 1911, the short-lived Republic that succeeded it and the first twenty-eight years or so of the People's Republic. The bulk of the entries concern important personalities, dynasties and events, but some information is also given on historical trends, analytical concepts, social and economic history, and technology.

A book of this size can clearly contain only a fraction of the possible topics, and although I have attempted to select the most significant and most frequently encountered ones, I am very well aware of the number that have been left out. Inevitably certain periods and areas of study are treated more fully than others, but I hope that this corresponds to the needs of the general reader.

The importance of Chinese history cannot be overstated. In addition to providing the context for Chinese literature and the arts, it is vital to the understanding of China today. No country can possibly be more conscious of its heritage than China or be more deeply involved in its past. Many political campaigns in the People's Republic first make their appearance as historical controversies. The Cultural Revolution, for example, began with an academic argument about the merits of a 16th-century official, Hai Jui, and political argument in the early 1970s centred on a campaign to vilify Confucius.

Historians in other fields are increasingly coming to realise the comparative value of Chinese history, a history which provides both sharp contrasts with the European past and a surprising amount of common ground. I hope that this dictionary will help to make the comparison and the understanding of China and its history a little easier.

Author's Note

Romanisation   Chinese is, of course, written in characters and there are a number of ways of representing the sounds of the words in Roman letters. The two most important systems are the Wade-Giles, which is rather old-fashioned but still widely used, and the *Hanyu Pinyin* which was developed in the People's Republic and is gradually replacing Wade-Giles. Many place names are romanised in neither of these but in the Post Office system, e.g.

Post Office	Peking
Wade Giles	Pei-ching
Hanyu Pinyin	Beijing

In this Dictionary I have adopted the form most commonly found in English books, and cross-referred where necessary. This means that most names and terms appear in Wade-Giles which is still the most commonly used. Town and province names are likely to be in the Post Office form, and hardly anything is in *Pinyin* as this has not yet gained universal acceptance.

Alphabetical Order   Different romanisations produce problems in alphabetical order. In this Dictionary hyphenated Chinese words, e.g. Ching-t'ien, are considered as one word, and apostrophes, e.g. Ching, Ch'ing, are ignored for the purposes of alphabetical order.

Names   Chinese people have a surname which comes first and is followed by a given name of which one individual may use several —childhood name, family name, style, pseudonym. Names are entered here under the one by which individuals are most commonly known.

The names of emperors are even more complicated. They may be referred to by a family name, temple name, posthumous or tomb name or a reign title. Once again entries here are under the name most usually used in English. In practice, Ming and Ch'ing emperors are referred to by their reign titles, e.g. Hung-wu, but earlier rulers are known by their posthumous titles, e.g. T'ai-tsu.

Cross-References   Cross-references have been kept to a minimum and (qv) only added where a further reference is likely to clarify. Individuals and events commonly known by different names are included under all the variations where possible. No cross-references are given for dynasties as nearly all are included, or for central figures such as Mao Tse-tung or Chiang K'ai-shek.

Abbreviations The only abbreviations used throughout the Dictionary are CCP for Chinese Communist Party and KMT for Kuomintang (Nationalist Party). Other abbreviations have been used within a particular entry, e.g. APC for Agricultural Producers' Co-operative, but these have been explained in the entry.

Chronological Table of Dynasties

Hsia	?2205 —	?1766 BC
Shang	?1766 —	?1122 BC
Chou	?1122 —	256 BC
Western Chou	?1122 —	771 BC
Eastern Chou	770 —	256 BC
Spring and Autumn	722 —	481 BC
Warring States	403 —	221 BC
Ch'in	221 —	207 BC
Han (Former or Western)	206 BC —	8 AD
Hsin (Wang Mang Interregnum)	8 AD —	23 AD
Han (Later or Eastern)	25 —	220
Three Kingdoms	220 —	265
Western Chin	265 —	316
Northern and Southern Dynasties	420 —	581
Sui	581 —	618
T'ang	618 —	907
Five Dynasties and Ten Kingdoms	907 —	960
Sung (Northern)	960 —	1126
Liao	907 —	1125
Chin	1115 —	1234
Sung (Southern)	1126 —	1279
Yuan	1271 —	1368
Ming	1368 —	1644
Ch'ing	1644 —	1911
Republic	1912 — 1949	(1949 — on Taiwan)
People's Republic	1949 —	

A

Abahai (1592–1643) Manchu leader and eighth son of Nurhachi. On the death of his father he was one of eight Banner princes, but he gradually concentrated power in his own hands. He extended the power of the Manchu state before the conquest of China by making Korea into a vassal state after attacking it in 1627 and 1636–7, and defeating the Inner Mongols in his expeditions into North China between 1629 and 1638. In 1636 he proclaimed the Ch'ing Dynasty at Mukden, although it is usually dated from the collapse of the Ming house in 1644. His reign and particularly his relationship with the Chinese who surrendered to him laid firm foundations for the Ch'ing dynasty.

Academia Sinica Founded in 1928 by the Nationalist Government to co-ordinate and advise on scientific affairs. Known in Chinese as the Central Research Academy (*Chung-yang yen-chiu yuan*) it included institutes specialising in the natural and social sciences and technology. After 1949 its name was changed to the Chinese Academy of Sciences (*Chung-kuo k'o-hsueh yuan*) but it continued in its co-ordinating role operating over a hundred research institutes on behalf of the State Science and Technological Commission. The Academia Sinica continued on Taiwan after 1949.

Afro-Asian Conference see *Bandung Conference*

Agricultural Producers' Co-operatives Co-operative farming units organised during agricultural collectivisation in the 1950s. Agricultural Producers' Co-operatives or APCs were first formed by the amalgamation of permanent Mutual Aid Teams (qv) in 1954 but most came into being during the 1955 High Tide of Socialism and by the end of 1956, 96% of all peasant households were members of APCs. They were regarded as semi-socialist because although agricultural land was pooled and managed centrally it was still privately owned, and the income of the peasants depended both on their work contributions and on the amount of land owned. APCs often coincided with existing villages and might include thirty to forty families. As the pace of collectivisation speeded up, APCs were combined to form Higher Producers' Co-operatives (qv) which in turn were later amalgamated into Communes (qv). See also *Collectivisation* and *Land Reform*.

Ah Q   The hero of *The True Story of Ah Q*, a long short story written by Lu Hsun (qv) in December 1921 and published in his collection *Outcry* in 1923. Ah Q (his name was pronounced Ah Quei but Lu Hsun called him Ah Q as he did not know which of the Chinese characters pronounced Quei his name was written with) was an itinerant agricultural labourer at the time of the Revolution of 1911 (qv) whose life of oppression, humiliation and self-deception symbolised the state of China to Lu Hsun. Ah Q ended his life the bewildered and innocent victim of both the revolutionaries whom he had hoped to join and the landlords who had bullied him. The story gained an international reputation and Ah Q has been compared with the Czech *Good Soldier Švejk*.

Aigun, Treaty of (1858)   Treaty signed between Russia and China on May 16, 1858 to determine the borders in the North East. Territory on the left bank of the Amur river was accepted as Russian, and territory on the right bank as far downstream as the Ussuri river was recognised as Chinese. The future of the land between the Ussuri and the sea was left to be settled at a later date. It was in fact given to Russia by a supplementary treaty signed after the Convention of Peking in 1860 and became the Maritime Province. Chinese grievances over the loss of land caused by this unequal treaty played a significant part in the Sino-Soviet dispute of the 1960s.

Alcock Convention (1869)   The convention, which derived its name from Sir Rutherford Alcock, British Consul in Shanghai and later Minister in Peking, emerged from a review of the Treaty of Tientsin (qv) and proposed an increase in the import duty on opium and the export duty on silk which would have favoured the Chinese economy. It also provided for a Chinese consulate in Hong Kong, but was never ratified by the British Government because commercial interests were opposed to it. This rejection disappointed and embittered the Chinese, particularly the Tsungli Yamen (qv) who felt betrayed, and it ushered in a new wave of anti-foreignism.

All China Federation of Trades Unions (ACFTU)   One of the semi-government nationwide Mass Organisations (qv) that emerged in the period 1949–1953. Its literature constantly emphasised the importance of labour discipline and provided guidance, encouragement and education for non-CCP trade unionists. The main functions of the federation, apart from the ideological, were to co-ordinate contracts between labour and management, administer welfare benefits, and increase production.

All Men Are Brothers see *Water Margin*

Altan Khan (1507–82) The most powerful leader of the Eastern Mongols in the 16th century. He organised a raiding band and ransacked large areas of Shansi province in 1541 and 1542 after requests for peaceful trade had been refused by the Chinese, and later attacked the area around Peking, in spite of the defence works and beacon towers built by the ruling Ming dynasty. Fairs for trading horses for silk were held as he proposed in 1551 but suspended when the Mongols asked for grain as well as silk. Altan Khan was aided by Chinese sympathisers and established an administration of his own at Kuei-hua just outside the Great Wall. His Chinese title, Shun-i Wang, which means Obedient and Righteous Prince, was bestowed on him in 1570 when he made peace with the Chinese rulers. He then referred to himself as a vassal of the Ming and sent tribute to the emperor, although in fact he remained completely independent. Altan Khan was a convert to and sponsor of the revival of the reformed or Yellow Sect of Lama Buddhism and was host to the third successor of Tsong-kha-pha, the founder of the sect, who arrived in Mongolia in 1580. It was from Altan Khan that this incarnation of Tsong-kha-pha received the title of Dalai (all-embracing) Lama.

Amherst, Lord (William Pitt, Earl Amherst, 1773–1857) The leader of an embassy to China in 1816. Dissatisfaction over the Canton system (qv) of trade and the failure of the Macartney embassy (qv) caused Lord Amherst, ex-governor of India, to be sent to Peking to negotiate freer trade and more diplomatic representation. The delegation left Portsmouth on February 8, 1816 and sailed direct to Peking to avoid hindrance at Canton. After a protracted argument over whether he should perform the *kowtow* and other misunderstandings, the embassy was expelled without imperial audience. The failure of the mission, recorded in Amherst's dispatches, was one of the factors that led to the Opium War (qv).

An Lu-shan A T'ang dynasty general of barbarian origin who was adopted by Yang Kuei-fei the consort of emperor Hsuan-tsung. Through her patronage he came to command almost 200,000 troops as head of the three regional commanderies along the North-Eastern frontiers, and his ambition to control the central government led him to revolt in 755. He captured the second city of Lo-yang and then the capital, Ch'ang-an; the emperor Hsuan-tsung fled to Szechwan, was forced by his soldiers to execute Yang Kuei-fei, and then abdicated in grief. An Lu-shan was killed by his own son in 757, but his rising had made it impossible for the T'ang government to control the provinces as firmly as had been done previously. Regional Commanders were appointed throughout the country and many of them revolted against the emperor. The period after the An Lu-shan revolt is generally felt to have been one of weak government and political and economic confusion.

Analects A work attributed to Confucius (qv) but probably written either by his disciples or by their pupils. It consists of answers that Confucius gave to questions put to him and is the basic source for the main concepts of Confucianism, although it has gone through many editions and annotations. Most of the quotations are brief and often enigmatic. They illustrate the life of Confucius, his mission as a teacher and the main principles of his philosophy — the concepts of humanity, filial piety and the conduct of the gentleman.

Ancestor Worship The most important ritual for the cohesion and sanctification of the family in the Confucian tradition. Although regarded as a vital part of Confucian belief, ancestor worship predated Confucius by many centuries and seems to have existed in China since prehistoric times, as many questions on the oracle bones (qv) of the Shang period relate to ancestors. The rituals were later integrated into Confucianism and were also promoted by Buddhists and Taoists. The ceremony — praying, burning incense and making offerings of food — was usually performed before the ancestral altar and tablets in the main hall of great houses or in the ancestral temples of the lineage in the villages. Offerings were frequently made daily but there were more formal ceremonies at the New Year and particularly during the festival of Ch'ing Ming (qv).

Ancient China see *Periodisation*

Ancient Text Movement (*ku-wen*) Opponents of the Modern Text School (qv) in the interpretation of the Confucian classics. Ancient text scholars supported the editions of the classics recovered in an early form rather than new transcripts made in the Han period and generally saw Confucius as a great man whose teachings could be used and adapted whereas the Modern Text School held them to be unchangeable.

Anfu Clique One faction that emerged when the Peiyang warlord clique split in 1917. The Anfu clique, which controlled the Peking Government in the early 1920s was notoriously pro-Japanese and regarded as traitorous by many Chinese because of its acceptance of the conditions of the Versailles settlement and the Twenty-One Demands (qv). See also *Warlords* and *Peiyang Army*.

Anti-Confucian Campaign A post Cultural Revolution campaign against the ideas of Confucius and his followers who were compared unfavourably with the Legalists (qv). The campaign began on August 7, 1973 with a *People's Daily* article by Yang Jung-kuo, professor of philosophy at Chung-shan University in Canton, stating that Confucius's ideas of 'benevolence' were a mask for his support of a declining slave-owning society at a time when feudal landlords were a progressive force. Criticism of Confucius was later linked to attacks on contemporary Communist officials, notably Lin Piao (qv), who was accused of wanting to 'restore the rites' in the manner of Confucius, that is of wanting himself made head of state. Although the title is reserved specifically for this campaign, criticisms of Confucian philosophy have been part of the ideological armoury of the CCP since its inception. Ch'en Tu-hsiu made many attacks on Confucian ideas, as did the writer Lu Hsun.

Anti-foreignism Xenophobia during the second half of the 19th century, aimed principally at foreign missionaries who penetrated deep into the Chinese countryside, converted villagers, tore down temples and built churches. This anti-foreignism was also directed against businessmen and officials and towards the end of the century xenophobic elements merged with traditional anti-dynastic secret societies in the Boxer Rebellion (qv).

Anti-Japanese War (1937–45) The war of resistance against Japan that began with the Japanese invasion of China in 1937 and ended with the surrender of the Japanese after the bombing of Hiroshima and Nagasaki in 1945. Japanese expansionism had begun with a gradual increase in Japan's control of Korea which came under its influence after the Sino-Japanese War of 1894–5 (qv) and was annexed in 1910. Thereafter Japan became increasingly involved in Manchuria and in 1931 after the Mukden incident (qv) the whole of Manchuria came under Japanese control. On July 7, 1937 after a clash between Chinese and Japanese forces the Japanese armies invaded China without a formal declaration of war. North China was overrun in the autumn of that year by the use of 'blitzkrieg' tactics and by November Shanghai and the Yangtze valley had fallen to the Japanese. Nanking fell in December and Hankow and Canton in October 1938. The Japanese occupied all the main cities in East China and controlled most of the railway lines. The Nationalist Government of Chiang K'ai-shek was forced to retreat to Chungking, but units of the KMT armies, with American and British arms, did resist the invasion. Tougher resistance was offered by the guerrilla units of the Communists from their bases mainly in the North. They were able to mobilise large numbers of peasants against the invaders, a factor which contributed to their victory in the 1946–49 civil war. In 1941 after the Japanese attack on Pearl Harbour the anti-Japanese War became part of the Second World War.

Anti-Rightist Movement   After the Hundred Flowers period (qv) of 1956–57 had revealed more discontent than the authorities had expected, a campaign was launched based on an article by Mao Tse-tung called 'On the Correct Handling of Contradictions among the People'. This campaign against 'rightist elements' who had revealed themselves in the Hundred Flowers period accused them of attacking the whole party and state structure. Many of the critics of government policies were sent to labour camps or were forced to sign a socialist self-reform pact to indicate their allegiance to the state.

Anyang   A town in northern Honan province which was the centre of the Bronze Age culture of the Shang dynasty and the site of earlier Neolithic Black Pottery and Painted Pottery cultures (qv). Oracle bones (qv) dating from the Shang period were discovered in Anyang as early as 1888 and systematic excavation by archaeologists of the Academia Sinica between 1929 and 1933 revealed large quantities of inscribed bones, bronzes, burial sites with the bones of humans and animals and the remains of war chariots, weapons and foodstuffs. These excavations established for the first time the existence of the Shang dynasty which had until then only been recorded in documentary evidence regarded by sinologists as inaccurate.

Anyuan Colliery Strike (1922)   The Anyuan Colliery in Pinghsiang county in Kiangsi was a large enterprise under the indirect control of Japanese interests. The newly-formed CCP began part-time Marxist education classes at the mine, organised a trade union in May 1922 and then formed a branch of the Socialist Youth League. The strike broke out on September 10, 1922 after the owners had tried to dissolve the union and had withheld wage payments. Troops were sent to suppress the strike but some were won over and on the fifth day the workers, led by Liu Shao-ch'i and Li Li-san, were granted their demands.

Ao   The capital of Chung-ting, tenth king of the Shang dynasty, which was built some time in the 15th century BC. What is believed to be the site has been excavated near the present-day city of Cheng-chou in northern Honan province, and contains evidence of work-shops for pottery, bone-working, bronze, jade, leather and silk.

Arab Traders   Trade routes from China were dominated by Persians and Arabs from the T'ang dynasty onwards. Arab traders established themselves in special quarters of the port cities enjoying privileges similar to those later known as extra-territorial, and there are records of many hundreds of Arabs living in Yang-chou and Canton in the 8th and 9th centuries. During the Yuan dynasty Arab commerce increased still further, both by caravan via Baghdad and by ship to the port of Ch'üan-chou which was known to the Arabs as Zayton. Towards the end of the Ming dynasty Arab influence declined and the newly-formed European East India Companies (qv) took over the bulk of the trade from China to the West.

Arrow War   The name given to the second Opium War (qv) between Britain and China in 1856. The ostensible *casus belli* was the refusal of the Chinese to apologise for an insult to the British flag on board the *Arrow*, a Chinese-owned vessel with Chinese rig and a foreign hull. When the *Arrow* entered the Pearl River at Canton in October 1856 it was boarded by a Chinese patrol in search of pirates. Twelve men were arrested and the British flag, used to enable the ship to sail into all Chinese coastal ports, was lowered. The British consul at Canton, Harry Parkes, lodged a protest and a demand for the return of the arrested Chinese sailors. When this was rejected, Canton was occupied by about a thousand British troops. The British and French authorities used the hostilities to negotiate a revision of the Nanking and other treaties, which led to the Treaty of Tientsin of 1858 (qv).

Autumn Grain   One half of the Double Tax (qv) levied by the state during the Ming dynasty. Autumn Grain was collected in the second month as a tax on the produce grown during the previous summer and harvested in the autumn. It was far larger than the Summer Tax (qv) levy.

Autumn Harvest Insurrection   A peasant rising organised by the CCP in the Hunan-Kiangsi border area in September 1927. The rising was under the overall direction of Ch'ü Ch'iu-pai but led in some areas by Mao Tse-tung and was carried out by units of the Red Army, workers from the Anyuan (qv) and Pinghsiang mines and peasant militia. It failed because of insufficient support, lack of arms and poor co-ordination, but the experience, coupled with his earlier investi-gations in Hunan, convinced Mao of the importance of the peasant movement in the Chinese Revolution.

B

Backhouse, Sir Edmund (1873–1944) Sinologist and translator best known for his books on the Empress Dowager and the Imperial Court and for his bequest of Chinese printed books to the Bodleian Library in Oxford. An enigmatic figure and Peking recluse, he was revealed long after his death to have led a double life. Many of his writings were based on documents of highly dubious authenticity and he was shown to have perpetrated frauds of enormous proportions in contracts he was supposed to be negotiating between the Chinese and Westerners.

Backyard Furnaces An experiment in small-scale iron and steel production which began during the Great Leap Forward (qv) in 1958. In keeping with plans to increase steel production and the policy of local self-reliance, many communes set up small-scale industries, notably the backyard furnaces which were intended to convert locally available ores and scrap metal into pig iron and then steel. Much of the steel produced in the villages was found to be of such poor quality that it was unsuitable for industrial use, but the experiment did give communes useful experience in organising small-scale local industries some of which have continued to the present day.

Bandit Extermination Campaigns see *Encirclement Campaigns*

Banditry A common phenomenon throughout the whole of Chinese history. Bandits were generally dispossessed peasants or unemployed labourers who drifted into inaccessible moutainous areas and lived by brigandage. Bandit groups often formed the nuclei for peasant rebellions (qv) and the dividing line between bandits and revolutionaries was always blurred from early times right up to the formation of the Red Armies (qv) in the 1920s which incorporated a number of brigand groups. Banditry was also a popular subject in fiction, particularly the exploits of Sung Chiang and his men in the novel *Water Margin* (qv).

Bandung Conference (1955) A conference of Afro-Asian statesmen from twenty-nine states held in Indonesia in April 1955. In spite of differences between pro-Western countries, neutrals and pro-Communists, resolutions opposing colonialism and supporting economic and cultural co-operation were agreed on. Chou En-lai represented China and laid the foundations for diplomatic relations and economic co-operation between China and a number of Asian countries. The Bandung Spirit moved China to offer low interest loans and grants to some Asian states.

Banners Military and administrative units organised by the Manchus. After 1601, companies of 300 warriors were grouped under four banners, yellow, white, blue and red. Four more were later added, using the same colours with borders of red (white for the red banner). The banner organisation superseded previous tribal organisation and eventually all Manchus were enrolled in a banner to which they had to pay taxes and owed military service. Appointed officers and clerks headed the banners, replacing hereditary tribal chieftains. This system which was the creation of Nurhachi (qv) succeeded in unifying the Manchus who had been previously divided into tribal formations. It was a necessary prerequisite for the Manchu conquest of China and played a vital role in the consolidation of the conquest and the organisation of the subsequent Ch'ing dynasty, and Manchu bannermen constituted the most important military units in provincial China. Eight Mongol and eight Chinese banners were later formed to incorporate allies of the Manchus into their military organisation. The banner forces were used throughout the 17th and early 18th century in campaigns to dominate continental East Asia, but by the 1750s corruption, poor supplies and inadequate training had brought demoralisation and the system fell into a decline.

Barbarians Non-Han Chinese (qv) peoples living in, or on the borders of, China. Relations with barbarian peoples, particularly on the northern frontier, were an important question of state policy throughout the history of the empire and the Chinese states that emerged were often a synthesis of nomadic barbarians and agricultural Hans. Several Chinese dynasties in the north like the Chin and Liao were almost entirely the result of barbarian conquest as were two dynasties that ruled the whole of China, the Yuan and the Ch'ing. Important barbarian peoples included the Ch'iang, the Hsien-pi, Hsi-hsia, Hsiung-nu, Khitan, Manchus, Mongols and Tibetans (qqv) and the first Westerners to reach China were regarded as being in the same category as these. China's inability to see that Western barbarians were superior in technology if in nothing else led to conflicts over trade and representation and China's failure to resist Western domination. See also *Minorities, National*.

Barefoot Doctors Folksy name for modern communist paramedical personnel with basic first aid and diagnostic training who act as part-time medical auxiliaries while continuing in a normal job of work. They are the foundation for the provision of basic medical services throughout China, and their part-time work may in the future be paid and developed into full-time medical work.

Beg, Yakub   see   *Yakub Beg*

Bell, Adam Schall von   German Jesuit who from 1630 was director of the Imperial Board of Astronomy, serving the last Ming emperor and the Ch'ing emperors Shun-chih and K'ang-hsi. In 1642 after a request to improve Chinese weaponry, he had guns cast, wrote a book on the manufacture and operations of weapons and taught armoury to a number of Chinese. He also translated and wrote many works on astronomical subjects but on presenting the young K'ang-hsi emperor with a two hundred year calendar he was accused by Chinese astronomers of predicting the downfall of the dynasty in two hundred years. He was thrown into prison and his life spared only because of the intercession of the then empress dowager. He was released in 1665 but died a year later. His grave was among those desecrated by the Boxers in 1900.

Bethune, Norman   Canadian surgeon and communist who worked at the front in the Spanish Civil War in 1936 and headed a medical team in Yenan in the spring of 1938. He spent nearly two years as a medical officer to the Communist armies and died in November 1939 of blood-poisoning contracted while he was operating on wounded soldiers.

Big Sword Society   Secret society that originated in Shantung as part of the Boxer (qv) movement. In 1898 it circulated posters urging patriotic Chinese to kill foreigners and Chinese traitors.

Black Pottery Culture (Lung-shan)   A neolithic culture possibly dating from before 2000 BC, so named because of the characteristic shiny black pottery it produced. Also named Lung-shan, after the location of a type-site in Shantung, it is distinguished from what is probably its near contemporary, the Painted Pottery Culture (qv) by more settled agriculture and improved techniques including the introduction of rice cultivation. Common animal and crop usage, systems of divination and pounded earth walls suggest it as an immediate precursor of the Shang dynasty. Sites identified with this culture are found throughout present-day Honan, Shantung, Kiangsu and Anhwei.

Blooming and Contending   Abbreviation of Mao Tse-tung's call to "let a hundred flowers bloom, a hundred schools of thought contend" that launched the Hundred Flowers Movement (qv) in 1957 by harking back to the philosophical controversies of the Warring States period (qv). The term was subsequently used for all kinds of criticisms and expressions of opinion.

Blueshirts   Special gendarmerie organised by a group of nationalists in the 1930s to spy on and suppress the CCP. The Blueshirt Society (Lan-i she) began in 1926 as an anti-communist group of officers from the Whampoa Military Academy and in 1931 and 1932, with Chiang K'ai-shek's approval, it created a tightly-controlled secret organisation along Fascist lines. The Blueshirts pledged obedience to Chiang as the supreme leader and acted as his personal police force, shooting or imprisoning anyone considered undesirable without concern for legality.

Boards, Six   see   *Ministries, Six*

Bogue   The principal mouth of the Pearl River to the south of Canton. The name is a corruption of the Portuguese Boca Tigre which translated the Chinese Hu-men (Tiger Gate).

Bogue, Supplementary Treaty of (1843)   One of the unequal treaties. It fixed the details of tariff regulations which had been agreed in principle in the treaty of Nanking (qv).

Book of Changes or Classic of Changes (I-ching)   One of the Five Classics (qv), a handbook of divination developed as an alternative to scapulimancy (see *Oracle Bones*) and based on the sixty-four combinations of whole and broken lines known as hexagrams. Selection of a hexagram was originally made probably by drawing odd or even numbers of the stalks of a plant. The I-ching could then be consulted for that sign and would yield some omen or piece of wisdom. The philosophy of the work is based on the concept of constant change within a unified cosmos and the hexagrams correspond to typical human situations and patterns of change. Some parts of the book are believed to derive from the early Chou period but other parts were probably added later, during the 7th century BC.

Book of Documents or Book of History (Shu-ching)   One of the Five Classics (qv). It contains semi-historical documents and speeches, oaths and injunctions dating from the early Chou period (1122–771 BC), although a large part of the text is now known to be a 4th century reconstruction. Its traditional associations with Confucius, who was alleged to have selected the documents to transmit to posterity the ways of an ideal age, gave it great influence on later historical writings and it was not till the Sung period that scholars began to doubt its authenticity. The part of the work now considered authentic has strong affinities with the style of bronze inscriptions (qv) of the Chou period.

Book of Filial Piety (Hsiao-ching) A reworking of parts of the Record of Rituals (qv) which became very popular as an elementary textbook throughout East Asia from the 3rd or 2nd century BC. It was allegedly written by Tseng Tzu, a disciple of Confucius, and is in the form of a discussion between the two. In the work Confucius puts forward the view that revering and obeying one's parents is the basis of all virtue.

Book of History see *Book of Documents*

Book of Lord Shang (Shang chün shu) The oldest known legalist work, attributed to Shang Yang, a great Ch'in statesman who died in 338 BC. It was probably compiled shortly after his death, possibly from his own writings, and lays heavy emphasis on the need for government by law rather than human will.

Book of Songs or Book of Poetry or Book of Odes (Shih ching) An anthology of verse dating from the 11th to the 6th century BC, including folk songs, love songs, political poems and longer ritual hymns, many of which were sung or chanted in Chou dynasty ceremonies. Tradition attributes the selection and compilation of the anthology to Confucius but this is considered unlikely although he knew and valued the work. It became one of the Five Classics (qv) in the 3rd century BC.

Border Disputes, Sino-Soviet Arguments about the definition of the border between Russia and China date back to the Tsarist unequal treaties (qv) of the 19th century such as the Treaty of Aigun (qv) which Lenin had promised to revoke. The border became an issue during the Cultural Revolution at the height of Sino-Soviet tension and the culmination was an armed clash on the Ussuri river (qv) over the ownership of the Damansky or Chen-pao Island on March 2, 1969. Further clashes in the same area and also on the Sinkiang border led to the hasty setting up of border talks which began in Peking on October 20, 1969. These have gone on intermittently ever since. See also *Sino-Soviet Dispute*.

Border Region see *Shen-Kan-Ning Base Area*

Borodin, Mikhail Markovich (Michael) 1884–1951   Comintern agent
in China in the 1920s. Born Michael Grusenberg of a Jewish family
in Lithuania in 1884, he emigrated to the U.S.A. in 1907 and lived
there until 1917. He worked in the Comintern from 1919 until 1923
when he became adviser to Sun Yat-sen with the task of reorganising
and revitalising the KMT. He drafted a new KMT programme based
on co-operation between the KMT, the Soviet Union and the CCP
which was adopted at the First National Congress of the KMT in
January 1924 at Canton. By 1927 he was mobilising left wing
nationalist support for the Wuhan government against Chiang K'ai-
shek who had taken control of the KMT. In July 1927 he was expelled
from China and sent back to Moscow during Chiang's purge of
Communists. He spent the rest of his life in journalism in the Soviet
Union and was editor-in-chief of the Soviet Information Bureau from
1941–49.

Boxer Protocal   Agreement signed by Li Hung-chang on September
7, 1901 after Boxer resistance had crumbled under the breakthrough
of allied troops to the legations in Tientsin and Peking. As part of the
terms, the Chinese government agreed to pay 450 million taels
(approximately £67 million) in reparations over a period of forty
years, to report on its punishment of officials who had been responsible for attacks on foreigners and to restrict arms supplies.

Boxer Rebellion   A confused millenarian mixture of anti-dynastic
and anti-foreign rebellions at the very end of the 19th century,
inspired principally by the I-ho-t'uan, the Righteous and Harmonious
Corps, which derived from the I-ho-ch'üan or Righteous and
Harmonious Fists, the Boxers. The roots of the rebellion lay in the
unemployment, hardship, bankruptcy of village handicrafts and
decline of domestic commerce that beset China in the late 19th
century. Added to these problems, which were blamed on foreign
domination of the Chinese economy, came a series of natural
disasters including the flooding of the Yellow River and a major
change in its course, and a severe drought in north China in 1900.
Foreign railways and other constructions were also blamed for these
as they were said to have disturbed the natural harmony of man and
nature, and there was much resentment at the German seizure of
Kiaochow in 1897 and the acquisition by Russia of Port Arthur and
by Britain of Weihaiwei. The I-ho-ch'üan was an offshoot of the
Eight Trigrams sect and associated with the White Lotus secret
society (qqv). It is first recorded in 1808 in Shantung, Honan, Kiangsu
and Anhwei and by 1818 had spread to Chihli. In the 1890s its
policies became primarily anti-foreign rather than anti-dynastic and

its members set out to exterminate the foreigner. As well as the political aspect, Boxer ideas involved legendary and historical military and rebellious figures, magic and incantation, and some members claimed immunity to bullets and the ability to fly. Many of the rebels were young and among the most prominent units were organisations of young girls known as the Red Lanterns. It became convenient for sections of the court and some local officials to support the Boxers in the 1890s and spurred on by this, the rebels laid seige to foreign legations and other buildings in Peking and Tientsin. Foreign troops fought back and a multi-national relief force took Tientsin on July 14, 1900 and advanced on Peking on August 4. The capital was taken ten days later and looted by the foreign armies. The Empress Dowager, the Emperor and a small entourage fled and Li Hung-chang (qv) was recalled to negotiate a peace settlement which was formalised in the Boxer Protocol signed on September 7, 1901.

Brainwashing   see   *Thought Reform*

Braun, Otto (Li Teh) (1900–   ) German communist sent by the Comintern to assist the Red Army in its resistance to the Nationalist encirclement campaigns (qv) in the 1930s. Braun, who was born near Munich, escaped from prison where he had been sent because of his work with the underground German Communist Party, and went to Moscow, where he was given military training before being sent to China as military adviser to the Central Committee of the Chinese Communist Party. He arrived in late 1932 or early 1933 with Po Ku and other CCP members who intended to replace Mao's leadership, and after the failure of his positional warfare strategy against the KMT encirclement campaigns, he took overall charge of the evacuation that led to the Long March. At the Tsunyi Conference (qv) Braun's military ideas were discredited and his influence disappeared. He returned to East Germany after the Second World War.

Bronze Age   The Bronze Age in China lasted from about the 18th century BC to the 6th century BC and included the dynasties known as the Shang and the Chou. The techniques of smelting and casting bronzes were developed by craftsmen attached to the palaces of the Shang aristocracy. They produced powerful weapons and elaborate vessels for use in ceremonies and ritual sacrifices. Bronze vessels of the Shang and Chou periods are highly esteemed for their fine angular animal designs. See also *Periodisation*.

Bronze Inscriptions   Inscriptions, often lengthy, cast as integral parts of bronze vessels from the Chou period onwards which recorded royal actions and title deeds and together with Shang oracle bones (qv) are the earliest examples of written Chinese.

Bucharest Conference (1960)   Congress of the Rumanian Communist Party held on June 20, 1960 at which the CCP was attacked by Khrushchev. This was an early salvo in the Sino-Soviet dispute (qv) and set the stage for the final break between Moscow and Peking at the Conference of Communist Parties that took place in Moscow in November of the same year.

Buddhism   Developed from the teachings of Gautama who lived in northern India at about the same time as Confucius, was transmitted to China at about the beginning of the Christian era, but began to play an active part in Chinese culture from the 4th and 5th centuries AD. Buddhist monasteries used the services of artists and craftsmen and were later able to provide capital for various investments. Indian missionaries were replaced by Chinese converts, many of whom like Fa-hsien and Hsüan-tsang (qqv) made pilgrimages to India in search of scriptures which they brought back and translated. At first the new religion made more progress in the north, but it spread southwards particularly in the period up to the 8th century which was the great age of Buddhism in China. It later declined as a significant politico-religious force after persistent persecution but remained important as a popular religion right up till the 20th century. See also *Lama Buddhism*.

Burning of the Books   An attempt made in 213 BC by the first emperor of the Ch'in dynasty, Shih Huang-ti, to suppress all non-legalist literature and so secure his own ideological position. The demand that all owners of proscribed works burn them or face heavy penalties was made at the suggestion of his chief minister Li Ssu. It is not known how thoroughly the decree was enforced but there was some burning and scholars are reported to have been executed for disobeying the command.

Butterfield and Swire   Trading firm which began in Shanghai in 1867, expanded to include Hong Kong and with Jardine, Matheson (qv) became one of the two most important import-export firms in China during the early 20th century.

Buyantu (reigned 1311-20)   Yuan emperor of China with a keen interest in Chinese poetry and scholarship who reintroduced the civil service examinations and so ensured the sinicisation of the Mongol administration.

C

Cadres Party and government officials of all ranks in the People's Republic and in the liberated areas before 1949. The development of a cadre (or body of cadres) has been one of the most important tasks in the consolidation of Communist control since 1949. Increasing the number of cadres who are women or from one of the minority nationalities has been a particular problem.

Cairo Declaration The outcome of the Cairo Conference held in November 1943 when Chiang K'ai-shek met Franklin D. Roosevelt and Winston Churchill to discuss the demand for the unconditional surrender of Japan and to lay down guidelines for post-war policies. A joint statement was issued on December 1 promising the eventual restoration to China of all territories lost to Japan, but this was later modified in the case of Manchuria by the Yalta Pact (qv) of 1945.

Cambaluc see *Khanbaligh*

Cantlie, Dr James Teacher of Sun Yat-sen and Dean of the College of Medicine for Chinese in Hong Kong. Dr. Cantlie advised Sun to flee to Japan in 1895 when the British authorities in Hong Kong complied with a Chinese government request to ban him for five years, and later arranged lodgings for him when he arrived in London in 1896. Here Sun Yat-sen was kidnapped and detained illegally in the Chinese legation. It was only when Dr. Cantlie brought the case to the attention of the Foreign Office and the London newspaper *The Globe* that Sun was eventually released.

Canton Commune A Communist-led insurrection that took place on December 11, 1927. In spite of the failure of the Autumn Harvest Rising (qv) and other insurrections, a hurried takeover was organised in Canton while Nationalist generals were at loggerheads. The rising had some trade union support but its main force was a rebelling Nationalist training regiment. A local soviet government and military command were set up in the public security offices, but on the same day a concerted Nationalist counter-attack was launched. On December 13 the Commune collapsed when the public security offices were captured. Chinese historians today see the Commune as an adventurist but heroic attempt to seize power. Its failure marked the effective end of the Communist movement in the towns and the turn to the peasantry.

Canton Coup   Chiang K'ai-shek's seizure of power in the KMT on March 20, 1926. Before the bloodless coup, the KMT was in disarray after the death of Sun Yat-sen, and Chiang K'ai-shek had a military but not a political power base. He consolidated his political power by moving his troops to arrest all pro-Communist and Communist elements in the KMT. Wang Ching-wei, the most important KMT left-winger, resigned, and Chiang K'ai-shek was formally declared head of the party, the Military Council, the Political Department, the arsenal and the military academies. He was now virtually dictator and was in a position to launch the National Revolutionary Army's Northern Expedition (qv) to unify China.

Canton System   Imperial China's way of controlling trade with the West. In 1757 Canton, which had been opened to Western trade at the end of the 17th century, became the only port legally open for foreign trade and all business had to be carried out through a member of a small group of officially approved merchants, the Cohong (qv). Western traders objected strongly to this restriction and one of the most important results of the Treaty of Nanking (qv) signed in 1842 after the Opium War was the opening of other ports to foreign trade.

Capitalism, Sprouts of   The question of the development of early capitalist forms of production. In the 1950s a controversy developed among historians over the periodisation (qv) of Chinese history and particularly about the extent of early forms of capitalism. Mao Tse-tung had stated that Chinese feudal society had contained within it the elements of capitalist organisation and would eventually have developed into a capitalist society even if there had been no foreign influence, and historians followed this up with a long series of exegetical articles examining the level of capitalist organisation in various periods. Some scholars found embryonic capitalism in the T'ang and Sung periods but most looked to the 16th century and particularly to the reigns of the Chia-ching and Wan-li emperors (qv), although there was considerable disagreement over the level of development of these 'sprouts'.

Capitalist-roaders   The derogatory term applied to supporters of Liu Shao-ch'i's policies during the Cultural Revolution. It is an abbreviation for 'top party persons in authority taking the capitalist road'. The 'capitalist road' was considered to include policies that advocated wage incentives and placed economic and technical priorities above political ones. See also *Two Lines*.

Cathay The name used for China by Marco Polo and by mediaeval Europeans in general. It probably derives from the word *Khitai*, a variant of the name of the Khitan (qv) people who ruled north China in the 10th century. The Russian word for China, *Kitai*, comes from the same word.

Catholicism, Roman Introduced into China as early as the 13th century during the Yuan dynasty by Franciscan monks sent by the Papal authorities on missions that were both diplomatic and evangelical. The first Roman Catholic outpost in Peking was established by John of Montecorvino (qv) in 1304 and many converts were baptised. Missions progressed during the late Yuan period, declined during the Ming dynasty but reappeared at its close when the Jesuit Matteo Ricci (qv) established himself at Peking in 1600. Jesuits (qv) remained influential at court till the early 18th century and made some converts. Roman Catholic missions increased along with those of other denominations during the 19th century and many missionaries became victims of militant Chinese nationalism during the Boxer Rebellion (qv).

C.C. Clique A right-wing faction within the KMT, named after its leaders Ch'en Li-fu and Ch'en Kuo-fu. The group was intransigently opposed to any collaboration with the CCP in the period after the Japanese surrender in 1945 and to the negotiations arranged by General Marshall.

CCP see *Chinese Communist Party*

Censorate An office of the Imperial government given the task of investigating official corruption, oppression or injustice and also controlling possible subversion. Individual investigators were appointed as early as 106 BC, but the system was institutionalised under the T'ang dynasty. The T'ang censorate had a controller, two assistants and three subdivisions: one responsible for official impeachment, one for inspecting palace procedures, and the third acting as an inspectorate. The Sung dynasty maintained the system, but added officers specially responsible for criticising the senior state officials. Under the Ming the principle remained the same in spite of some reorganisation and the Ch'ing rulers followed the Ming model. The power of the censorate derived from its direct access to the emperor and its ability to investigate officials of all ranks. Its importance enabled censors to criticise the palace or even the emperor himself.

Central Committee The main forum for debating policy issues within the CCP. The Central Committee has approximately two hundred members and during its infrequent plenary sessions discusses basic policy lines that have been decided on by the Politburo (qv) which is selected from the Central Committee. Reports from Politburo members involved in particular issues are followed by small group sessions and a final plenary session which may seek clarification or modification before agreeing on a final wording of the proposals under discussion. The Central Committee is composed of delegates from all provinces of China and plays a vital role in policy transmission and acceptance, but its size prevents it from taking detailed decisions. The Central Committee is elected after each party Congress (qv) and the full meetings are referred to as, for example, the Third Plenum of the Eighth Central Committee, that is the third full meeting of the Central Committee elected by the Eighth Party Congress in 1956.

Chaghadai Second son of Chinggis Khan and Khan of Chaghadai (Djaghatai) in Turkestan from 1227–1242 under the Mongol Empire.

Chahar Originally the name of one of the strongest tribes of Inner Mongolia, Chahar was the name given to the eastern part of the region when it was made a province by the Republican government as part of its divide-and-rule policy towards the Mongols after 1911. Chahar was occupied by the Japanese during 1937–45 and is now part of the Inner Mongolian Autonomous Region.

Champa Rice   see   *Early Ripening Champa Rice*

Ch'an Buddhism More familiar in its Japanese reading of *Zen*, Ch'an is a meditative sect of Buddhism, introduced, according to tradition, by Bodhidharma in the early 6th century. Its stress on enlightenment through intuition and anti-textual, anti-scholastic bias were close to the tradition of Taoism (qv) and this enabled it to become one of the strongest of the Buddhist sects in China. All Chinese Buddhism was eventually absorbed into either the Ch'an or the Pure Land sect (qv) and the two later merged, in the popular religion, into an indistinct mixture of beliefs.

Chan-kuo ts'e   see   *Intrigues of the Warring States*

Chang Ch'ien Military officer sent by the Han emperor Wu-ti in 139 BC to make an alliance with the Central Asian peoples known as Yüeh-chih against the Hsiung-nu (qqv). Chang Ch'ien was captured by the Hsiung-nu and after years in prison finally found the Yüeh-chih but was unable to secure an alliance. He returned to China in 126 BC with much detailed knowledge of Central Asia and the lands to the west. His second embassy to the Wu-sun of the Ili region of 115 BC was no more successful but further increased Chinese knowledge of the western frontiers.

Chang Ch'un-ch'iao Journalist who rose to be director of propaganda in the Shanghai Party Committee in the 1960s. He helped Chiang Ch'ing to promote revolutionary operas and films, became a member of the group that directed the Cultural Revolution and was the inspiration behind the short-lived Shanghai Commune (qv) of January 1967. He became chairman of the subsequent Shanghai Revolutionary Committee that was formed on February 24, 1967 and towards the end of Mao's life was one of the influential radical group which included Chiang Ch'ing, Yao Wen-yuan and Wang Hung-wen (qqv), was often called the Shanghai Mafia, and was later castigated as the Gang of Four (qv) by the new leadership of Hua Kuo-feng.

Chang Hsüeh-liang Known as the Young Marshal. He succeeded his father Chang Tso-lin (qv) as governor and warlord of Manchuria when the latter was killed by a bomb in 1928. He controlled the north-eastern provinces till he was ousted by the Japanese invasion of 1931. He had pledged allegiance to Chiang K'ai-shek's government in 1928 and his armies fought with the Nationalists against Japan. In 1936 he arrested Chiang K'ai-shek in the famous Sian Incident (qv) to try and force him to end the civil war and organise co-ordinated resistance with the Communists against the Japanese. He released Chiang K'ai-shek after negotiations in which Chou En-lai played a vital role and was himself imprisoned by the Nationalist leader. He remained in prison on Taiwan till 1962.

Chang Kuo-t'ao (1897–   ) Founder member of the CCP and important leader in its early days, Chang came from central Kiangsi, was involved in the 1911 Revolution and from 1916 attended Peking University where he came to know Ch'en Tu-hsiu, Li Ta-chao (qqv) and other radicals. He joined the May 4th demonstrations in 1919 and represented Peking Marxists at the first CCP Congress in Shanghai in 1921. He was active in the labour movement and in Comintern affairs, attending the Toilers of the East Congress in Moscow in 1922. An opponent of Communist participation in the KMT, he nevertheless became a member of the Nationalist central executive committee during the first United Front (qv). He spent more time in Moscow between 1928 and 1931 and on his return to

China was sent to direct political work in the Communist base on the borders of Hupeh, Honan and Anhwei. His units evacuated Kiangsi ahead of the main Long March column and set up a small base area in north Szechwan, eventually arriving in Yenan with sadly depleted forces. Old differences with Mao Tse-tung who had replaced him as head of the CCP Organisation Bureau in 1924 had never healed, and Chang left the Yenan area in 1938 and was expelled from the CCP in the same year. He found refuge in Hankow, then the Nationalist capital, and moved with the government to Chungking where he took part in government and KMT affairs. In 1949 he moved to Hong Kong to spend most of his time working on his autobiography.

Chang Tso-lin (1873–1928) The Old Marshal and warlord of Manchuria from the 1911 Revolution until his death in a Kwantung Army (qv) bomb plot in 1928 when he was succeeded by his son Chang Hsueh-liang (qv). In 1924 Chang Tso-lin established himself in Peking and became notorious for a raid on the Soviet embassy in 1927 which resulted in the capture and execution of the communist leader Li Ta-chao.

Ch'ang-an Capital of China during the Han, Sui and T'ang dynasties (on the site of present-day Sian) and a rival to the city of Lo-yang (qv). Defensive walls were built around Ch'ang-an from 194 BC onwards, nine market-places were established in and around the town, and great palaces were built to house the Han emperors and their families. The court moved to Lo-yang after the interregnum of Wang Mang, but Ch'ang-an was again chosen as capital by the newly established Sui dynasty in 582, on a new site that was later developed by the T'ang emperor. The new Ch'ang-an was a systematically planned town on a grid pattern, with eleven streets running north to south and fourteen from east to west, a plan which facilitated the enforcement of curfews and the supervision of public places. This model was extensively copied both by other Chinese towns and by foreigners, notably the Japanese, who built the cities of Nara (in 710) and Hei-an (from 793 — modern Kyoto) on the design of Ch'ang-an.

Chao Kao Chief eunuch of the first Ch'in emperor. In 210 BC he conspired with Li Ssu (qv), the chief minister, to conceal the death of the First Emperor, Shih Huang-ti, until he had engineered the suicide of the heir apparent, and then put a young, weak son on the throne as Second Emperor (qv), whose confidant he became. He became Prime Minister, had Li Ssu put to death, and finally caused the Second Emperor to commit suicide.

Ch'en Dynasty (557–589)   State based on Nanking during the period known as the Northern and Southern Dynasties. It was founded by Ch'en Pa-hsien but wiped out by the Sui Empire after thirty-two years.

Ch'en Ch'eng (1897–1965)   Nationalist general who led important operations against the Communists in the encirclement campaigns (qv) of the early 1930s. He commanded the Wuhan Defence Area in the Sino-Japanese War and was commander-in-chief in the Manchurian theatre of the Civil War for a short period in 1947. He was governor of Taiwan at the time of the Nationalist evacuation of the mainland in 1949 and became vice-president of the Republic of China in 1954. Documents and publications captured by his men during the campaign against the Kiangsi Soviet provide an invaluable collection of source materials for research on the 1930–34 period and are known as the Ch'en Ch'eng Collection.

Ch'en Po-ta (1904–   )   For many years served as private secretary, speech-writer and adviser to Mao Tse-tung. He was elected alternate member of the Politburo after the Eighth Party Congress in 1956, and became Director of the Central Committee's Cultural Revolution Group (qv) in 1966 after having been Deputy Director of the Party's theoretical journal. He was removed from the leadership in 1970 for his association with the May 16th Group (qv).

Ch'en Sheng   Leader of one of the rebellions at the end of the Ch'in dynasty that led to its downfall and replacement by the Han. Ch'en Sheng, also known as Ch'en Sheh, was an ambitious farm labourer who led a group of conscripts to desert and revolt rather than face death for arriving late at the garrison. He made himself General and Wu Kuang his chief commander, and then set himself up as King of Ch'u. Ch'en Sheng was killed after only six months as king, but was regarded by the Han emperors as one of their predecessors.

Ch'en Tu-hsiu (1879–1942)   Founder of the CCP and leader of the literary and cultural revolution that culminated in the May 4th Movement. Ch'en Tu-hsiu was editor of *New Youth* and Dean of the Peking University Faculty of Letters. He became a Marxist and organiser of the Shanghai group that formed the nucleus of the CCP. From 1921 to 1927 he led the Party, but in 1930 he was expelled and went on to form a Trotskyist opposition which he led till his arrest by the Nationalist government in 1932. He was imprisoned till 1937 and spent the rest of his life studying and writing. His most important writings from the early period were those in which he popularised the ideas of Western progress in his characters Mr. Democracy and Mr. Science, and launched powerful attacks on Confucianism and the social structure it espoused. His break with the CCP in 1930 came with his criticisms of the disastrous policies of alliance with the KMT and the ill-prepared uprisings that the Comintern had forced on the Communists. For a time he supported Trotsky's view of a permanent revolution but later left political life entirely.

Ch'en Yi (1883–1950) Originally an officer in the army of the warlord Sun Ch'uan-fang, Ch'en Yi joined forces with Chiang K'ai-shek's Nationalists after the Northern Expedition. He served as governor of Fukien from 1934 to 1941 and in 1945 was appointed to administer Taiwan where he was responsible for suppressing the Taiwan Uprising of 1947. He was governor of Chekiang in 1948–9, dismissed in 1949 after contacts with agents of the CCP, and executed by the Nationalists as a traitor and conspirator in June 1950.

Ch'en Yi (1901–72) Outstanding communist military commander in the Red Army and later the New Fourth Army in the 1930s and 1940s. He joined the Chinese Socialist Youth League in France in 1921 where he was taking part in the work-study programme, and the CCP in 1923 in Peking. His military career began at Whampoa Military Academy under Chou En-lai and he saw distinguished service in the Kiangsi Soviet period and during the Anti-Japanese War. After 1949 he became Mayor of Shanghai and then foreign minister in 1958.

Ch'en Yung-kuei Secretary of the model Tachai (qv) production brigade. A native of Shansi, Ch'en Yung-kuei moved to Tachai at the age of six and began work as a labourer when he was eleven. In 1964 he was a delegate to the National People's Congress and during the Cultural Revolution he became vice-chairman of the Shansi Provincial Revolutionary Committee and a member of the Central Committee of the Chinese Communist Party.

Ch'eng Brothers Ch'eng Hao (1032–1085) and Ch'eng I (1033–1108). Two brothers who made important contributions to Sung Neo-Confucianism (qv). Both were reformers and the precursors of the neo-Confucian synthesiser Chu Hsi (qv).

Cheng Ho Moslem court eunuch from Yunnan and the leader of a series of maritime expeditions undertaken between 1405 and 1433 that brought a number of South and South East Asian states into the tribute system (qv). The voyages were only possible because of the development of the maritime compass (qv), and improved navigational and shipbuilding techniques. In the first voyage of 1405-7, sixty-two vessels reached India. Two other expeditions were mounted to India in 1407 and 1409 and two expeditions to Aden and the Persian Gulf in 1413 and 1417. A sixth voyage took place in 1421 and in the final venture that reached the Persian Gulf and East Africa between 1431 and 1433, seven Chinese visited Mecca. The motives for the voyages are still largely unknown, and it is not clear whether they were intended to stimulate overseas trade or to expand the area of Chinese political influence. Neither is it clear why the expeditions ceased in 1433, although the great cost of equipping them, higher priority given to expeditions against the Mongols, and the opposition of officials to eunuch-controlled enterprises all seem to have played a part. Whatever the reason, the voyages were never followed up commercially and Ming governments remained indifferent to foreign trade and commercial activity in general.

Cheng Kuan-ying Compradore (qv) who managed Li Hung-chang's (qv) cloth mill in Shanghai in 1882-4. In 1875 he had published a short work *Remarks on Change* in which he called for the development of free trade and industry without the interference of officials and it was republished in 1893 as *Warnings to a Prosperous Age*.

Ch'eng-hua, Ming Emperor (reigned 1465-87) Succeeded his father the T'ien-shun emperor at the age of seventeen. He avoided public appearances and dealings with officials, and eunuchs dominated the court.

Cheng-te, Ming Emperor (reigned 1506-21) Succeeded his father the Hung-chih emperor at the age of thirteen and acquired a reputation for irresponsibility and adventure. Eunuchs once again controlled the court and their exactions provoked a revolt by one of the imperial princes.

Cheng-t'ung, Ming Emperor (reigned 1435-49) Succeeded his father the Hsuan-te emperor at the age of seven and was dominated by the eunuch Wang Chen who imposed a reign of terror. Squandered resources, floods and famines and unsuccessful military action against the Mongols damaged the stability of China and in 1449 the emperor was captured by Oirat invaders under their leader Esen. He was replaced by his younger brother who ruled as the Ching-t'ai emperor but returned to power in 1457 and reigned again till 1464 as the T'ien-shun emperor.

Chen-pao Island or Damansky Island   An island on the Ussuri river at the disputed border between Russia and China where fighting broke out in March 1969. See *Border Disputes*.

Ch'i   Peripheral state in the Shantung peninsula region, during the Warring States (qv) period, one of a number that sprang up after the collapse of the Chou regime. It increased its territory considerably during the 6th and 7th centuries BC and under Duke Huan and his adviser Kuan Chung or Kuan-tzu, modernised its administrative structure to include a uniform system of taxation, a central army and possibly salt and iron monopolies. Ch'i and the other states were eventually defeated by the state of Ch'in and incorporated into the first Chinese empire.

Ch'i Pai-shih (1863–1957)   Probably the modern Chinese artist best known outside China, a painter noted also for his calligraphy and seal engraving. He travelled widely in China and developed a simple and vigorous style of painting that was much admired. After 1949 his name was on the roll of many national and international cultural organisations.

Chia-ching, Ming emperor (reigned 1521–67)   Chu Hou-ts'ung (1507–67), the eleventh Ming emperor. The early years of his reign were spent in controversy over his succeeding his cousin and in his search for everlasting life through Taoism. He retained his own power and authority throughout his reign, unlike many other Ming emperors who were dominated by eunuchs, and his reign saw the growth of great economic wealth and power, particularly in the lower Yangtze area. From this wealth came leisure and the demand for luxury goods, the arts and entertainment; commerce and crafts flourished. Throughout the reign there were Mongol raids on the northern frontier, the worst in 1550 when Altan Khan (qv) threatened the capital. Chu Hou-ts'ung was succeeded by his third son Chu Tsai-hou who ruled as the Lung-ch'ing emperor.

Chia-ch'ing, Ch'ing Emperor (reigned 1796–1820)   Yung Yen (1760–1820), the fifth son of the Ch'ien-lung emperor, was the fifth Ch'ing emperor and ascended the throne on his father's abdication, although he did not achieve real control until after the death of his father in 1799. His reign was a time of rebellion and costly pacification. The emperor tried to reduce the expenditure of his own household but was unable to control corruption among officials. In 1816 he prepared to meet the Amherst Mission (qv) from England but was prevented from doing so by official trickery. He died after a journey to the summer palace at Jehol and was succeeded by his second son Min-ning, the Tao-kuang emperor.

Ch'iang   Group of Tibetan peoples who overran part of north China in the early part of the 4th century after some two centuries of pressure on the frontier. The name originally applied to one group of a shifting confederation of nomadic peoples which later took up settled agriculture on the western grasslands; the name Ch'iang subsequently came to be used for all Tibetans.

Chiang Ch'ing (1914–   )   Third wife of Mao Tse-tung. A former actress, then known as Lan P'ing, Chiang Ch'ing came to Yenan in 1937 where she met and married Mao against the opposition of senior party officials who were unhappy about his divorce from Ho Tzu-chen. Chiang Ch'ing took no part in politics, but became head of the film office of the Central Committee propaganda department in 1948. Throughout the 1950s and 60s, Chiang Ch'ing was active in artistic and cultural circles and in 1963–4 launched a movement to reform Peking Opera and ballet and to make it more revolutionary. She built up a large following in Shanghai, particularly in cultural and journal-istic circles, and in 1966 became Deputy Head of the Central Cultural Revolution Group in which she seems to have played the leading role. After the Cultural Revolution her power and prestige remained high because of her closeness to Mao but after his death in 1976 she was arrested along with other Shanghai associates, the Gang of Four, and attacked for numerous counter-revolutionary crimes.

Chiang K'ai-shek (1887–1975)   Leader of the Kuomintang and head of state of the Chinese Nationalist government in China until 1949 and on Taiwan until his death. After a classical education in Ningpo he decided on a military career, studied in a military school in Japan from 1908–1910 and spent a year training with a Japanese regiment. He returned to China when news of the Wuchang revolt became known and took part in the Republican revolution of 1911 in Shanghai. In 1918 Chiang was appointed to the staff of Sun Yat-sen's Kwangtung Army and enjoyed Sun's patronage, securing an appoint-ment as commandant of the Whampoa Military Academy in Canton in 1924. He built up the Nationalist army and also developed the KMT and on Sun Yat-sen's death in 1925, his military position enabled him to rise to power (see *Canton Coup*), which was con-solidated after his successful leadership of the Northern Expedition. In 1928 after factional disagreements within the KMT he emerged as leader of the National Government which ruled from Nanking until the Japanese invasion of 1937 forced the removal of the capital to

Chungking. His policies in the Nanking decade were primarily concerned with national unity, winning over the warlords, and with suppressing the CCP, but after the Japanese invasion survival became the priority. Chiang K'ai-shek was much criticised for conserving his troops and particularly his officer corps for the civil war he knew would follow Japan's defeat and leaving resistance to the CCP and the war against Japan to the Americans. When he lost this civil war and retreated to Taiwan in 1949 his main problems were concerned with suppressing Taiwanese discontent at Nationalist policies. He was later able to preside over an economy that was booming with American support, but never lost sight of his overriding goal — the reconquest of the mainland.

Chiang-nan (Kiangnan) 'South of the (Yangtze) River'. Originally the name of one of the administrative circuits of the T'ang dynasty. Although the region was later broken up and administered by separate provinces, the name was retained and often used to refer to south central China below the Yangtze. It was a prosperous rice-growing area and its flourishing craft and commercial activities in the Ming dynasty made it one of the key economic areas of China.

Ch'ien-lung, Ch'ing Emperor (reigned 1736–96) Hung-li (1711–99) was the fourth son and successor of the Yung-cheng emperor. The reign of Ch'ien-lung and that of K'ang-hsi are regarded as high points of the Ch'ing dynasty. Ch'ien-lung was able and conscientious and as a result the administration was stable. He made six tours of the southern provinces. He was a painter, poet and patron of the arts, although his reputation in this was marred later by the literary inquisition (qv). His government was successful in pacifying the border areas but towards the end of his reign factionalism and corruption set in and the army became demoralised and unable to cope with the White Lotus Rebellion (qv) that broke out in the last year of his reign. He abdicated in 1796.

Chien-wen, Ming Emperor (reigned 1398–1402) Successor to the Hung-wu emperor, Chien-wen was a practical statesman and knew how to keep eunuchs and court factions under control. He reduced the power of his uncle, the Prince of Yen, who was the fourth son of Hung-wu and had been passed over in the succession, and eventually the prince revolted. In 1402 the rebellion was successful and although Chien-wen is presumed to have perished in his burnt palace, rumours persisted that he had escaped disguised as a Buddhist monk. The Prince of Yen ruled as the Yung-lo emperor.

Chihli Province under the Ming and Ch'ing dynasties roughly equivalent to present-day Hopei.

Ch'i-min yao-shu see *Essential Techniques for the Common People*

Chin Dynasty (1122–1234) Regime established by the Jurcheds (qv) in the northern part of China. The Jurcheds were a Tungusic people from the forested river valleys of north and east Manchuria where they lived by hunting, fishing and farming. Originally vassal tribes of the Khitan Liao dynasty, they became united under A-ku-ta, who led them to revolt and seized both the East and Supreme capitals to establish the Chin (Golden) dynasty named after a river in the Jurched homeland. The Chin expanded into north China, capturing the Sung capital of Kaifeng in 1126 and eventually ruled the north of China as far south as the Huai river, the approximate northern limit of rice cultivation. Their main capital was at Yen-ching on the site of modern Peking, but they were forced to move their government south to Kaifeng under Mongol pressure in 1215. The dynasty was extinguished by the expanding Mongol empire in 1234.

Ch'in Dynasty (221–207 BC) Ch'in began as one of the Warring States (qv) in the far western Wei valley, the former seat of Chou power. Political and military reforms by Shang Yang the leading official, and highly developed cavalry made it into the most powerful of the states that arose when Chou rule disintegrated. By 318 BC it had crushed the five northern states and in 312 defeated the southern state of Ch'u. By 221 BC China was unified under its first Imperial system. This was carried out by Shih Huang-ti (qv), First Emperor, with the aid of his great official Li Ssu, a former disciple of Hsün-tzu. The main achievements of the new empire were the application of a centralised system of weights and measures and carriage and wagon axle lengths and standardisation of the style and system of writing. On the debit side Li Ssu organised a literary inquisition which has come to be known as "the Burning of the Books", (qv) and scholars who opposed this were said to have been executed. Shih Huang-ti organised the consolidation of border defences into what became known as the Great Wall (qv). On his death he was succeeded by the Second Emperor, a virtual puppet of the chief eunuch Chao Kao (qv). Poor leadership, lingering regional loyalties and oppressive demands for labour service precipitated a number of rebellions by peasants and soldiers. Ch'in collapsed in 207 BC and one rebel band, led by Liu Pang (qv), was powerful enough to take control as the Han dynasty. The name of Ch'in lives on, of course, in 'China'.

Chin P'ing Mei   see   *Golden Lotus*

China Aid Act   Act passed in April 1948 by the United States Congress after intense Republican criticism of proposals for financial aid to the ailing regime of Chiang K'ai-shek. Large sums of money were allocated for reconstruction projects with the hope of saving China for the Nationalists, and although a Chinese-American Joint Commission on Rural Reconstruction was set up to increase food supplies it was overtaken by the Communist victory and soon confined to Taiwan.

China Merchants' Steam Navigation Company   First Chinese company to utilise steam-ships. It was founded in 1872 with the approval of Tseng Kuo-fan and Li Hung-chang and with capital from both public and private sources, a *kuan-tu shang-pan* (qv) enterprise. Rapid expansion followed and after purchasing the American-owned Shanghai Steam Navigation Company in 1877 it had thirty ships and a virtual monopoly of trade. Under the management of Sheng Hsuan-huai (qv) it brought in large revenues but gradually became more and more dependent on official support.

China Proper   China within the Great Wall (qv) as distinct from areas such as Manchuria, Turkestan (Sinkiang) and Tibet which were drawn into the Chinese Empire at various periods of its history.

China's Destiny   Influential work by Chiang K'ai-shek in which he expounded his political philosophy. It was written in late 1942 and early 1943 by one of his personal secretaries but the ideas and final presentation were Chiang's own. He analysed Chinese history and anthropology and advocated national reconstruction based on traditional Confucian virtues. Foreigners were blamed for war-lordism, opium imports and the chaos of the birth of the Chinese Republic. The book sold half a million copies before being "withdrawn for revision" as it was an embarrassment when an alliance with the West against the CCP became a necessity for the Nationalists.

Chinaware   Porcelain (qv), the alternative name indicating the pre-eminence of Chinese porcelain. See also *Ching-te chen.*

Chin-ch'uan Rebels   Mountain aborigines who lived on the upper Yangtze, the River of Golden Sand, near the Szechwan-Yunnan border. In the middle of the 18th century they expanded and built thousands of stone forts in the rocky defiles of their homeland. Two campaigns were mounted by the imperial Ch'ing armies against them, one in 1747–9 and a second in 1771–6 which cost 70 million taels of silver.

Chinese Communist Party (CCP)   The Chinese Communist Party was formed on July 21, 1921, stimulated by the success of the October Revolution in Russia and the growth of a radical nationalism in China after the disappointment at the Versailles settlement (qv). At the first congress in 1921 which was held in the Po Wen Girls' School, Szechwan Road, in the French Concession of Shanghai, Ch'en Tu-hsiu was elected chairman *in absentia* by twelve delegates who represented fifty-seven members belonging to seven regional groups. Between 1921 and 1927 the CCP, in accordance with Comintern policy, co-operated with the KMT (qv) in the First Revolutionary Civil War, which was directed against the warlord-dominated Peking government. The collaboration was made possible by Sun Yat-sen's sympathy with the October Revolution and the USSR, and made necessary by the fact that the CCP was too small to act effectively alone. Communists took part in the Northern Expedition that Chiang K'ai-shek mounted against the Peking government when he took over the leadership of the KMT after the death of Sun Yat-sen, and spent much time organising trades unions in the towns and peasant associations in the countryside. The co-operation ended on April 12, 1927 with the Shanghai Coup (qv) when Chiang K'ai-shek attempted to wipe out Communists and their organisations. After a brief flirtation with the Wuhan government of Wang Ching-wei (qv) the CCP was forced out of the cities to its first rural base in Chingkangshan (qv) in 1928. Under the leadership of Mao Tse-tung and Chu Teh the base expanded into the Kiangsi Soviet (qv) which lasted from 1930 until 1934 when it was crushed by the Encirclement Campaigns (qv) of Chiang K'ai-shek. The Communist armies were forced to make a strategic withdrawal — the Long March (qv) — to the north-western stronghold of Yenan.

In the Yenan period from 1935 to 1949 the CCP consolidated the area under its control, developed policies of agrarian reform and in the period after the Japanese invasion of north China expanded both its population and area. A second period of co-operation with the Nationalists against the Japanese in this period was short-lived. The expansion of the party necessitated a Rectification Campaign (qv) in 1942 which reaffirmed party control over Yenan and the primacy of Mao Tse-tung's philosophy in the party. The Liberated Areas (qv) under CCP control grew in size during the resistance against the Japanese, and in the Civil War that followed the Japanese defeat the Communist armies gradually overwhelmed the Nationalists so that the CCP was able to take power in 1949.

Once in power the Party had to reorganise itself to administer such a sizeable nation, and a number of policy conflicts developed over the speed and nature of political and economic development (see *Great Leap Forward*). These culminated in the Cultural Revolution (qv) of 1966 which resulted in a full-scale shake-up of the party apparatus and a necessary restructuring afterwards. See also *Congresses of the CCP, Central Committee, Politburo*.

Chinese Eastern Railway Company formed in 1896 by the Russo-Chinese Bank (an organisation backed by French banks but staffed by Russian officials) to build a Trans-Manchurian railway which was finished in 1903. The company was also empowered to work mines in its territory. See also *South Manchurian Railway*.

Chinese Socialist Youth League Formed in France in February 1921 from Chinese students taking part in the work-study programme (qv) but changed its name to the French Section of the CCP in July 1922 acting on instructions from the CCP in China. Many senior CCP members including Teng Hsiao-p'ing, Chou En-lai, Ch'en Yi and Li Fu-ch'un (qqv) were involved in the French section.

Ch'ing Dynasty (1644–1911) The last dynasty of Imperial China. It was founded by the Manchus (qv) on their conquest of China after the collapse of the Ming house in 1644. In utilising the institutions of the Ming to control the empire, the Manchus first ruled through a Manchu-Chinese dyarchy but eventually became assimilated and practically indistinguishable from the Chinese. The most important periods of the dynasty were the reign of the enlightened K'ang-hsi (qv) in the 17th century who both enlisted the help of the hostile scholar class and proved willing to learn from the Jesuits, and the Ch'ien-lung (qv) emperor's domination of intellectual life in the 18th century. The dynasty entered a period of decline at the end of the 18th century and in the 19th century saw the coming of Europeans as traders, missionaries and officials. China came off worst in the Opium Wars (qv) against Britain after which it fell more and more under the domination of all the European powers. Attempts to remedy this were made during the Tung-chih Restoration (qv) by the Foreign Matters Movement (qv) and in the Hundred Days reform (qv) but to no avail. The dynasty and the empire were so weak by 1911 that both collapsed after the Wuchang Rising (qv) to be replaced by a Republic.

Ch'ing Ming Festival The festival of the tombs during which family graves are tidied and ceremonies held before them to commemorate both recently dead relatives and ancestors long passed away. It falls on April 4 or 5 and was the setting for the T'ien-an men Square riots (qv) of 1976 sparked off by memorials to Chou En-lai who had recently died.

Chinggis Khan (?1167–1227) Unifier of the Mongols and Great Khan of the Mongol Empire. Chinggis (also rendered Genghis, Jenghiz) Khan was born Temüjin, of aristocratic family, but was orphaned at an early age and brought up in humble circumstances. From being a vassal of a minor chieftain he mastered the art of tribal politics and was able to overthrow his lord and then subjugate one tribe after another. At a *khuriltai* or great meeting of Mongol tribes on the Kerulen River in 1206 the chieftains of all the Mongol tribes committed themselves to his leadership. Under Chinggis Khan the scattered clans and tribes were forged into the most powerful military state on earth. Between 1205 and 1209 he subjugated the Hsi Hsia kingdom (qv) in Central Asia. In 1211–1215 he destroyed the Chin (qv) capital and in securing the service of north Chinese administrators gained valuable knowledge which was later useful in the Mongol conquest of China. He took over the Kara Khitai (qv) empire in the west and then the Turkish empire of Khorezm in 1219–21 and then divided up this vast empire among his sons, as was the tribal custom, being succeeded as Great Khan by his third son Ögödei (qv).

Chingkangshan Mountain fastness to which Mao Tse-tung and Chu Teh retreated in 1927 after the massacre of Communists in Shanghai and other cities by Chiang K'ai-shek. The barren ridge on the Hunan-Kiangsi border, which later became a powerful symbol of the revolutionary spirit of the party and the Red Army, was the setting for early experiments in agrarian reform, the establishment of basic principles of guerrilla warfare and military conduct and the jumping-off point for the formation of the great Kiangsi Soviet (qv) in 1930.

Ching-t'ai, Ming Emperor (reigned 1450–7) Younger brother of the Cheng-t'ung emperor who was captured in battle in 1449. The Ching-t'ai emperor succeeded him and relied on able officials to defend the capital. When Cheng-t'ung was released he was imprisoned by the Ching-t'ai emperor but staged a coup d'etat in 1457 and took the throne again as the T'ien-shun emperor. The Ching-t'ai emperor died, possibly murdered, within a month.

Ching-te chen Source of practically all top quality porcelain in the Ming and Ch'ing dynasties. Ching-te chen, situated in a mountainous part of north-east Kiangsi which was rich in porcelain clays and pinewood fuel, produced pottery as early as the Han period and porcelain from the T'ang dynasty to the present day. One of the earliest industrial centres in China, the town was a conglomeration of small businessmen who owned kilns and workshops which were backed by commercial capital. Imperial depots in Ching-te chen supervised and shipped imperial porcelain to the capital. Imperial patronage and the expansion of markets in the Ming period stimulated Ching-te chen's economy. The production of vast quantities of imperial porcelain during the 16th century was matched by equally large orders for export ware from Europe in the early 17th and 18th centuries. In the late 18th and 19th centuries the town and its industry declined because of the lack of modernisation and produced nothing to compare with its earlier glories.

Ching-t'ien system   see   *Well-field System*

Ching-t'u Sect   see   *Pure Land Sect*

Ch'i-ying (died 1858)   High Manchu official and diplomat, imperial clansman and probably a descendant of Nurhachi. He held many official posts in the Imperial Household, the customs service and the Six Ministries from 1806 onwards and in 1838–42 was military governor resident in Mukden in the north-east where he was engaged in suppressing the opium trade and fortifying the coast against possible British raids. In 1842 he was put in charge of negotiating peace after the Opium War, after which he was appointed governor-general of Kiangsu, Kiangsi and Anhwei. His continued diplomatic activities made him one of the principal Chinese signatories to nearly all the unequal treaties of the second half of the 19th century and his consideration for the foreigner's point of view was a new departure for Chinese officials. Repeated difficulties in negotiating with the British culminated in Ch'i-ying's trial for deserting his post and his suicide by poison at the command of the emperor.

Chou, Duke of   Traditionally the brother of Wu, king of Chou (qv) whose trusty adviser he became. He is said to have consolidated the empire and built an effective administration which remained a model for generations. The *Ritual of Chou* (qv) is often ascribed to him although it dates from a much later period.

Chou Dynasty (12th Century–771 BC)   The Chou people who conquered Shang came from the Wei valley to the west of the great bend in the Yellow River. Before their conquest they had established a capital at Hao near modern Sian (Ch'ang-an) which was on the fringes of Shang civilisation and near to the sheep-herding peoples of the west and north. After they had overrun Shang, the Chou kings took the old Shang title of *wang*, king, and delegated authority to the rulers of various vassal states. Chou society was sharply divided between aristocratic warriors and the peasants and slaves that they ruled, and the hereditary lords seem to have had unlimited power in their domains. Imposing bronze sacrificial vessels were cast on the model of the Shang. Chou's supremacy came to an end in 771 BC when the barbarians and Chinese rebels sacked the capital at Hao and although a new capital was founded at Lo-yang, the regime that lasted till 256 BC never managed to control the rival states that were springing up. This period, known as the Eastern Chou, saw profound changes that laid the basis for much of what became the distinctive civilisation of China. Iron came into general use, agriculture was improved by irrigation and trade and towns developed. The break-up of Chou power was followed by two periods of division known as the Spring and Autumn (qv) and the Warring States (qv).

Chou En-lai (1898-1976)   Communist political leader, head of the State Council and Premier of the Chinese People's Republic. Chou En-lai was born into a family of officials in central Kiangsu province and studied at Nankai University and in Paris where he joined the Chinese Socialist Youth League. Returning to China in 1923 he became CCP secretary for Kwangtung and then head of the Political Section at the Whampoa Military Academy. He was a member of the Politburo of the CCP from 1927 onwards and played a prominent role in the negotiations over the Second United Front (qv) against the Japanese and in securing the release of Chiang K'ai-shek after the Sian incident (qv) of 1936. He became head of the State Council in 1949 and remained in power, virtually uncriticised, until his death. He was a pragmatist, able to reconcile the often conflicting demands of ideological correctness and economic and technological progress, and a cultivated man, more at home with foreign visitors than any other Communist leader. He is, however, best remembered for his statesmanlike qualities. He had a wide basis of support in China and the T'ien-an men Square riots (qv) of 1976 were sparked off by attempts to remove wreaths commemorating him.

Chou Yang (1908–   )   Literary critic and Communist official responsible for literary policy until 1966. Chou Yang was born in Hunan, studied in Japan in the 1920s and became a member of the Communist Party and the League of Left Wing Writers in the 1930s on his return to Shanghai. He was Director of Education in Yenan and headed the university there in the 1940s and after 1949 held many posts including the Deputy-directorship of the CCP Propaganda Department. He translated Tolstoy and other Russian writers into Chinese and wrote a number of works in which he propounded his belief that literature must be primarily a political weapon and that a post-May 4th Movement (qv) literary revolution was needed to make literature accessible to the masses. He fell from power in 1966 during the Cultural Revolution after accusations that he was a hypocrite and had opposed Mao Tse-tung's literary policies.

Chou-k'ou-tien   Site where the remains of palaeolithic Peking Man (qv) were discovered in 1927, in a cave about thirty miles south-west of Peking. In 1933 skeletons dating from a much later period were also discovered. Fragments of another fossil skull of Peking man and stone implements were unearthed near Chou-k'ou-tien in 1967.

Christianity   First introduced into China by Nestorians (qv) during the T'ang dynasty and flourished in the 8th century capital, but was wiped out in the religious persecutions of 841–845. Papal envoys introduced Catholicism (qv) into China during the Mongol dynasty and a number of converts were apparently made in the late 14th century. Jesuits (qv) first became established in China with Matteo Ricci's arrival in 1600 and remained attached to the imperial court till the early 18th century, though few converts were made. The most serious attempt to introduce Christianity was made by missionaries (qv) of all denominations who flocked to China in the second half of the 19th century after the commercial and military 'opening' of China had paved the way. Thousands of converts were made in spite of hostility to foreign religions such as that manifested in the Boxer rebellion (qv) but the influence of Christianity was probably greatest through education. The earliest modern schools in China were run by foreign missions and the great Yen-ching university was a Christian institution. Under the People's Republic, Christianity remains legal but is rarely practised, partly because it is unacceptable to the CCP, and partly because of the association of foreign religions with imperialism.

Ch'u   One of the Warring States (qv) that grew up after the decline of Chou power. It occupied the middle Yangtze region, was regarded as barbarian and became a power in its own right by the 8th century BC, rejecting the claims of Chou to kingship over it. Ch'u wiped out the south-eastern state of Yueh in 334 BC but succumbed itself to the Ch'in which eventually incorporated it into the first Chinese Empire that it founded in 221 BC. Ch'u regional feeling remained alive however, and there was an attempt to set up a Ch'u emperor in the period of rebellions between the collapse of the Ch'in and the establishment of the Han dynasty in 206 BC. Even as late as the 10th century AD the name and memory of Ch'u was invoked by a small dynasty in Hunan during the period of division at the end of the T'ang, known as the Five Dynasties.

Ch'ü Ch'iu-pai (1899–1935)   Communist writer who succeeded Ch'en Tu-hsiu as general secretary of the CCP in 1927 but was criticised for his part in the failures of that year and removed from office in 1928. He remained prominent as a writer, translator and organiser in the League of Left Wing Writers till his capture and execution in 1935. He was an essayist and critic and translated Gorky, Tolstoy and theoretical Marxist works into Chinese.

Chu Hsi (1130–1200)   Unifier and synthesiser of Neo-Confucian (qv) thought during the Sung dynasty. Chu Hsi was a statesman, historian and commentator on the classics who systematically brought together many of the elements of Confucian thought and forged them into a state orthodoxy. By 1313, it was his commentaries on the classics that were prescribed for the state examinations, and his work had raised the *Analects, Mencius, Great Learning* and *Doctrine of the Mean* to the status of canonical classics. The intellectual straitjacket that this produced hindered philosophical development in later years.

Chu Teh (1886–1976)   Communist military and political leader who was born into a well-to-do farming family in Szechwan and graduated from the Yunnan Military Academy. After taking part in the 1911 revolution he travelled to Germany and joined the CCP in Berlin in 1922. He led the Nanchang rising in 1927 after the split with the KMT, and with Mao Tse-tung organised the Red Army. Indeed so close were they that many people thought the Communist Army was led by one man — Chu Mao. Chu Teh took part in the Long March (qv) with Mao and was one of the key military leaders in the defeat of the KMT during the Civil War of 1946–49. After the victory of the CCP he was appointed Commander-in-Chief of the Chinese armed forces and also Chairman of the Standing Committee of the National People's Congress.

Chu Yuan-chang   see   *Hung-wu Emperor*

Ch'uan-chou (Chuanchow)   Known to Arab traders as Zaytun, the most important port in the Sung and Yuan dynasties. It was later rivalled by its near neighbours, Shanghai and Ningpo, and then superseded in the Ch'ing period by Canton.

Chuang-tzu   Taoist (qv) text probably written in the 3rd century BC and attributed to a man of the 4th century BC after whom it is named. Chuang-tzu, whose real name was Chuang Chou, lived from about 369 BC to about 286 BC. He was for a short time a minor official but seems to have preferred independence. His writings developed the ideas of Lao Tzu (qv) on life and death and freedom and extended them considerably. Like all Taoist texts his work is full of paradox and cryptic construction; it is also a literary masterpiece. The most famous passage in the book describes how Chuang-tzu dreams that he is a butterfly and wakes unsure whether it was he dreaming or whether he is a butterfly dreaming that he is Chuang-tzu.

Chu-ko Liang (died 234)   Premier and noted political strategist of the Shu Han kingdom (qv) during the Three Kingdoms and a popular hero in Chinese historical fiction.

Ch'ung-chen, Ming Emperor (reigned 1627–44)   Last Ming emperor and brother of the T'ien-ch'i emperor whom he succeeded at the age of seventeen. His reign was marked by increasing internal disorder and the growth of Manchu power in the north. He committed suicide as the rebel Li Tzu-ch'eng (qv) massed his troops outside Peking ready to take the capital.

Chungking Government   Administration of Chiang K'ai-shek in the remote mountain city of Chungking in Szechwan province. When the Japanese invaded China in 1937 Chiang was forced to move his government away from the front line. Japanese planes regularly bombed Chungking which was in communication with the Allies during the Second World War. Chiang is widely regarded as having spent too much of the Chungking period in cultivating his officer corps and too little in actively resisting the Japanese. The government moved back to its former seat at Nanking on the cessation of hostilities in 1945.

Civil Service   Administrative arm of the imperial government, distinguished by its open competitive examination system (qv). It included the various offices of the imperial household, the Six Ministries (qv) and local government in the provinces, prefectures and *hsien* (qqv) or districts.

Civil War   see   *Revolutionary Civil Wars*

Clan or Lineage Federation   All those who could trace descent from a common ancestor, bore the same surname and were not allowed to intermarry. The size of the lineage could be from a few hundred up to ten thousand and included kinship and family groups which were important because of their clan membership. Clans often united to provide defence or relief against poverty or misfortune and many had large land holdings. Richer clans frequently founded charitable trusts to provide food or shelter for widows or education for orphans. Some schools were managed by and for the clan. The clan was also able to act as a countervailing force against formal official power, to prevent injustice or oppression, but equally was often relied on to police its own members and maintain peace and order locally. The influence of the clan can be seen in the fact that many north Chinese villages bear clan surnames such as Wang Family Village (Wang-chia ts'un). The government of the People's Republic is the first not to rely on the clan to consolidate its own power or maintain order. No attack has been made on the clan but its authority and power have disintegrated because its economic and social functions have been taken over by other agencies. The lineage however remains important among overseas Chinese.

Classics   see   *Five Classics* and *Thirteen Classics*

Cohong   Guild organised by the Hong merchants to strengthen their monopoly of European trade in Canton. The Cohong (the Cantonese form of *kung-hang*, 'officially authorised firms') which adopted a code of thirteen articles to regulate prices, the volume of trade and business practices, consisted originally of sixteen Hong merchants. However new members could join on payment of one thousand taels and a reserve fund was set aside against possible insolvency. The Cohong was a private organisation that served as a useful buffer between the government and foreign traders. It collected customs duties for the government, paid fees for and was responsible for the conduct of foreign merchants and completely monopolised the Canton trade. In the face of opposition from Chinese and foreign merchants the guild, first formed in 1720, had to disband after a year. It was revived in 1760 but disbanded in 1771 under pressure from the East India Company, reformed in 1782 and then survived till the Treaty of Nanking (qv) in 1842, although by then it had lost much of its former power. Even when the Cohong as such did not exist, the Hong merchants (qv) monopolised the Canton trade.

Collected Statutes (*hui-tien*)   Compendia of administrative regulations compiled during the Ming and Ch'ing dynasties from existing statutes and used as a guide by officials throughout the empire. The *Collected Statutes of the Ming (Ta Ming Hui-tien)* was printed in

1511 and issued in an enlarged edition in 1587. The *Collected Statutes of the Ch'ing (Ta Ch'ing Hui-tien)* went through five editions in 1690, 1732, 1764, 1818 and 1899.

Collectivisation   Communist policy of gradually transforming the private ownership of land into collective ownership, with the aims of improving agricultural productivity and establishing a firm power base for the party in the rural areas. Experiments in collectivisation were begun on a small scale in both the Kiangsi Soviet and the Yenan border region in the 1930s and 1940s, but it was not until after 1949 that a large-scale transformation could be attempted. The CCP avoided the Soviet Union's mistakes of herding peasants into state farms and adopted a gradualist policy that went through the stages of Land Reform, Mutual Aid Teams, Agricultural and Higher Producers' Co-operatives to Communes (qqv).

Commanderies (*chün*)   Name given to large administrative units under the Ch'in dynasty governed by civilian and military officials and divided into *hsien* or counties. The system was brought in to replace the fiefs of the Chou period and continued under the Han. Commanderies were abolished by the Sui emperor Wen-ti who divided the country into prefectures (*chou*) and sub-prefectures or counties (*hsien*). The name commandery has also been used to translate *wei*, the organisation of Mongol and subsequently Manchu tribal units which were absorbed into the Ming army in order to control them.

Commercial Revolution   The spectacular growth of the Chinese economy during the 11th and 12th century. Population expanded rapidly and many significant technical advances were made including the development of explosives, medical science, mining technology and the introduction of early ripening Champa rice (qv). Private trade grew rapidly, breaking out of the government straitjacket. It spread beyond the small areas of towns designated for official markets and great cities began to develop which were primarily centres of trade and not just centres of political administration. Inter-regional trade flourished, specialist wholesalers and brokers developed, as did an inn system for housing travelling merchants. Trade guilds became important, foreign trade developed quickly, imports of raw materials and exports of handicraft manufacture increased. The most significant indicator of the economic growth was the increased use of currency which replaced barter in many business transactions. The minting of copper coinage increased and paper currency was also developed.

Commercial Tax (*shang shui*)   Local business tax levied by the Ming government on all merchandise transported by land and water, paid by the merchants and administered by provincial officials. It was a forerunner of the *likin* (qv) as it had the same minimal rates, broad coverage and duplicated collection.

Communes   People's communes were created during the first half of 1958 as part of the Great Leap Forward (qv), by amalgamating existing Agricultural Producers' Co-operatives. They were officially endorsed by the Party Central Committee on August 29, 1958 and by November there were 26,000 communes embracing 98% of the farming population. An average commune consisted of about thirty co-operatives, 5,000 households, say 25,000 people with nearly all land owned publicly. Communes are the basic rural administrative organ, controlling agricultural and industrial resources, collecting taxes, running schools, banks, nurseries, old people's homes, clinics and other public services. They are made up of production brigades and production teams (qqv) and in the early 1960s it was decided that the commune was too large to take all local decisions, and in a process of decentralisation, decision-making powers were devolved to the smaller units (see also *Collectivisation*). Urban commune experiments were also tried, notably the Red Flag Commune based on the Chengchow Spinning and Weaving Machinery Factory which stressed collective living and public mess-halls. These however were less successful and many were abandoned.

Communist Party   see   *Chinese Communist Party*

Communist Youth League   Junior branch of the CCP, catering for young people between the ages of about fourteen and twenty-five. Younger children join the Young Pioneers. The league was formed in 1957 from the existing New Democratic Youth league and was designed to educate young people in Communist ideology and prepare them for future membership and leadership of the Communist Party. It was effectively replaced in 1966 by the Red Guard (qv) organisations that mobilised youth during the Cultural Revolution.

Commutation of Taxes   see   *Corvée*

Compass, Invention of   The phenomenon of magnetic polarity was recognised in China as early as the 3rd century AD. By 1119 the maritime compass was being used on the ships trading between China and south-east Asia, several decades before it was introduced into Europe by the Arabs. The compass was one of the factors that made possible the great voyages of Cheng Ho (qv) in the early 15th century.

Compradores Merchants who acted as intermediaries between foreign businesses and Chinese firms. From the Portuguese *compradore* — buyer. See also *Hong Merchants*.

Comprehensive Mirror for Aid in Government (*Tzu-chih t'ung-chien*) A full chronicle of Chinese history from 404 BC up to the establishment of the Sung dynasty in 960, written by the greatest historian of the Sung period, Ssu-ma Kuang (qv). In the breadth of its sources and objectivity it set new standards for Chinese historical scholarship and was continued by scholars in later dynasties.

Concessions Specific areas reserved for foreign residences in the treaty ports (qv) in which local administration, police, sanitation, roads, building regulations etc. were in foreign hands and financed out of taxes levied by the foreign authorities. In Tientsin, Hankow and Canton, large areas were appropriated or purchased by the Chinese government and leased in perpetuity to a particular power, Britain, France, Germany, Japan, Russia, Belgium, Italy or Austria-Hungary. In Shanghai the foreigners purchased land directly with the title deeds guaranteed by the Chinese government. No Chinese were legally permitted to own land in the concessions though some did through foreign agents.

Confucianism Official ideology of the traditional Chinese state, deriving from the teachings of Confucius and his later interpreters, notably Mencius and the Neo-Confucians (qqv). It was expressed in institutions such as schools, shrines and temples to Confucius which were supported by the local gentry and in ethical principles which rulers were supposed to follow. See also *Four Books, Five Classics, Five Relationships*.

Confucius (?551 BC–?479 BC) The greatest and most highly revered of all traditional Chinese philosophers. Confucius (K'ung-fu-tzu or K'ung-tzu, Master K'ung) was a native of the state of Lu (modern Shantung) in the period known as Spring and Autumn. An educated man from the lower aristocracy, he was dissatisfied with the minor official posts he held and wandered from state to state in search of a position suitable for his talents, before returning to Lu to die. He preached that government should be based on ethics, rather than just practical politics, and harked back to the early days of the Chou period and the rule of King Wen and the Duke of Chou as a golden age. His ideal was a gentleman (*chün-tzu*) who possessed the five cardinal virtues: he should be upright, righteous, conscientious, altruistic and humane, and also be cultured with a proper understanding of etiquette. Confucius believed that humanity or goodness (*jen*) should be the supreme principle of human conduct. The *Analects* (qv) attributed to him were probably sayings collected and recorded out of their original context by his disciples, and his ideas stimulated the writing of *Great Learning* and the *Doctrine of the Mean*.

Congresses of the Chinese Communist Party In theory, the supreme policy-making body of the party, although in practice, long gaps between congresses have meant that they sometimes merely ratified existing policies.

First Congress: 12 members attending the founding congress which was probably held on July 1–5, 1921 in the Po Wen Girls' School in Szechwan Road, Shanghai. Confused ideological debate was mainly between supporters of open 'legal Marxism' and those unwilling to co-operate with any existing parties. The congress took a hostile attitude to the KMT. Ch'en Tu-hsiu was elected Secretary-General.

Second Congress: (Shanghai, July 1922) Delegates ratified a manifesto calling for a democratic united front in the revolutionary movement, in line with Comintern policy, but insisted on the necessity of maintaining the independence of the proletariat and its party. The question of collaboration with the KMT was raised.

Third Congress: (Canton, June 1923) Delegates considered a proposal by Maring (qv) made in August 1922 that the CCP become part of the KMT. The proposal was accepted in spite of opposition from a group led by Chang Kuo-t'ao who wished to retain the party's independence. Mao Tse-tung and Ch'ü Ch'iu-pai who were elected to the Central Committee were later described as supporters of the co-operation.

Fourth Congress: (Shanghai, January 11–12, 1925) Twenty delegates representing 980 members and 2,635 members of the Youth Corps endorsed the alliance with the KMT and recognised the special importance of peasants in the Chinese revolution. Party authority and the training of activists were tightened up.

Fifth Congress: (Wuhan, April 27, 1927) The party had a theoretical membership of 57,967 but this was almost meaningless after Chiang K'ai-shek's Shanghai Coup (qv). 80 delegates attended and M. N. Roy (qv) was the representative of the Comintern. Emphasis was still on alliance rather than revolution. Mao is said to have opposed this and retired from the conference.

Sixth Congress: (Moscow, July–September, 1928) Held in Moscow for security reasons, to coincide with the Sixth Congress of the Communist International, and illustrates the CCP dependence on Moscow at this time. There were 84 delegates representing a theoretical membership of 40,000; Bukharin and Pavel Mif (qv) also attended. The congress analysed the reasons for the failure of the alliance and stressed peasant struggles and guerrilla warfare as part of the mass movement. Mao Tse-tung was elected to the Central Committee and Li Li-san (qv) became head of the Politburo.

Seventh Congress: (Yenan, April 23–June 11, 1945) Party membership was 1,211,128 and the congress was attended by 544 delegates and 208 other members. Mao's *On Coalition Government* was adopted as the party programme and the CCP's independence was firmly established. Mao was elected Chairman of the Central Committee and this confirmed him as the sole leader of the party. The Seventh Congress was effectively the first congress of the present CCP.

Eighth Congress: (Peking, September, 1956) The first Congress since liberation sought to legitimise the consolidation of the People's Republic. Mao's role was played down in line with criticisms of the 'cult of the personality' in the Soviet Union, Mao Tse-tung Thought was written out of the Party Constitution and cautious, conservative policies were adopted, that Mao was later to reverse in the Great Leap Forward. The struggle between the Two Lines (qv) can be discerned in the differing attitudes of the cautious Liu Shao-ch'i and Mao's radical policies supported by Teng Hsiao-p'ing. A second session of the congress was held in May 1958 to ratify the policies of the Great Leap.

Ninth Congress: (Peking, April 1969) Planned for the early 1960s but postponed till 1969 by which time Liu Shao-ch'i had been removed from office. It was an attempt to rebuild and stabilise the post-Cultural Revolution CCP, had a large proportion of military delegates, and elected a compromise radical Central Committee. The congress was notable for the pride of place given to Mao Tse-tung Thought and for its attacks on the 'New Tsars' of the Soviet Union.

Tenth Congress: (Peking, August 1973) Another congress, like the Ninth, called to consolidate the CCP, this time after the Lin Piao affair. The leadership that emerged was a collective one with political leaders as different as Wang Hung-wen and Chou En-lai in the Central Committee.

Constitution of the People's Republic of China   The first constitution was drafted by a committee in January 1953 and approved by the first National People's Congress in September 1954. It had many similarities to the 1936 constitution of the Soviet Union and included

104 clauses on ownership, rights and duties of citizens, policy towards different classes, the structure of central and local government and the judicial system. The CCP was mentioned only in the preamble. The draft of a new constitution was circulated in 1969–70 but not approved till 1975 when the fourth National People's Congress met. The 1975 constitution has only 30 articles but the leading role of the CCP and Marxism-Leninism-Mao Tse-tung Thought is written in, and there is no provision for a president or chairman as head of state.

Constitutional Movement (1905–11)   Impressed by the discovery that nearly all Western Powers had constitutional governments, Chinese reformers, notably Liang Ch'i-ch'ao, advocated a constitutional monarchy to save China and the empire. The movement had some support from the Empress Dowager Tz'u-hsi who hoped it might put off revolution. She approved fact-finding missions abroad which returned favouring the Japanese constitution rather than European models. In September 1906 it was announced that constitutional government would be eventually introduced. Dozens of Constitution Protection clubs sprang up in a tide of public opinion that forced the court to issue an Outline Constitution in August 1908. The Outline provided for a purely consultative Constitutional Assembly with no decision making powers and stipulated a nine-year preparation period before the reforms were to be enacted. After Tz'u-hsi's death on November 15, 1908, provincial assemblies were established by Prince Chün, acting as regent for three-year-old emperor P'u-i, but he ignored petitions from them to convene a parliament. The movement was superseded by the overthrow of the Ch'ing in the Republican revolution of 1911.

Copper Coinage   Appeared as early as the late Chou, but was first standardised in the Ch'in and Han empires and made only by government-controlled mints. Single denominations were used, cast round or square with a central hole for threading on a string or leather thong, as coins of multiple denomination proved unpopular. Standard exchange rates were fixed between copper coins and ingots of gold or silver used for major transactions. Coins circulated widely in the Han empire and later under the T'ang government when increased production of copper cash could not keep up with the demand. The government's monopoly of copper mining and restrictions on the private use of copper for casting vessels were enforced to maximise production. Demand was eventually met by the issue of paper money in the 9th century.

Corvée   Statutory forced labour services required by the state from its subjects. A peasant farmer in Ch'in or Han times might spend a month each year working on local roads and canals or palaces and imperial tombs and some time on military duties. Han corvée was less burdensome than that of the Ch'in. Corvée was the main tax after land tax under the early T'ang and amounted to twenty days' labour per annum for the central government and extra for the local authorities. It was sometimes commuted into textile or money payments. The corvée and its associated militia system declined in the first half of the 8th century when tax-grain transport up the Grand Canal was transferred to hired men and the militia replaced by professional soldiers. The government did not rely so heavily on corvée after this, substituting paid workers and mercenaries which required new taxes and forms of income. Wang An-shih (qv) in the 11th century commuted the remaining corvée services which fell on the poor into taxes on the rich, but forced labour was reintroduced by the Mongol dynasty. The Ming continued to impose a corvée tax, but in the Single-Whip (qv) reforms of the 16th century most corvée labour service was commuted to a cash payment. The Ch'ing government officially abolished corvée in the 17th century but some forced labour continued even after this.

Creation Society   One of a large number of literary societies that mushroomed in the cultural ferment that followed the May 4th movement (qv) in 1919. It was founded in 1921 by Chinese students in Japan but was later based mainly in Shanghai. Members of the society, notably Kuo Mo-jo and Yu Ta-fu had common interests in foreign literature, modernism and romanticism and concentrated on the individual and social conditions. After committing itself to social progress and revolution the society was banned in 1929.

Creations of Nature and Man (*T'ien-kung k'ai-wu*)   Illustrated handbook of agricultural and industrial technology written by Sung Ying-hsing and printed in 1637, near the end of the Ming dynasty. It describes the methods, raw materials and tools used to produce rice, silk, salt, pottery and porcelain, metals, coal, paper, weapons and many other products.

Cultural Revolution   Political upheaval that began officially in July 1966. The full Chinese name is the Great Revolution in Proletarian Culture and it was in the cultural field that battle was first joined. A play published in 1961 by Wu Han (qv) the historian and deputy mayor of Peking entitled *Hai Jui Dismissed* (qv) and ostensibly about an honest mid-16th-century official dismissed by an obstinate Ming emperor, was seen as an indirect attack on Mao's dismissal of P'eng

Teh-huai (qv) in 1959. This criticism was added to by Teng T'o and Liao Mo-sha, journalists and high party officials who made satirical attacks on the Great Leap (qv) and other policies in the 'Evening Chats at Yenshan' column in the *Peking Evening News* and in the journal *Frontline*. Unable to retaliate satisfactorily in Peking, Mao went to Shanghai, a stronghold of his wife Chiang Ch'ing, in the summer of 1965. On November 10 the first article attacking *Hai Jui Dismissed* was written by Yao Wen-yuan (qv), editor of *Liberation Army Daily* in Shanghai.

Although Wu Han rapidly confessed the error of his ways, the struggle did not stop there. On March 26, 1966 P'eng Chen, the mayor of Peking, was dismissed. Far deeper policy disagreements were involved: the conflict between the demands of ideology and specialist expertise, with Mao the head of the former and Liu Shao-ch'i (qv) of the latter; these later became known as the Two Lines (qv). Mao returned to Peking which had now been made secure by the army and Lin Piao (qv) on July 18, 1966. The 11th plenum (full meeting) of the Central Committee met on August 1, adopted Lin as first Vice-chairman, decided to attack "those in authority within the party who take the capitalist road", and announced the creation of the Red Guards (qv) to attack old bourgeois and bureaucratic habits in the party.

Liu Shao-ch'i was attacked as a revisionist, although not stripped of the state chairmanship till October 1968, and many other important leaders such as Teng Hsiao-p'ing, Chu Teh and Chou Yang were attacked. From summer 1966 onwards, power seizures, struggles between rival groups of Red Guards and between radical Maoists and their opponents plunged the cities into administrative chaos. In January 1967, after radicals had taken over in Shanghai, Mao ordered in the army to restore order. Lin Piao and the People's Liberation Army were able to fill the power vacuum that had been created and by January 1968 with army aid the radicals had won control of about a third of the country. Clashes continued, sometimes violent, till the end of 1968 when preparations for the Ninth Party Congress to rebuild the CCP were underway.

The Cultural Revolution has been analysed in many ways: as a simple power-struggle between party factions led by Mao and Liu Shao-ch'i; as an attack on bureaucracy by Mao; as an attempt to revitalise the party with a new revolutionary spirit; as a controlled experiment in mass democracy that got out of hand; as an attempt to change human nature and socialist society. It contained all these elements, though in what proportions it is difficult to say. Its immediate results were chaos in the cities and economic disruption. In the long term, the power struggle was still not resolved. See also *Gang of Four*.

Cultural Revolution Group   Group of seventeen members around Mao that directed the Cultural Revolution. It was a loose coalition within the Central Committee of the CCP, chaired by Ch'en Po-ta with Chiang Ch'ing as first Vice-chairman.

Customs Duty . see   *Imperial Maritime Customs*

D

Dairen   see   *Port Arthur*

Dalai Lama   Leader of the Yellow sect of Lama Buddhism. The title of Dalai (Ocean or All-Embracing) Lama was bestowed on the third reincarnation of the Tibetan Lama Tsong-kha-pa in 1380 by the Mongol Prince Altan Khan (qv). Tsong-kha-pa was considered retroactively to have been the first Dalai Lama. The fourth reincarnation happened to be the grandson of Altan Khan. The Dalai Lama gradually achieved temporal power in Tibet, with the help of Mongol and Manchu support, as well as religious authority over the Yellow sect. The fifth Dalai Lama (1617–82) established diplomatic relations with the Ch'ing government in 1652 and built the great Potala palace in Lhasa the capital of Tibet. The current reincarnation of the Dalai Lama fled Tibet in 1959 after the CCP took control following the rebellion.

Damansky Island   see   *Chen-pao Island*

Decrees   see   *Edicts*

Democratic League   Liberal democratic party opposed to the authoritarianism of the Nationalists and Chiang K'ai-shek in the 1940s. It was supported by many intellectuals but had no military backing and was proscribed in 1945 and its members driven into exile. It was driven into a coalition with the CCP and today continues to exist in Peking, although its members have little real power.

Dixie Mission   United States Army Observer Group which was based in Yenan, the Communist capital, in 1944. The eighteen-man mission, under the command of Colonel David D. Barrett, a Chinese language officer and former military attaché in Peking, arrived in Yenan on July 22 to learn about the military potential of the Communists and their possible contribution to the war effort against the Japanese. The Americans were impressed by the guerrilla fighting they saw and wanted to incorporate the CCP forces into the war against Japan. Chiang K'ai-shek's opposition prevented this and the mission was withdrawn. Subsequent opposition to this kind of co-operation with the CCP cost Col. Barrett his promotion prospects.

Doctrine of the Mean (*Chung Yung*)   One of the Four Books (qv) of Confucianism, an essay emphasising moderation and sincerity and dealing with the character and duties of a true gentleman, social obligations and the ideal institutions of the Sage Kings.

Dorgon (1612–1650) or Dorgan   Fourteenth son of Nurhachi (qv) and Manchu conqueror of north China. Dorgon refused to accept the title of emperor on the death of Abahai (qv) in 1643 but became regent, in conjunction with Jirgalang, a nephew of Nurhachi, to Abahai's six-year-old son Fu-lin who became Shun-chih emperor on October 30, 1644. In April 1644 Dorgon had accepted the invitation of Wu San-kuei to join him in suppressing the rebels led by Li Tzu-ch'eng after the suicide of the last Ming emperor. The Manchu armies poured through the gates of Shanhaikuan; Dorgon buried the Ming emperor with honours and declared the Manchus to be the saviours of China. On the accession of Shun-chih as the first Ch'ing emperor Dorgon became known as Uncle Prince Regent. In late 1644 he reduced Jirgalang to assistant-regent and dismissed him in 1647. Dorgon's titles became more and more extravagant: Imperial Uncle Prince Regent in 1645 and Imperial Father Prince Regent by 1649. He became the most powerful man in the country and even chose the empress who was to marry Shun-chih. He directed the Ch'ing armies in the conquest of China and earned the hatred of Chinese by enforcing the wearing of the pigtail and by enclosing Chinese farms to be given to Manchu princes, nobles and bannermen. After his death which occurred while he was hunting near Karakorum in 1650, the fourteen-year-old Shun-chih began to govern personally. Jirgalang returned to power, and a campaign was begun to vilify Dorgon. It was not till the Ch'ien-lung reign that his positive contributions were recognised again.

Double Tax   The agricultural taxes of Summer Tax and Autumn Grain. In 780 Yang Yen (727–781) a T'ang statesman consolidated existing land, personal and household taxes into the Double Tax levied in the sixth and eleventh months and calculated according to land areas farmed rather than on the number of peasants farming the land. Land areas were to remain the basic units of agricultural taxation throughout the rest of Chinese history and tax collection was thus simplified. The reform also altered the pattern of land ownership as the owners of large estates were unwilling to pay the heavy taxes levied on them. Aristocratic estates were broken up and replaced by a system of landlordism with the tenants paying taxes directly. The Ming system of agricultural taxation followed a similar pattern. The Summer tax was collected in the eighth month on supplementary crops, especially winter wheat grown during the winter and harvested in early summer. The Autumn Grain was collected in the second month as a tax on summer-grown produce harvested in the autumn, especially the south and central China rice crop. It was far larger than the Summer Tax.

Double Tenth The anniversary of the Wuchang Rising (qv) which took place on October (the 10th month) 10 1911.

Dowager Empress see *Tz'u-hsi*

Downward Transfer see *Hsia-fang*

Dragon Boat Festival (*tuan-wu*) Festival of south Chinese origin held at the summer solstice. Races of decorated Dragon boats symbolised the struggle of heavenly dragons who made the rain needed for the newly transplanted rice. As well as being a celebration the festival, like the New Year, was a time for settling debts.

Dragon Bones see *Oracle Bones*

Dream of the Red Chamber Best known of the classic Chinese novels. Its title in Chinese is *Hung-lou meng* (Dream of the Red Chamber) but it has also been translated as *The Story of the Stone*. It was written around 1760 by Ts'ao Hsüeh-ch'in (qv) (Cao Xueqin in the Pinyin form) whose family had held important official posts under the Ch'ing emperors but had later declined in fortune. On one level the novel is the story of the frustrated love between two cousins, Pao Yu and Tai Yu, but it is also a semi-autobiographical account of the complex relationships in and the gradual collapse of the Ts'ao family (the Chias in the novel) and a powerful description of the whole Chinese family system.

Dutch Traders The Dutch East India Company (*Vereenigde Oost-Indische Compagnie*) was formed in 1602 and gradually took over the East and South-East Ocean trade from the Portuguese (qv), initially by capturing Portuguese ships. The Dutch established themselves on Taiwan in 1624 after failing to take Macao (qv) from the Portuguese. They soon became the most important European nation trading with China (and also with Japan) and remained so until Britain and other European powers gained a foothold in the Canton trade during the 18th century. Their hold on Taiwan came to a sudden end in 1661 when they were driven out by Koxinga (qv). After assisting the Ch'ing government to seize Amoy and Quemoy from the rebels the Dutch were given permission to trade in Kwangtung and Fukien where they were soon in competition with the English and French East India Companies.

Dyarchy   Descriptive term for the Ch'ing government system after 1644 when China was administered jointly at the higher levels by roughly equal numbers of Chinese and Manchus. For example three members of the Grand Secretariat (qv) were Chinese and three Manchus. The system was intended to integrate the two ethnic groups without allowing any one official to establish an entrenched position.

Dynastic Cycle   Traditional Chinese interpretation of Imperial history as a series of repetitive dynastic cycles. According to this interpretation, in each dynasty the empire rose to a peak of glory, slowly declined then collapsed when it lost the Mandate of Heaven (qv) and was replaced by a new dynasty which had the mandate and which then followed the same cycle. The underlying assumption of this view of history denies any progress and on its own such a cyclical interpretation is unsatisfactory in explaining economic, social and technological developments.

Dynastic Histories or Standard Histories   Histories of the preceding dynasty written by official historians of its successor. The first of these, the *Records of the Grand Historian* (qv) covered the period up to the Han dynasty and was taken as a model by later compilers. The histories vary but all contain the basic annals of the court, tables, biographies and monographs on particular topics. In the 18th and 19th centuries there were twenty-four Standard Histories. A new History of the Yuan Dynasty accepted in 1921 brought the number up to twenty-five. The Twenty-sixth, the *Draft History of the Ch'ing Dynasty* has not yet been officially accepted as standard. The quality of the histories varies greatly but taken together they provide remarkably accurage coverage of two thousand years of Chinese history, seen however from the official point of view. On the debit side much information is omitted; there is, for example, very little information on technology or social conditions as these were of no concern to the compiling officials.

Dzungars   Western Mongol tribe, led by Galdan Khan, which controlled large areas of Turkestan round Lake Balkash and the Ili river in the 17th century. The power of the Dzungars was destroyed in a battle fought south of Urga when Galdan Khan was marching towards Peking. Emperor K'ang-hsi fielded 80,000 troops with artillery support and wiped out Galdan's army. Turkestan, present-day Sinkiang, was also known as Dzungaria after the Dzungars.

E

Early Ripening Champa Rice   Fast-maturing strain of rice introduced into south China from Champa in South Vietnam in the 11th century. As a result, rice yields in south China may well have doubled between the 11th and 12th centuries. A sharp population rise was made possible and the position of the Yangtze region as China's key economic area was confirmed. The rice required only about a hundred days to ripen after transplantation and later strains only sixty days, and it was also drought-resistant. Double cropping could be extended and triple cropping was possible in some areas.

East India Companies   European merchant companies formed to trade with India and lands further east. The East India Company was formed in England in 1602 by a charter granted by Queen Elizabeth I and a new charter from James I in 1609 gave it the royal authority to trade with China. The Dutch East India Company was founded in 1604 with authority from the Dutch government to maintain troops, colonise overseas territories, declare war and conclude peace with countries in the East (see also *Dutch Traders*). A French *Compagnie de la Chine* was also formed in 1604 but went through several incarnations, ending up as the *Compagnie des Indes* in 1719. These companies were restricted to Canton and monopolised the trade with Europe.

Eastern Forest Party   see   *Tung-lin Party*

Economism   The offer of material incentives to workers and peasants by local authorities trying to counter Maoist policies during the Cultural Revolution. Economism was originally an evil against which Lenin warned in *What is to be Done*, the danger of separating the struggle for economic betterment from political agitation. The Shanghai Municipal Committee was accused by supporters of the Cultural Revolution who replaced them after the January Storm (qv) of having tried to buy the support of workers' organisations in December 1966 by giving extra bonus payments and agreeing to demands for higher wages.

Edicts   or **Decrees**   Orders issued by or on behalf of the emperor indicating the action to be taken on a particular issue or in some cases formally approving actions already carried out. Edicts which were often issued in response to a memorial (qv) submitted to the emperor were usually the only policy decisions made and the promulgation and authentication of them was in the hands of a select group of senior officials close to the emperor.

Educated Youth Going to the Countryside   see   *Hsia-fang*

Education Through Labour (*lao-chiao*)   Standard three-year terms of imprisonment under the People's Republic for those who have committed political errors rather than crimes; criminals undergo Reform Through Labour (qv). Unlike criminals those undergoing Education Through Labour retain their civic rights during their sentences.

Eight Immortals (*pa-hsien*)   Group of legendary personages who became immortal through the practice of Taoist ideas. They appear in folklore in the Yuan dynasty and were popularised in the drama of that period.

Eight Kings, Revolt of the   Civil war that tore apart the short-lived Chin dynasty in 290 AD during the Three Kingdoms period (qv).

Eight Trigrams Rebellion (1813)   The Eight Trigrams Sect (*Pa-kua chiao*) also known as the Heavenly Reason Sect (*T'ien-li chiao*) was a secret society with a large following in north China, and a branch of the White Lotus Society (qv). Its leaders practised astrology and divination and in 1812 one of them, Li Wen-ch'eng, announced that he was a 'True Lord of the Ming' and designated 1813 as the year of action. A plot to attack the Imperial Palace during the Chia-ch'ing emperor's absence on a hunting-trip was uncovered, the rebels were goaded into action prematurely and more than twenty thousand members of the sect were killed during the subsequent suppression.

Eighth Route Army   Name given to the 30,000-strong Red Army (qv) of the Communists in 1937 during the Second United Front (qv) period. The Communists were waging guerrilla war behind the Japanese lines in collaboration with the armies of Chiang K'ai-shek who were responsible for positional warfare. It was later renamed the Eighteenth Route Army, although it is better known as the Eighth Route Army, and was commanded by Chu Teh and P'eng Teh-huai. It was then incorporated into the People's Liberation Army (qv) in 1946.

Elder Brother Society (*Ko-lao Hui*)   Ancient secret society that rose to prominence after the collapse of the Taiping Rebellion and was particularly influential in the army. It was fiercely anti-Manchu during the Ch'ing dynasty, and participated in the 1911 revolution. In the 1920s and 1930s its members often fought alongside the Communists, some society members being also Red Army commanders. In 1936 Mao made an open appeal to the Elder Brother Society to form an alliance with the CCP in the resistance to Japan. It later declined in importance. See also *Secret Societies*.

Elgin, Lord (James Bruce, 1811–63) Succeeded his father as 8th Earl in 1841. A former governor-general of Canada, sent by Palmerston as leader of an expedition to China in 1857. He was instructed to obtain compensation for British losses in the recent fighting (see *Arrow War*), diplomatic representation in Peking and principally to extend British trade. Elgin arrived with his troops in Hong Kong in September 1857 after a diversion to take part in the suppression of the Indian Mutiny. When the governor-general of Kwangtung, Yeh Ming-ch'en refused direct negotiation and the immediate payment of an indemnity, the combined Anglo-French forces under Elgin and the French diplomat Baron Gros, stormed Canton on December 28, captured Yeh, and installed an Allied Commission under Harry Parkes (qv) which ran the city until 1860. Elgin was involved in the negotiations that led to the Treaty of Tientsin (qv) and the Shanghai Tariff Conference (qv). In 1860 he reluctantly undertook his second mission to China, during which he dictated the Treaty of Peking and ordered the burning of the Summer Palace. In 1862 he became the second Viceroy of India but died after only a year in office.

Elliot, Captain Charles Son of the governor of Madras and master attendant in charge of British ships in the Bogue (qv) in 1833. He became Chief Superintendent of Trade in 1836 and fought for direct and equal communication with the Canton authorities in which he was partially successful. In 1839 it was Elliot who authorised British traders to surrender their opium to him when traders and other foreigners were detained in the factory compounds by Lin Tse-hsü (qv), hoping to relieve the stagnant trade and hold the Chinese responsible for the cost. He then delivered the chests of opium to Lin who had them destroyed. On being freed, Elliot and the whole British community left for Macao on May 24, 1839. In June 1840 he became second-in-command of the British Expeditionary Force at the beginning of what became known as the Opium War (qv). His cousin, Rear-Admiral George Elliot, commanded the force. Charles Elliot later replaced his cousin as leader of the expedition on the latter's illness. He achieved the cession of Hong Kong to Britain but was reprimanded by Palmerston for disobeying his instructions and not getting better terms and was dismissed in 1841.

Elliot, Admiral George Commander of the British Expeditionary Force that began the Opium War in June 1840, and cousin of Captain Charles Elliot (qv) who replaced him on November 29, 1840.

Embryonic Capitalism see *Capitalism, Sprouts of*

Emperor The authority of Chinese emperors derived from historical precedents, Confucian philosophy and practical politics. Their political position was made legitimate by the formula that the Mandate of Heaven (qv) had been conferred on them, which also gave them spiritual authority. The power of the emperor was his by virtue of his position at the head of an administrative structure and at times it was limited by this body of officialdom. Many major policy decisions were taken after a memorial (qv) had been submitted to the emperor. The emperor would consider the question possibly with the aid of senior advisers and then issue a decree or edict (qv) which had the force of law. A strong emperor could dominate the political scene by choosing his senior ministers carefully, while a weak one could be manipulated by his advisers or by intriguing factions in the court.

Empress Dowager see *Tz'u-hsi*

Encirclement Campaigns or Bandit Extermination Campaigns Series of five military exercises mounted by Chiang K'ai-shek and the Nationalist armies in an attempt to wipe out the Kiangsi Soviet (qv) base of the Communists. In the first campaign, which began in October 1930, 100,000 Nationalist troops were defeated and forced to retreat by 40,000 regular Communist troops, under the command of Chu Teh (qv). The second campaign in May 1931 had a similar result, the Communists losing 4,000 men to nearly 200,000 Nationalist losses. Chiang K'ai-shek took personal command of the third campaign in July 1931 from a headquarters at Nanchang, but the Nationalist armies again retreated northwards, partly because of defeats by the Communists and partly because of the Japanese occupation of Manchuria. The fourth attack on the Red Bases in June 1932 pushed the Communist forces back from Hankow and the Yangtze valley, but was otherwise no more successful than the first three. The fifth and decisive campaign was launched in April 1933. With far better preparation, almost 800,000 men and supporting air

E

power, the Nationalists squeezed the soviet bases till the Communists were forced to withdraw in October 1934. This was the start of the Long March (qv) to the Yenan base in the north. See also *Braun, Otto.*

Encyclopaedias The tendency towards encyclopaedic compilation which was to typify one branch of Chinese scholarship was already marked by the beginning of the T'ang dynasty, when organised collections of excerpts began to appear. The *Comprehensive Compendium* (*T'ung-tien*) appeared in 801 and the *Assembled Essentials on the T'ang* (*T'ang hui yao*) which included much material on T'ang government and economics was completed in 961. Better known than these is the *Encyclopaedia of the Yung-lo Period* (*Yung-lo Ta-tien*) of the Ming dynasty. This was a compilation of all the principal works on history, government, ethics, geography, etc. inherited from earlier periods. It was compiled in 1407 by more than 2,000 scholars in 11,095 volumes — 22,000 chapters — and was too large to print. Two more manuscript copies were made, but only about 700 volumes survive. Many specialist compilations were also produced such as the *Creations of Nature and Man* (qv) by Sung Ying-hsing and the great materia medica compiled by Li Shih-chen (qv). There were also encyclopaedias of institutions which provided guides to administrative practices of the past, others which served as primers or textbooks for the imperial examinations, and encyclopaedias for a popular audience which gave information on more practical matters such as trade routes, popular superstitions and outlines of the bureaucratic structure. See also *Gazetteers.*

Ennin Japanese Buddhist pilgrim who travelled widely in T'ang China and recorded graphic and detailed observations in his diary. He was in China between 838 and 847 as an official member of a Japanese embassy and his diary records how impressed he was by the prosperous, well-ordered society with meticulous bureaucracy and strong control that he found. His visit coincided with attempts to suppress Buddhism in China (842–5) and his diary was an important stimulus to the development of Buddhism in Japan.

Equal Field System (*chün-t'ien*) System in which all adult ablebodied farmers were supposed to be allocated agricultural land. It was first introduced by emperor Hsiao-wen of the Northern Wei. The system was elaborated under the Sui and T'ang dynasties and every adult male between 21 and 59 was supposed to have about fourteen acres of land. However this was applied mainly to newly-cultivated land and not to the large holdings of the great families and there is no evidence that peasants had landlords' land allotted to them. The measures were an attempt to keep some land out of the hands of the private estates and to establish units for tax payment. The system broke down in the middle of the T'ang period as taxation on individual peasants was so high. See also *Manorial System*.

Equal Inheritance   Practice of fragmenting large estates on the death of the owner by dividing them equally among male heirs. With the impossibility of amassing enormous estates as in Europe, by the 19th century rural China had become predominantly a world of smallholders.

Equal Service (*chün-yao*)   Form of corvée introduced by the Ming to supply labour for official establishments. In some cases cash payments were substituted.

Esen   Oirat (qv) chieftain who became leader of his people in 1439 and gradually extended his control over the frontier tribes as far east as Korea. In late 1449 he mobilised his forces and advanced on northern Shansi. The Chinese forces led by the eunuch Wang Chen and the Cheng-t'ung emperor were defeated and the emperor captured. Esen later advanced on Peking where a new emperor had been enthroned but withdrew to Mongolia after releasing his captive and soon resumed trade with the Ming.

Essential Techniques for the Common People (*Ch'i-min yao-shu*) Handbook written between 533 and 544 AD by Chia Ssu-hsieh and much reprinted. It contained details of agricultural techniques, papermaking and other arts.

Etsingol Han Records   Wooden slips used in administration and dating, discovered in the region of Etsingol (Edsingol) by Folk Bergman in 1930. They mainly concern Han dynasty border and military administration. 10,000 were found at the main site and since 1930, another 2,000 or so have been found in the same area.

Eunuchs   Originally employed by the court to guard and administer the imperial harem, eunuchs gradually acquired other functions. As men of low social origin with no descendants to rival the imperial line, they were natural allies for emperors and empresses against ambitious officials and were frequently involved in factional disputes with the bureaucracy. They often obtained high posts in the imperial household, commanding palace guards or even frontier armies, and were uniformly condemned in the Chinese histories for misrule. At the end of the Han dynasty eunuchs helped purge the court of powerful families who were rivalling the emperor and some T'ang rulers were virtual puppets of their eunuchs. Eunuchs had great power during the Ming period as military commanders and imperial commissioners in the provinces: the celebrated navigator Cheng Ho was a eunuch. As their duties proliferated they gradually permeated the entire Ming administration. In the 1420s a palace school was set up for them. They ran an office in Peking in which they kept files, accessible only to the emperor, on officials. The Ming emperor Cheng-t'ung was dominated by a eunuch clique under Wang Chen who led the Chinese to defeat by the Oirat nomads. The zenith of eunuch power was in the period 1624–7 when Wei Chung-hsien (1568–1627) imposed a reign of terror in the capital and in the provinces. He had a small army of eunuchs and a network of spies and informers throughout the empire. His manipulation of the throne came at the end of the degenerating Ming dynasty and the succeeding Ch'ing rulers, with the lessons of the Ming before them, did all they could to keep eunuchs out of positions of power.

Evening Talks at Yenshan Series of 153 articles written by Teng T'o (qv) that appeared in the *Peking Evening News* between March 1961 and September 1962. The articles were remarkably outspoken and criticised the leadership and its policies either directly or through historical analogies. The tone of the writings was sarcastic and satirical: for example one compared the Great Leap Forward with building castles in the air. In the Cultural Revolution Teng and others were attacked for their opposition to the policies of Mao and the Central Committee.

Ever Normal Granaries (*ch'ang-p'ing ts'ang*) Stores of grain maintained in each prefecture or district during the Ch'ing period under the supervision of the local magistrate. The intention was to stabilise rice prices by selling to residents at a price lower than the high market price in the spring when stocks were low, and using the revenue from the sales to replenish stocks in autumn when the grain would be cheaper. Interest-free loans were available in times of famine. In practice, only people living near to the district seat ever benefited as temporary stations for sale in the rural districts were rarely set up although required by the regulations. Corruption was also rife and officials and brokers often stockpiled grain for themselves or demanded extra payments.

Ever-Victorious Army 'Foreign Legion' raised in Shanghai in 1860 by businessmen to help the government put down the Taiping

Rebellion (qv). The original army of deserters and discharged seamen was augmented by 4,000 to 5,000 Chinese soldiers drafted in by Frederick T. Ward, an American. After Ward died he was succeeded by an adventurer, Henry A. Burgevine, who was soon replaced by Charles (Chinese) Gordon, later famous as General Gordon of Khartoum. The title 'Ever-Victorious' was bestowed on the army by the emperor in March 1862 when it repulsed the second Taiping attack on Shanghai. In 1863 it supported the Huai Army (qv) in an attack on the Taiping stronghold of Soochow which surrendered. The example of the Ever-Victorious Army showed Tseng Kuo-fan, Li Hung-chang and others the superiority of Western guns and ships.

Examination System   System of entry into the career civil service which involved the rote learning of the Confucian classics and their style, and the reproduction of the style and contents in a series of competitive examinations which led to the highest offices in the bureaucracy. In the Han dynasty by the year 1 AD, one hundred men a year were passing through the examination system. The Sui house continued the system which was expanded by the T'ang and conducted by the Ministry of Rites. A talented bureaucracy was created in the T'ang and Sung periods though admission could never be entirely on merit as preparation for the examinations required a considerable investment of time and finance which was normally only possible for the sons of wealthy families. The system was also adopted by the barbarian Liao dynasty after 998 and eventually by the Mongol conquerors. As refined by the Ming the system continued until the twentieth century. There were three levels: the district level which conferred the *hsiu-ts'ai* (flowering talent) degree, the provincial level which conferred the *chü-jen* (recommended man) degree and the metropolitan examination in the capital which conferred the *chin-shih* (presented scholar) degree. The examinations took place at regular intervals, the candidates sitting in rows of specially-made examination cells, and the last took place in 1905 when the system was formally ended.

Extraterritoriality   System agreed in the treaties of the 1840s in which foreign governments were allowed to rule the concessions (qv) granted to them and administer them according to their own law. This encroachment on Chinese sovereignty which was greatly resented by nationalist opinion can be traced back to the methods used to control the Persian and Arab trading communities of the T'ang period. Extraterritorial jurisdiction was exercised by consular officials in the Treaty Ports and by diplomatic officials in Peking.

F

Factories Merchant trading depots established by foreigners at first in Canton and after the unequal treaties, in the treaty ports. Few factories in the sense of large manufacturing units were built in China until the 1920s.

Fa-hsien Buddhist pilgrim who left for India in company with nine other monks by way of Central Asia in 399 in search of scriptures. He returned to China by sea in 414 and settled at Chien-k'ang, now Nanking, to translate the scriptures he had brought. He left a carefully dated record of his travels, the *Record of Buddhist Kingdoms* which is the oldest known travel book in Chinese literature and which has been invaluable in establishing Indian and Central Asian chronology. His more famous successor was Hsüan-tsang (qv).

Fang Chih-min (1900–35) Communist martyr. Fang was born in Iyang, Kiangsi, educated in Nanchang and Kiukiang and then in Shanghai where he came into contact with the CCP. He returned to Kiangsi in 1922 and organised the peasant movement in his native area in 1924. In 1928 he was elected to the Central Committee of the Chinese Communist Party and in 1929 he headed the Hsin River (later North-East Kiangsi) Soviet and the Tenth Army of the Chinese Red Army. In 1934 he was forced out of Kiangsi by Nationalist troops and ordered by the CCP to push north to the Yangtze. His forces were encircled by the Nationalists in January 1935 and he was captured, imprisoned in Nanchang and executed on July 6, 1935. He was married to Miao Min who has written an account of his career, and he left behind several essays and letters. Mao regarded him as one of the Communist leaders who had followed correct policies in the 1930s.

Fang La Rebellion Revolt in Chekiang in 1120 which accelerated the collapse of the Northern Sung dynasty. Although it was suppressed in the following year it weakened the imperial rule which was forced to move south to Hangchow after the invasion of the Chin nomads in 1126.

Feng Hsüeh-feng (1906–   ) Poet and literary critic purged during the anti-rightist campaign of 1957. Feng wrote lyrical nature and love poetry in the 1920s and polemical essays in the 1930s after joining the CCP. He was a friend of Lu Hsun, took part in the Long March and was imprisoned by the KMT in 1941–2. After 1949 he edited the important *Wen-i pao* (Literary Gazette). Although a Marxist he believed that literature should involve spontaneity and emotion as well as direct political messages and his call for more creative freedom resulted in his expulsion from the CCP.

Feng Yu-hsiang (1882–1948) Army commander with the Chihli warlord forces who mutinied and occupied Peking on October 23, 1924. He reorganised his forces as the Kuominchun or National People's Army and invited Sun Yat-sen to a conference on nationalist unification. Unlike many of the warlords, he, in common with Yen Hsi-shan, more or less supported the Nationalist enterprise, and after Sun's death proposed a second Northern Expedition (qv) which brought the Peking area fully under the control of the Nanking government in 1928. He was strongly anti-Communist and supported the expulsion of the CCP from the Wuhan Government (qv) in 1927 and the reconciliation of the Wuhan and Nanking regimes. His support earned him the post of vice-president of the executive Yuan (effectively the cabinet) of the 1928 Nanking government. This did not prevent him from retaining his own political and military base in the northern and north-western provinces as one of the New Warlords backed by his National People's Army. From this base he attacked government forces in 1929, challenged the power of Chiang K'ai-shek and co-operated with Wang Ching-wei in a rival government in Peking. Feng was reinstated in the KMT in 1931 and held office, but without power, until his death. He acquired the soubriquet 'Christian General' because of his nominal conversion to the Protestant church.

Feng-shui see *Geomancy*

Festivals Everyday life in traditional China revolved around a series of annual festivals, many dating back centuries. Among the most important were the Dragon Boat, the New Year, and the Ch'ing Ming (qqv).

Feudalism According to current Communist historiography, the whole of Chinese history is characterised as feudal from the Warring States period to the middle of the 19th century when the penetration of foreign imperialism turned China into a semi-feudal, semi-colonial society. In the more limited sense of the term as used to describe early mediaeval European society, feudal has been used to describe the decentralised rule of the Chou dynasty. In the modern Chinese usage, the terms 'feudal' and 'feudalism' are employed to describe, in a pejorative sense, the peasant economy controlled and exploited by the emperor, nobility and landlords. They do not imply the complex legal and contractual system that existed in feudal Europe or in Japan in the Middle Ages.

Field Armies   Units of the People's Liberation Army first designated in February 1949. Troops of the Shantung Column and associated forces in Jehol, Chahar and Manchuria were placed under the command of Lin Piao (qv) in 1945. This body of 100,000 men was expanded, retrained and reorganised into the North Eastern Field Army, which was designated the Fourth Field Army in February 1949 when the numbered Field Army system came into existence. The five Field Armies, with their main areas of operation in the Civil War before 1949 are:

First — commanded by Ho Lung and based in north-west China and Sinkiang.

Second — commanded by Liu Po-ch'eng and operating in the west and south-west China.

Third — commanded by Ch'en Yi and Su Yu and fighting in east China, notably in the Huai-Hai campaign (qv).

Fourth — commanded by Lin Piao and operating in north-east China before moving to Kwangsi and Kwangtung.

Fifth — an unofficial title for the North China Field Army which fought in north China and Inner Mongolia but never received an official number.

All these field armies had fought independent campaigns before 1949 and after liberation they became firmly established as political and military powers in the regions of their operations. Their commanders assumed control of regional military and administrative committees and thus acquired local power bases. Although mobility of units to fight in the Korean War eroded some local power, Field Army loyalties have remained important in factional politics within the upper echelons of the CCP and People's Government.

Filial Piety   Putting loyalty to parents first in all things. The most admired of Confucian virtues and part of the complex philosophical system that tied the authoritarian family to the imperial state. The idea goes far back into Chinese tradition and was incorporated into a set of maxims called the *Book of Filial Piety*.

Firewood Gatherers' Sect   One of a number of rebellious groups that rose among the poorest people in the Hunan hills in 1851 and later joined the Taiping Rebellion (qv).

Five-Anti Campaign   One of a series of campaigns mounted in the early 1950s by the new People's Government (see also *Three-Anti Campaign* and *Su-fan Campaign*). The Five-Anti Campaign launched in 1952 was aimed at eliminating bribery, tax evasion, fraud, theft of government property and the leakage of state economic secrets and was a more specific attack on the kind of corruption that had come to light in the earlier Three-Anti Campaign.

Five Classics   Collective name for the Book of Songs (*Shih ching*), the Book of Documents (*Shu ching*), the Book of Changes (*I ching*), the Spring and Autumn Annals (*Ch'un Ch'iu*), and the Record of Rituals (*Li chi*). See also *Four Books* and *Thirteen Classics*.

Five Dynasties and the Ten Kingdoms   Period of disunion between the fall of the T'ang (907) and the rise of the Sung dynasty (960). The Five — the Liang (907–23), the Later T'ang (923–936), Later Chin (936–947), Later Han (947–951) and Later Chou (952–960) — were would-be dynasties in the north of China which followed each other in rapid succession. The Ten Kingdoms were independent regimes, mainly in the south of China, which resurrected local or historical names such as Ch'u, Min and Shu. The five ephemeral northern dynasties were concerned mainly with controlling barbarian pressure on the borders. They were replaced by the Sung in 960 when Chao K'uang-yin, guard commander of the Later Chou who had been sent to stop a Khitan incursion, seized the throne and unified the empire.

Five Emperors   Sequence of legendary rulers and Chinese culture heroes of the pre-Hsia period. The most famous were Huang-ti, Yao and Shun. Huang-ti, the Yellow Emperor, was credited with defeating the barbarians during his reign that is reputed to have begun in 2697 BC. Yao (traditional reign dates 2357–2256 BC) regulated agriculture and, passing over his unworthy son, nominated Shun to succeed him. Shun, the last of the five, is said to have reigned between 2255 and 2205 BC. A devoted son to his parents, he was transformed from poor peasant into model ruler.

Five Pecks of Rice Band   Szechwan Taoist rebels at the end of the Han dynasty led by Chang Hsiu and then Chang Lu and named after the dues paid by their supporters. Chang Lu was bought off by Ts'ao Ts'ao (qv) in 215 but the Han never recovered from the disruption caused by this and the Yellow Turban (qv) rebellions. The cult which the band followed had been founded by Chang Ling, known as T'ien Shih or Heavenly Master, around the middle of the 2nd century.

Five Principles of Peaceful Co-existence Principles initiated by Peking at the Bandung Conference of Afro-Asian leaders (qv) in 1955. They were: (1) Respect for sovereignty and territorial integrity (2) Mutual non-aggression (3) Non-interference in each other's internal affairs (4) Equality and mutual benefit (5) Peaceful co-existence. These were endorsed by the United States during the visit of President Nixon in February 1972.

Five Relationships The five relationships central to Confucian philosophy: between ruler and subject, father and son, husband and wife, elder brother and younger brother, friend and friend. They were first established in *Mencius* and apart from the last were all relationships of authority and obedience.

Five Year Plans Basic economic planning units in the People's Republic following the model of the USSR. The first plan, 1953–57, called for a massive expansion of heavy industry paid for by extracting surpluses from agriculture and with help from the Soviet Union. A 6–7% growth rate was achieved, double the Indian performance in the same period. The second plan, 1958–62, envisaged a gradual speed-up in agricultural production and an increase in industrial plant, but its targets and projections were made obsolete by the radical policy changes of the Great Leap Forward in 1958. The third five-year plan began in 1966, delayed because of the readjustments needed after the Great Leap and the economic chaos of 1959–61, but the targets were not even announced before it too was overtaken by political upheaval — the Cultural Revolution.

Flying Horse of Kansu Unique statue of a bronze galloping horse stepping on a flying swallow which was found in Kansu province in 1969. It dates from the Eastern Han dynasty (25–220 AD) and comes from a tomb of that period uncovered in Leitai in Wuwei county which also yielded many precious items of gold, jade, lacquerware and other bronze and stone statuettes.

Footbinding First introduced among upper class women in the Sung period. The feet of young girls were wrapped tightly and gradually bent till the arch was broken and the toes turned under, which produced a foot of about half the normal size. Women with bound feet were crippled and economically useless and it was an indication of their declining status. They were, however, status symbols for their families, emphasising the wealth of the man who could afford such handicapped women. Bound feet developed strong erotic associations and the practice spread through all social classes.

Right up to the 20th century families felt that unless their daughters' feet were bound they had poor marriage prospects. The practice began to die out in the present century and was outlawed after 1949.

Forbidden City Imperial palace and its surrounds in central Peking, created by the early Ming emperors, and protected from the outside world by high walls and a moat. A similar palace city was constructed in Nanking.

Foreign Matters Movement (*Yang-wu yun-tung*) Part of the self-strengthening movement (qv) that followed China's defeat in the Opium Wars. Although defence remained a chief preoccupation, between 1872 and 1885 enterprises directed to profit such as shipping, railways, mining and telegraphs became more important and these were known as foreign affairs or foreign matters.

Formosa see *Taiwan*

Formosan Incident (1868) Gunboat diplomacy. After a dispute between the Taiwan authorities and a British firm over the Taiwanese monopoly of the camphor trade, British gunboats attacked Anping, a port in northern Taiwan, killing seventeen Chinese soldiers.

Four Books Four short texts which became the supreme embodiment of the Confucian philosophy. The *Analects* (qv) of Confucius, the *Mencius* (qv), the *Great Learning* and the *Doctrine of the Mean*, the latter two being chapters from the *Record of Rituals*. Their importance dates from the commentaries on them by the Sung philosopher Chu Hsi.

Four-Class Alliance Formula coined by Stalin for the temporary alliance between the workers, peasants, petty bourgeoisie and national bourgeoisie at a certain point in the revolutionary struggle, and taken up later by Mao. The idea is fundamental to the theory of the people's democratic dictatorship as a transitional period on the road to socialism. Implicit in the theory of the alliance is its transitoriness as eventually the workers and peasants would find themselves in conflict with the bourgeoisie and the alliance would end.

Four Treasuries, Complete Library of the Great manuscript library of the Ch'ien-lung period 1736–95 which brought together in one collection all the important works in the four 'treasuries' or branches of literature: classics, history, philosophy and belles lettres. The compilation took nearly twenty years and involved 350 scholars and

15,000 copyists. Some works were copied in their entirety, others merely commented on, and the compilers began with the 11,095 volumes of the Yung-lo encyclopaedia (qv). The Four Treasuries Library when complete comprised more than 36,000 volumes and included 3,450 complete works. An additional catalogue commented on a total of 10,230 titles. Seven original manuscripts were made. Two lodged at Yangchou and Chungkiang were destroyed during the Taiping rebellion and one at Hangchow was partially destroyed. The Anglo-French expedition destroyed one when it burned the Old Summer Palace outside Peking in 1860. Two sets were preserved in Peking and one at Mukden and some parts have now been printed. The aim of the compilation was to produce a definitive Imperial Library and weed out anti-Manchu writings. It is important because of the quality of the annotations and its comprehensiveness. See also *Literary Inquisition*.

Franco-Chinese War   Dispute over control of the Chinese tributary state of Annam (Vietnam). France had tried unsuccessfully to trade with Annam in the 17th century and in 1874 imposed a treaty on the Annamese court, securing the right to trade and propagate Christianity and gaining effective control over the south of Annam which it called Cochin China. The Ch'ing court wished to assert its suzerainty over Annam but was unwilling to fight the French and tried to negotiate a compromise by which it would be administered as a joint protectorate. When Chinese troops refused to withdraw from Tongking as set down in the 1884 Li-Fournier agreement (qv), fighting broke out between them and French troops. On August 23, 1884 French ships attacked Foochow, sank twelve Chinese vessels and destroyed the dockyard; the Chinese court declared war on France. France blockaded the Yangtze and key ports, and peace was finally negotiated between Li Hung-chang and the French minister in China in June 1885. China agreed to recognise the Li-Fournier agreement of 1884 (qv) and France to make no further demands. Annam was lost to China and became a French protectorate.

Fu Tso-yi (1895–   ) Nationalist General who negotiated the surrender of Peking to the Communists in 1949. A native of Shansi and an officer of the warlord Yen Hsi-shan, Fu fought against the Japanese in Inner Mongolia in 1936. In 1947, despite his dislike for Fu, Chiang K'ai-shek had been forced to invite him to take over the defence of Peking and Tientsin.

Fukien Revolt (November 1933) Insurrection engineered by the commanders of the Cantonese 19th Route Army which had been transferred from the anti-Japanese front in Shanghai to fight the Communists in Fukien. The rebels made an Anti-Japanese, Anti-Chiang pact with the Communists and set up a People's Revolutionary Government in Foochow in November 1933. Because of pressure by the Nationalists and indecision by the Politburo, Communist aid for the rebels never arrived. On January 20, 1934 Chiang K'ai-shek suppressed the Revolt and reorganised the 19th Route Army as the 7th National Army.

Fut'ien Incident (December 1930) Conflict between Mao and the leaders of the 20th Red Army in southern Kiangsi who were staunch supporters of Li Li-san (qv). In December several of the leaders were arrested on charges of being undercover agents of the Anti-Bolshevik league and imprisoned in Fu-t'ien in southern Kiangsi. A battalion rose in revolt to try and free the prisoners, and in the fighting that followed 2,000–3,000 officers and men lost their lives.

Gang of Four   Name given to Chiang Ch'ing, Chang Ch'un-ch'iao, Yao Wen-yuan and Wang Hung-wen, all prominent members of the Shanghai radical group during the Cultural Revolution. After the death of Mao Tse-tung in September 1976 they tried to assert their political power nationally but were thwarted by Hua Kuo-feng, and other party members conventionally termed 'moderates'. A campaign against the Gang of Four started on October 21, 1976 in which they were accused of trying to usurp the leadership of the party, of sabotaging the economy, dictating to literary and art circles, disrupting the army and isolating Mao from the party and leadership. Chiang Ch'ing was singled out for particularly venomous attacks and accused of all kinds of personal faults as well as political ones.

Gazetteers or Local Histories (*fang-chih*)   Histories of a particular locality compiled by members of the local elite and sponsored by officials. Gazetteers were produced for Provinces (*sheng*), Prefectures (*fu*) and Districts or Counties (*hsien*) and contain a wealth of information on local administration, economic systems and culture, and biographies of officials and other notable and admirable people. By the Ch'ing period when the format had become more or less standard, gazetteers contained a preface on the method of compilation, local maps and town or city plans, chapters on administrative units, topographical materials, famous places, official buildings, schools, temples, bridges, canals and irrigation works, officials and examinations, information on taxation, markets, local products and crops, local customs, chronicles of disasters, biographies of prominent local people — the longest section of all — and miscellaneous topics. Gazetteers derived from the practice of providing basic information on local conditions for the central government and the habit of collecting exemplary biographies. About thirty of the two hundred gazetteers compiled in the Sung period survive, eleven out of the sixty from the Yuan dynasty, and nine hundred from an unknown number written in the Ming period. There are at least 5,000 Ch'ing gazetteers extant. About 650 more were produced during the Republican period. In spite of the comprehensiveness of the compilations there are many gaps since generally speaking the only information collected was that which might prove useful to officialdom, and there is very little information about the lives of ordinary people.

Genghis Khan see *Chinggis Khan*

Gentry (*shen-shih*) Strictly degree holders, but commonly used to describe the ruling elite in the countryside. The gentry were always holders of degrees from the official examination system and almost always members of great landowning families. They provided an unofficial system of control in the regions and also a buffer and a means of communication between the officials and the mass of the people. Since the gentry were local people and officials came from all over China, the former were relied on to help with local dialects, customs and laws and to give information about local conditions. The origins of the gentry are in the decline of the landed and military aristocracy of the Han and early T'ang period. Many of the new gentry class were absentee landlords, living in the new cities and towns with the merchants and officials and they depended less exclusively than the old rural aristocracy on agricultural wealth. Educational attainments became all-important and inherited wealth less so, as the absence of primogeniture fragmented large landholdings. Nevertheless there were gentry families which included degree holders generation after generation and landholding was essential as an economic support for scholarly study. Degree holders and landlords overlapped considerably and the term 'gentry' is rather imprecise. Under the Ming dynasty, the gentry assumed many official functions, were responsible for schools, gazetteers and public works, presumably at some profit to themselves, and this practice continued under the Ch'ing.

Geomancy (*Feng-shui*, 'wind and water') Cosmic pseudo-science which when applied to the lie of the land indicated the correct sites for houses, graves etc. It was a set of rules for the relationship between man and nature which stemmed from a primitive animism in which the spirits of land and water were credited with an active role in the affairs of men. Temples, for example, should always face south with hills behind for protection and a watercourse nearby. In modern times, these beliefs often hindered the building of railways etc. Either people who deeply believed in geomancy opposed new building if it disturbed sites of graveyards for example, or the belief was used by people who were opposed to construction for other reasons.

Giles, Herbert Consular official in China between 1880 and 1893 and later Professor of Chinese at Cambridge University. He wrote many books on Chinese history and literature, compiled an important Chinese-English dictionary and with Thomas Wade (qv) was responsible for the standard Wade-Giles system of romanising Chinese.

Gobi Broad desert plain that occupies the greater part of Inner Mongolia and the Mongolian People's Republic. Its southern edge is skirted by a broad grass belt which is the main home of Mongolian nomads. The term Gobi Desert is, strictly speaking, a tautology, since *gobi* is the Mongolian word for desert.

God Worshippers Earliest organisation of the Taiping rebels (qv). The God Worshippers Society was formed in Kwangsi province by Feng Yün-shan, a neighbour of Hung Hsiu-ch'uan (qv). By 1849 the society had over three thousand members, mainly Hakkas, and after the rising organised by the Heaven and Earth Society in 1849–50 its numbers grew rapidly although its members took no part in the insurrection. In 1851 the God Worshippers rose in rebellion proclaiming Hung Hsiu-ch'uan Heavenly King of the Taiping kingdom.

Golden Lotus (*Chin P'ing Mei*) One of the greatest novels in Chinese, written in the late Ming period between 1582 and 1596 and first published in 1610 or 1611 in Soochow after circulating in manuscript form. Parts of it contain explicit erotic scenes and description — rendered into Latin in the standard English translation. The novel gives a valuable insight into Ming society, manners and family life through the story of Hsi-men Ch'ing and his pursuit of pleasure in everyday urban surroundings, and is important as a reflection of strictly non-Confucian views of life, and as the first Chinese novel not based primarily on existing stories from the oral tradition. Hsi-men Ch'ing's relationships with his wife and concubines and his infatuation with Golden Lotus are described with great insight.

Gordon, General Charles C. Known as 'Chinese' Gordon, but later more famous as Gordon of Khartoum. He led the Ever-Victorious Army (qv) against the Taipings and was friendly with Li Hung-chang (qv). He was called to China again in 1881 to assist with defences against a threatened attack from Russia, and counselled peace as he believed China would be defeated.

Government Administration Council Immediate predecessor of the State Council (qv) by which it was replaced under the 1954 Constitution. It was the effective cabinet of China but was not able to control military and economic agencies completely.

Governor (*hsün-fu*) Also called Grand Co-ordinator. Top official post in provinces under the empire. Originally the position was an *ad hoc* appointment to co-ordinate official policies and check on mis-government in a particular region. During the Ming dynasty, in the early 15th century, the appointments became more regular and some turned into residential posts with much longer tenure. Under the Ch'ing dynasty, the appointments were made permanent and incorporated into the statutory organisation of local government, so that every province, except Chihli and Szechwan which were under governors-general had its own governor.

Governor-General or Viceroy (*tsung-tu*) Like the post of governor, this was instituted as a temporary measure by the Ming authorities and later made permanent. Governors-general were originally delegated to supervise areas larger than one province, to deal with rebellion or invasion, to oversee flood control along the Yellow River, or supervise the transport of grain tax to the capital. Under the Ch'ing dynasty, governors-general were usually appointed to superintend two provinces, although one took responsibility for the three provinces of Kiangsi, Kiangsu and Anhwei. Szechwan and the metropolitan province of Chihli around Peking each had its own governor-general. In the early part of the Ch'ing period, two-thirds of the governors-general were Manchus and they administered the regions jointly with the governors who were mainly Chinese.

Grain Tribute Taxation system that supplied the capital and court with rice or other grains. Emperor Wu-ti of the Han dynasty began a canal system to assist the transport of tax grain from east China to the capital at Ch'ang-an, and the supply was improved by replacing corvée labour with professional transport workers in the T'ang period. Under the Yuan dynasty food supplies were organised by extending the Grand Canal (qv) to Peking and by the use of sea transport around the Shantung coastline. The Ming emperor Yung-lo improved the canal route when he moved his capital north to Peking, and then transferred the burden of shipments from the peasantry to the military transport divisions of local garrisons. A similar levy of tax grain was made throughout the Ch'ing dynasty. See also *Land Tax*.

Grand Canal System of waterways linking the northern and southern parts of the Chinese empire. A series of canals dug during earlier dynasties was unified by the Sui emperors into a single system that joined Hangchow to K'ai-feng in the north-west. The canal was used under the Sung but fell into disuse when China was split into

F

two empires during the latter half of the dynasty. The capital of the Mongol Yuan dynasty which succeeded the Sung was in the north-east rather than the north-west so a new system was developed. Coastal transport was tried, but abandoned because of the danger from pirates and typhoons, and a second Grand Canal which started in the Huai Valley and crossed the Yellow River on its way to Peking was completed about 1295. This canal served as the main north-south artery of communication until the advent of the railways in the late 19th and early 20th century, in spite of the silting to which it was subject.

Grand Co-ordinator see *Governor*

Grand Council (*Chün-chi ch'ü*) Literally Military Plans Office and sometimes called Privy Council. The top policy-making body of the Ch'ing period set up by the Yung-cheng emperor in 1729 to supersede the Grand Secretariat (qv) which he retained to handle the more routine business. The Grand Council worked in closer contact with the palace and the emperor on urgent or important matters and this meant a greater concentration of power in the hands of the emperor. There were usually five or six Grand Councillors, and two or three of these were usually concurrently Grand Secretaries, so there were strong links between the two bodies. The Council usually met the emperor daily at dawn and its business was handled quickly and secretly by a select group of secretaries.

Grand Secretariat (*Nei-ko*) Body set up during the Ming dynasty which acted as a kind of cabinet, superior to the six ministries and other administrative organs. The origin of the body lay in the Grand Secretaries who handled memorials and drafted edicts for the Hung-wu emperor in the 14th century. In the 15th century they became institutionalised as the Grand Secretariat, but remained informal and without statutory powers. No one Grand Secretary could act as a European Prime Minister might, except with the express permission of the emperor. During the Ch'ing dynasty, the Grand Secretariat was more formally established, with three Manchu secretaries and three Chinese. In 1729 its functions were taken over by a Grand Council, although it continued in existence to handle more routine matters.

Grass Cutters Sect One of a number of rebellious sects that rose in the Hunan hills in 1851 and joined in the Taiping Rebellion (qv).

Great Khan Title of the successors of Chinggis Khan (qv), Khans of East Asia with their capitals at Karakorum in Mongolia and senior Khans in the Mongol empire. The power of the Great Khan diminished in the 14th century because of internal disagreements, and the hold of the Mongols over China was weakened.

Great Leap Forward   Dramatic turn-round in policy in 1958 and the subsequent drive for rapid economic expansion. The Great Leap Forward movement was announced by the National People's Congress that met in February 1958 and called for a 19% increase in steel production, 18% in electricity and 17% in coal output in the following three years. It was even expected that China could catch up with or even surpass British industrial capacity within 15 years. All production quotas were raised and everyone was urged to participate in industrial production. By autumn 1958, 600,000 back-yard furnaces (qv) had sprung up throughout the country. Associated with the industrial drive was the commune (qv) movement to effect the socialist transformation of agriculture. By the end of 1958 the government was able to announce massive increases in the production of machine tools, coal, steel, oil and electricity although it was later admitted that in many cases quality had been sacrificed for quantity. Dissatisfaction with the policies of the Leap, combined with appalling harvests and natural disasters between 1959 and 1961 which drasti-cally reduced the level of agricultural production led to a severe retrenchment in the early 1960s and a retreat from the policies of the Leap Forward.

Great Proletarian Cultural Revolution   see   *Cultural Revolution*

Great Wall   Network of forts and defensive walls that delineated the border between China and the barbarian north. The last walls were built in the late Chou period when the states of north China began to erect frontier defences, and these were incorporated by Shih Huang-ti the first Ch'in emperor into a fourteen-hundred mile network of walls that ran across the south of Inner Mongolia to Manchuria. It was reasonably effective if manned properly as it could defend an area against a raiding party of horsemen long enough for an adequate force to be mustered. The wall was extended west-wards to Yü-men (Jade Gate) by the Han dynasty to facilitate its occupation of Central Asia, reconstructed by the Northern Wei in the 5th century and also by the Sui empire in the early 7th century. These later walls were sometimes to the north or south of the original ones and there was a great deal of reconstruction and new building until the 16th century, but the Great Wall remained essentially the defensive system created by the Ch'in.

Green Band or Green Gang   Traditional secret society formed in about 1725 which took an active part in the 1911 revolution but degenerated into a criminal gang and dominated the Shanghai underworld in the 1910s and 1920s. It controlled opium supply, prostitution and extortion and frequently acted in support of Chiang K'ai-shek and the Nationalists. Although the precise details of the connection between Chiang and the Green Band are not clear, the Band were certainly involved in the putsch against Communists and trades unionists in Shanghai in 1927.

Green Standard Army   Chinese army under the Ch'ing dynasty as distinct from the Manchu bannermen. It had suppressed the Three Feudatories revolt in 1673–81 when the banner forces were unable to do so. 600,000 men were enrolled in the Green Standard Army, which was stationed at strategic points throughout the empire. However the army, like the banners, was severely weakened by corruption and both the Chinese and Manchu regulars often left any fighting to locally-raised militia units. By the time of the Taiping rebellion the Green Standard Army and the bannermen were totally ineffective and were replaced by locally based forces like the Huai and Hsiang armies.

Guerrilla Warfare   Strategy and tactics adopted by the Red Armies and Mao Tse-tung from the 1920s to the 1940s. Faced with superior forces and often encircled, the Red Army tended to operate in guerrilla units in liaison with local militias. These strategies, similar to those of Sun Tzu, were flexible enough to allow positional warfare whenever the balance of strengths made this a practical proposition.

Guilds (*hang*)   Semi-official associations of merchants which grew originally out of the trade associations grouped in particular streets (*hang*) of the T'ang market-places. The *hang* (or *hong* in its Cantonese form) came to be the name for a licensed trading firm. In the Sung periods, guilds were organised under a head who was responsible to the government for the collection of taxes or fees from its members. The most important guilds were those which transported and sold grain, salt, tea, silk or other basic commodities, or engaged in currency storage or lending. In the Ming dynasty, during the 16th century, a number of regional guilds were established with guildhalls in major commercial centres to provide mutual aid for merchants from a common region. The guilds organised lodgings for merchants away from home, provided introductions, arranged finance and transport and provided guarantees for all transactions with the members of the guild, as well as representing the members in contacts with officialdom. See also *Landsmannschaften, Hong Merchants* and *Cohong*.

Gunpowder   Gunpowder was invented in the early T'ang period, but was at first used only for fireworks. By the 11th century gunpowder was being used in weaponry for mines, hand-grenades and other projectiles.

Güyüg Khan   Son of Ögödei, Great Khan of the Mongols from 1246–48 and an uncompromising and authoritarian ruler in his short reign.

H

Hai Jui (1513–1587) Ming official renowned for his integrity. After teaching in a school in Fukien he became a magistrate of Ch'un-an in Chekiang. He attacked corruption, equalised the burden of taxation and emphasised obedience to the law and strict Confucian teaching. After an appointment in Kiangsi, he became a secretary in the Ministry of Revenue in Peking and in November 1565 submitted a memorial to the throne criticising the Chia-ching emperor for not attending to public affairs, for permitting the spread of poverty, corruption and injustice and for his excessive involvement in Taoist prayer ceremonies. Hai was ordered to prison and tortured to exact a confession of conspiracy but released after the death of the emperor in 1567. He was promoted eventually to the governorship of southern Chihli, continued his fight against corruption but was again forced out by his opponents. He was however given a senior post in the Censorate in 1585 and died in office two years later. A play, *Hai Jui dismissed*, (qv) written by Wu Han in 1961, was much criticised at the beginning of the Cultural Revolution.

Hai Jui Dismissed Play about the dismissal of the Ming official Hai Jui (see above), written by Wu Han, the deputy mayor of Peking and a former university professor, which appeared in the January 1961 issue of *Peking Literature and Art*. Hai Jui was portrayed as an honest official who lost his post as governor because of his proposal to return to the peasants land that had been seized by rich landlords, and the connection with the dismissal of P'eng Teh-huai (qv) shortly after the Great Leap and the Commune movement was not lost on people. The fierce attacks on this play beginning with an article in the Shanghai paper *Wen-hui Pao* by Yao Wen-yuan are generally regarded as the starting-point of the Cultural Revolution.

Haikwan Taels Standard unit of account adopted by the customs (*hai-kuan*) in the late Ch'ing period.

Hakkas Minority people living in south and south-east China who are thought to have migrated there from the north in the 12th century. Although they are Chinese their language and customs set them apart from the indigenous minority people such as the Yao and Cantonese speakers who had settled there earlier.

Han Dynasty (206 BC–220 AD)   Usually divided into the Former or Western Han (206 BC–8 AD) and the Later or Eastern Han (25 AD–220 AD) separated by the Wang Mang (qv) interregnum. The Han dynasty was the heyday of the early Chinese empire, roughly contemporary with the Roman empire and paralleling it in power, prestige, and historical significance. Chinese still refer to themselves as 'men of Han'. The dynasty was formed after the collapse of the Ch'in when Liu Pang, the leader of a rebel band, declared himself emperor and made Ch'ang-an his capital. Emperor Kao-tsu, as Liu Pang was known posthumously, maintained strong central control over the area around the capital but did allow small kingdoms or marquisates to rule outlying areas of his empire. Much of the Han period was marked by conflict with the steppe nomads known as the Hsiung-nu, who invaded China periodically but the Han rulers were still able to establish a firm centralised government for a population larger than that of the Roman empire. A huge bureaucracy grew up in Ch'ang-an to staff the elaborate institutions that were used to administer the empire.

After the early period of consolidating the new rule, the reign of Emperor Wu-ti (141–187 BC) saw a great expansion in Chinese power. Wu-ti was a more severe ruler and he launched a programme of canal building to transport grain from the south to Chang-an. As well as his wars against the Hsiung-nu, he conquered many of the small native states in south China including those in Chekiang, Fukien and Nan-yüeh (Kwangtung, Kwangsi and North Vietnam) and brought parts of Kweichow and Yünnan into the Chinese sphere of influence for the first time. In 108 BC he conquered the state of Choson (in North Korea and South Manchuria) and consolidated his power to the west by extending the Great Wall into the deserts of Central Asia, hoping to outflank the Hsiung-nu in both east and west. During the Han period Confucianism gradually became the dominant philosophy of the Chinese court and the classic texts were revived. Ssu-ma Ch'ien's *Historical Records* (qv) written in Wu-ti's reign set the pattern for 2,000 years of historical writing in China and was closely followed by the *Han Shu* or History of the (Earlier) Han by Pan Ku.

A series of revolts that began in 22 BC set the scene for the decline of the Former Han. The throne was usurped by Wang Mang who carried out many economic reforms. Further rebellions, internal disunity and the failure of defences against the Hsiung-nu brought about the complete collapse of the government. It was revived in 25 AD by Liu Hsiu who suppressed the rebels and reconquered south China and Central Asia, but he was not able to organise such a secure economic base as that of the earlier Han. The dynasty finally collapsed in a number of court intrigues and further rebellions and the empire was divided into the Three Kingdoms. The Han period was noted for bronze sculptures and vessels, jade work, silk wall paintings, bronze mirrors, pottery vessels and figures.

Han Chinese Chinese people as distinct from the national minorities such as Mongols, Tibetans, Miao etc.

Han Fei-tzu or Han Fei Leading legalist philosopher of the Warring States period (died 233 BC). Han Fei, although a member of the Han state royal house served the Ch'in emperor till he was forced by Li Ssu to commit suicide. He was a disciple of Hsün Tzu and his ideas were expounded in the work known as the *Han Fei-tzu* in which he elaborated the work of Hsün Tzu and other legalists, particularly the political and legal aspects. He advocated a system of rewards and punishments to ensure the authority of the ruler and the military strength of the state, ideas that went completely against traditional ideas of chivalry and Confucian ethics.

Han Yü (768–824) Prose stylist and critic of Buddhism during the T'ang dynasty. Han Yü gave new prominence to the *Mencius* and the *Great Learning* and made them into two of the most important Confucian texts. He was a forerunner of the Neo-Confucian (qv) school of the Sung period.

Handicraft Workshops Most common form of large-scale manufacturing in pre-modern China. Unlike rural cottage industries which were usually family concerns, the workshops tended to be owned by a master craftsman and may have been quite large. They had masters, journeymen and apprentices in the same way as the workshops in mediaeval Europe and were often capitalised by merchants or merchant syndicates.

Hangchow The southern end of the Grand Canal (qv) in the Sui period and the capital of the Southern Sung, between 1135 after the Chin had captured Kaifeng and 1276 when it was taken by the Mongols. Hangchow, known then as Lin-an, was far grander than Kaifeng had ever been, and became a centre of playwriting and dramatic production under the Southern Sung. From the Ming dynasty onwards it was celebrated as a cultural centre as well as for its natural setting on the West Lake amid wooded hills and with many attractive temples.

Hanlin Academy Carefully selected body of scholars who expounded the classics for the court and compiled imperial utterances. Although it had its origins in the Sung period and continued right through to the Ch'ing, it was most influential in the Ming dynasty when, in the 1420s, it also controlled the eunuch school in the palace.

Hart, Robert (1835–1911)   Inspector General of the Chinese Imperial Maritime Customs (qv) under whom Western customs commissioners became important figures in all the treaty ports. He was a native of Northern Ireland and a graduate of Queen's University Belfast. In 1859 he left the British consular service to become deputy commissioner at the Canton customs under Horatio N. Lay (qv) and replaced him as Inspector General in November 1863. Hart developed the Chinese customs as an international force so that by 1875 it employed 252 British and 176 other Western officials. He was a man with great sympathy for China and constantly promoted progressive ideas and the opening of China to Western commerce, railways, mining and the telegraph. It was through Hart that the Chinese government invited General Gordon to assist in its defence against Russia in 1880. In 1896 he took charge of the Imperial Postal Service as well as the customs. He left Peking for England in May 1908 and while he retained the formal title of Inspector General till his death in September 1911, effective control passed to his successor Robert Bredon in 1908 and then to Francis A. Aglen who became Inspector General on Hart's death and served till January 1927.

Heaven And Earth Society (*T'ien-ti hui*)   Secret Society which rebelled in 1786–89 and later in 1849–50 in Kwangsi when it formed part of the great Taiping Rebellion (qv). After the failure of the rebellion, the Heaven and Earth Society continued underground, keeping alive the idea of national revolution against the Manchus. It was part of the Triad (qv) group of organisations.

Hegemons   Small power centres that grew up as the power of the Chou rulers began to wane during the period known as the Spring and Autumn (qv) (722–481 BC). Although Chou retained its spiritual authority, military power was taken over by small kingdoms, and alliances between them provided some stability. The hegemons were the precursors of the Warring States (qv) (463–221 BC), which were more independent.

High Level Equilibrium Trap   Concept developed by Mark Elvin to explain the lack of technological and economic development in early modern China, when compared with the great expansion during the Sung dynasty. It is suggested that input and output patterns in the late traditional economy had reached an equilibrium that could not be altered by internally generated forces. Agricultural productivity, water transport and other factors were as efficient as they could be without industrial-scientific inputs.

High Tide of Socialism   Great increase in the number of peasant households joining Agricultural Producers' Co-operatives (qv) in 1955. Opinion seems to have swung strongly in favour of co-operatives in the first half of the year and in July, Mao Tse-tung issued a directive for an upsurge or 'high tide of socialism' in the countryside by the end of which 60% of peasant households belonged to co-operatives.

Higher Producers' Co-operatives (HPCs)   Third stage of agricultural collectivisation, after Mutual Aid Teams and Agricultural Producers' Co-operatives (qqv). They appeared in 1956 and by mid-1957 more than 96% of all peasant households were members of HPCs. The transition to the higher stage involved both the amalgamation of APCs into larger units and the common ownership of all agricultural land, tools and livestock apart from some small private plots. Income for the members was now dependent solely on work points, no allowance being made for the amount of land previously owned in the APCs. Each HPC had somewhere between 100 and 300 families and was divided into Production Brigades corresponding approximately to the old APCs, and Production Teams of seven or eight families. In 1958 all HPCs were incorporated into communes (qv).

Historical Records   see   *Records of the Grand Historian*

Ho-Umetsu Agreement   Secret agreement signed by Ho Ying-ch'in, the Minister of War in the Nanking Government, and General Umetsu, the commander of Japanese forces in north China on July 7, 1935 during Japanese expansion in Manchuria. The Chinese government was forced to yield to Japanese demands that Chang Hsüeh-liang's Manchurian troops be withdrawn from Hopei and Chahar and that KMT offices in the provinces be closed. This was part of a larger Japanese plan as outlined in the somewhat suspect Tanaka Memorial (qv) to separate the five northern provinces of China (Hopei, Shantung, Shansi, Chahar and Suiyuan) from the rest.

Ho Lung (1896–   )   Red Army General in command of the Second Front Army in the 1930s. At the abortive Nanchang Rising of 1927 Ho Lung was the main military leader, with Yeh T'ing. He was then still a representative of the left wing of the KMT but was to join the CCP soon after the uprising. Ho commanded the 20th Army then, and during the Long March his forces were merged into the Second Front Army which he also led. The Second Front Army was prevented by Nationalist Armies from joining the main column of the Long March till 1936. Ho Lung led a division which fought the Japanese in Shansi from 1937 and by the end of the war his bravery and qualities as a commander had made him legendary. After similar successes in the civil war against the Nationalists, he served in the CCP's Military Affairs Commission and as head of the Sports Commission.

Ho Ying-ch'in   Senior military instructor at the Whampoa Military Academy in the 1920s. He commanded the Second Encirclement Campaign (qv) against the Communists in May 1931. See also *Ho–Umetsu Agreement*.

Hong Merchants   Proprietors of commercial firms — Hongs — in Canton which were authorised as the sole agents of foreign trade. Hongs (a corruption of *yang-hang*, overseas firms) originated during the Ming dynasty and in the 16th century there were thirty-six trading with foreign countries. Known as the Thirteen Hongs, from the number at the end of the Ming dynasty, their number actually fluctuated considerably. There were three groups specialising in trade with Europe and America, South East Asia and Fukien. Under the Ch'ing dynasty, the Hongs rose to power in spite of opposition from another group, the emperor's merchants (Huang-shang) who were eased out when the Hongs and English ships refused to deal with them in 1702. In 1720 the Hong merchants organised themselves into a guild, the Cohong (qv), to strengthen their position.

Hong Kong   Properly the island of Hong Kong ceded in perpetuity to the British crown under the Treaty of Nanking and the Convention of Peking (qqv), but commonly includes the tip of the Kowloon Peninsula also ceded in perpetuity, and the New Territories, lying behind Kowloon City, leased for ninety-nine years in 1898. The colony was attacked by the Japanese in December 1941 and occupied until 1945. Hong Kong is governed as a Crown Colony with a governor; today it provides a window on the world for the People's Republic and a convenient channel for commercial and political dealings, both official and unofficial. In 1998, failing further agreements, the leased territories should revert to China in which case the economy of Hong Kong would collapse, as more than half its manufacturing industry and its water conservancy projects are on leased territories.

Hoppo Superintendent of Canton maritime customs from the early Ch'ing period who negotiated with Western traders through the Hong merchants (qv). The name Hoppo is thought to be a corruption of Hu-pu (Board of Revenue) to which he belonged.

How to be a Good Communist Book written by Liu Shao-ch'i in 1939 criticised during the Cultural Revolution because passages on the importance of Mao Tse-tung Thought were not added to the 1962 edition.

Howqua or **Howkua** One of the best known and richest of the Hong merchants of the 18th and early 19th century (the suffix *qua* or *kua*, incidentally, being a corruption of the honorific designation *kuan*, official.) In 1834 he had built up a fortune of 26 million silver dollars, but he led a frugal life and was famed for his generosity. In March 1839 he was arrested by Lin Tse-hsü (qv) the commissioner charged with suppressing the opium trade and held as a hostage against the British. He pleaded with the British to comply with Lin's demands as he had been threatened with beheading, and he was later released.

Hsi Hsia Kingdom founded by the Tanguts, who were of Tibetan origin, in north-west China in 1038. The Tanguts had created a strong state in the Ordos, Kansu and western Inner Mongolia area by the early 11th century. In 1038 they adopted the Chinese dynastic name of Hsia (they were known by the Chinese as the Hsi Hsia or Western Hsia) and set out to conquer China. They were beaten off and made a treaty with the Sung government in 1044, so that between the Sung, the Hsi Hsia and the Liao (qv) in the north there was a three-way balance of power on the northern frontier. The Sung sent 'brotherly gifts' to the Hsi Hsia to ensure peaceful relations, and trade between the two developed, the Sung paying for Tangut horses with tea, silks, and other goods. The Hsi Hsia kingdom around its capital at Ning-hsin had a semi-oasis economy, combining irrigated agriculture with pastoralism and trade, notably on the central Asian trade route to the West. Their government was based on the Chinese model but the state religion was Buddhist. Between 1205 and 1209 the Hsi Hsia kingdom came under the control of Chinggis Khan and was finally destroyed by the Mongols in 1227.

Hsia Dynasty By tradition the predecessor of the Shang dynasty and the earliest of the Chinese dynasties. Its dates are usually given as from the 23rd to the 18th century BC and the names of a number of rulers have been passed down in legend, but there is as yet no archaeological evidence to justify accepting it as a dynasty. It is possible that future excavations will show that the Hsia existed, as happened in the case of the Shang, and the dynasty might even be linked with the Black Pottery or Painted Pottery cultures (qv).

Hsia-fang Rustication, downward transfer or going down to the countryside. The CCP policy in the 1960s and 70s of sending young college or university graduates and school leavers to rural districts for a period of farm work before appointing them to permanent posts. *Hsia-fang* also involved cadres, officials and intellectuals. The explanation given for the policy was that it brought educated youngsters into closer contact with the peasants, who were regarded as the backbone of China and the main force of the revolution, and removed any aversion they might have to manual labour. The ostensible reason was to remove the last traces of traditional values and reduce the formation of class barriers, but critics have suggested that the policy was needed to reduce urban underemployment and to help halt the mushroom growth of cities.

Hsiang Army Hunan Army (Hsiang is the traditional name for Hunan province) raised by Tseng Kuo-fan (qv) in 1852 to fight the Taiping rebels. 1,080 men in three battalions of 360 were recruited initially, all from Hunan and all owing allegiance to their officers. The army was enlarged to 13 battalions each of 500 men, all quite well paid. At first the force concentrated on bringing its home province of Hunan under control, but then fought the Taipings in Hupeh and Kiangsi and with the Huai Army (qv) which was formed later, was instrumental in putting down the revolt. The Hsiang army was not so successful against the Nien rebellion (qv) and parts of it were demobilised in 1864. The existence of powerful regional armies like the Hsiang Army, locally recruited with personal loyalties to their commanders, can be seen as a factor in the break-up of the unified empire and the growth of warlordism (qv) in the 20th century.

Hsiang Yü Powerful rebel in the area of the old Ch'u states at the end of the Ch'in dynasty. He was eventually defeated by one of his generals, Liu Pang, the eventual founder of the Han dynasty.

Hsiao Ching see *Book of Filial Piety*

Hsien District or County. The lowest unit of local government administration in imperial China and subsequently. It was the seat of a magistrate (qv) who was immediately subordinate to the prefect at the *fu* or prefecture. *Hsien* in the Ch'in period were large units, but the origins of the modern *hsien* are in the Sui and T'ang periods when the old commanderies were divided up. By the Ming dynasty there were 1,171 of them and these increased to about 1,470 under the Ch'ing. The *hsien* government was responsible for administering local taxation, keeping public order and maintaining public works.

Hsien-feng, Ch'ing Emperor (reigned 1850–61) Twenty-year-old successor to the Tao-kuang emperor who followed an even more intransigent foreign policy than his father, dismissing many advocates of appeasement. After the Chinese defeat in the Arrow War and the devastation caused by the Taiping rebellion he lost heart and retired to Jehol. He had always been a weak man and this, combined with self-indulgence, precipitated a fatal illness; he died on August 21, 1861.

Hsien-pei (Hsien-pi) Barbarian tribe, possibly proto-Mongolian, who invaded China early in the 4th century after having attacked the North China plain from as early as 281. In the 4th and 5th centuries they organised the Southern Yen, Northern Yen and Southern Liang states in north-east China, and the T'o-pa clan who founded the Northern Wei dynasty in 386 were largely of Hsien-pei origin.

Hsien-yang Capital of the Ch'in dynasty near the site on which the Han capital of Ch'angan was built.

Hsin ch'ing-nien see *New Youth*

Hsin-an Merchants Merchant syndicate from the Hui-chou prefecture (formerly called Hsin-an after its river and still often referred to by that name) in the southern part of Anhui province. During the Ming and Ch'ing dynasties they shared the bulk of Chinese commerce with the Shansi merchants (qv) from north China. During the Sung period the Hsin-an syndicate was involved with local trade. Their expansion into a nationwide network was partly due to the licences granted to them for the sale of salt during the Ming. From salt trading they moved on to dealing in the products of the great handicraft centres of south-east China: porcelain, tea, cotton, silk, and also timber and rice. Members of the syndicate worked as shopkeepers, warehousemen, pedlars, travelling merchants, and also ran pawnshops and other credit agencies. They became so important that eventually they were providing the financial backing for many small industrial undertakings.

Hsiung-nu Turkish-speaking tribesmen from Central Asia who may have been eastern relatives of the Huns. They founded their first steppe empire in the 3rd century BC and were conquered eventually by the Han dynasty. This first empire ranged from western Manchuria across Mongolia and southern Siberia into Chinese Turkestan as far west as the Pamirs. The Hsiung-nu threat was a constant problem for the Han rulers and the emperor Wu-ti sent army after army against the nomads. It was a war of attrition that cost the lives of thousands of Chinese soldiers, but gradually the power of the Hsiung-nu was reduced. By 127 BC they had been drawn out of the Ordos and in 119 BC they were pushed into the Gobi. Wu-ti sent an emissary, Chang Ch'ien (qv) to make alliances with other Central Asian peoples against the Hsiung-nu and so outflank them, but this attempt was unsuccessful. In 52 BC the ruler of the Hsiung-nu submitted to the Chinese authorities, but fighting continued with the others. In 23 AD they invaded China, sacked the capital and killed Wang Mang who had usurped the throne, but during the later Han they were less of a menace since they were no longer so united. Some Hsiung-nu tribes later settled in north China and in the 4th century AD after the downfall of the Han, founded the state of Chao.

Hsü T'e-li (1877–1968)   One of Mao Tse-tung's earliest teachers, at the First Normal School in Changsha. Hsü, who like Mao was Hunanese and from a peasant family had studied in Japan where he had joined Sun Yat-sen's T'ung-meng Hui. At the school he was a deliberate iconoclast and made a point of arriving on foot rather than in a rickshaw or a sedan chair like the other staff. In 1919, when over forty, he had enrolled as a worker student in Paris and in 1928 he studied at the Sun Yat-sen University in Moscow. He returned to China in 1930 to become Assistant Commissioner for Education in the Kiangsi Soviet, succeeding Ch'ü Ch'iu-pai as Commissioner in 1935 when Ch'ü was executed by the KMT. Hsü was committed to education and became Commissioner for Education in the Border Region Government set up by Mao in Yenan although he was over eighty. After 1949 he served the CCP as a deputy director of the Central Committee's propaganda department and was also a member of the Central Committee and the Standing Committee of the National People's Congress.

Hsüan-te, Ming Emperor (reigned 1426–1435)   Eldest son of the Hung-hsi emperor. He had served as imperial deputy in Nanking and shared his father's reputation for leniency and concern for the people. However his reign was the beginning of the decline of Ming power. Annam was lost in 1428, the navy declined, the northern defences against the Mongols deteriorated and the power of the eunuchs was growing steadily.

Hsüan-tsang (600–664) Most famous of all Chinese Buddhist pilgrims. Hsüan-tsang, like his predecessor Fa-hsien (qv) travelled from Ch'ang-an through Central China to India between 629 and 654, returning with scriptures which he spent the rest of his life translating into Chinese. On his return he was honoured by the emperor who bestowed on him the title Tripitaka (San Tsang). *Record of the Western Regions* is an account of his travels written in 648 at the emperor's command and the Ming novel *Journey to the West* (qv) (translated as *Monkey*) is based on his journeys.

Hsuan-tsung, T'ang Emperor (reigned 712–56) In 710 Hsuan-tsung eliminated the Empress Wu (qv) and her relatives, allowed his father to reign for two years and then took the throne for himself. His long reign, which lasted till the An Lu-shan rebellion, is regarded as a high point of the T'ang dynasty and a key period in the transition from mediaeval to early modern China. It was also a time of conflict between court factions, of population pressure, the deterioration of tax and military systems and the defeats of Chinese armies in Yunnan and Central Asia. In 745 Hsuan-tsung took as his concubine Yang Kuei-fei (qv), the consort of one of his sons, and under her influence neglected his imperial duties. Yang Kuei-fei became the patron of a young general of barbarian origin An Lu-shan (qv) who was given control of nearly 200,000 troops along the north-east frontier and subsequently rebelled against the empire. Hsuan-tsung fled to Szechwan, acceded to the execution of Yang Kuei-fei and then abdicated in favour of one of his sons. The rebellion eventually collapsed but the dynasty was much weakened.

Hsüan-t'ung, Ch'ing Emperor (reigned 1909–1911) see *P'u-I*

Hsün-fu see *Governor*

Hsün-tzu (298 BC–238 BC) Warring States (qv) philosopher and teacher noted for his refutation of the underlying principle of Mencius that man is by nature good. The style of his writings, a series of essays in his work known as the *Hsün-tzu* was a great advance over the dialogue form used by Mencius. He emphasised formal education, discipline, the study of the classics and proper conduct according to traditional rules and rituals. These ideas formed the basis of the Legalist (qv) school of thought and were developed by Han Fei-tzu (qv) and other disciples of Hsün-tzu.

Hu Feng (1903–   ) Left-wing writer and disciple of Lu Hsun who was the subject of a massive propaganda campaign in 1955 during which he was attacked as the ideological representative of the bourgeoisie for demanding more freedom from party control. Like Feng Hsueh-feng he had attempted to fuse Marxist ideas with a belief that literary creativity required subjective emotional commitment. His case was raised during the Hundred Flowers period when he became a symbol of student protest, but he never reappeared.

Hu Han-min Republican revolutionary and contributor to the *People's Tribune* (*Min-pao*) which the T'ung-meng hui (qv) published from 1905. In 1923 he drafted the manifesto for the reorganised KMT in collaboration with the communists and the following year was elected to the KMT's Praesidium of five. When Sun Yat-sen died in 1925 Hu Han-min led the right-wing faction of the KMT in opposition to Wang Ching-wei, and in 1927 he helped Chiang K'ai-shek to organise a government in Nanking in which he headed the Legislative Yuan. His split with Chiang in 1931 enabled the latter to become reconciled with Wang Ching-wei.

Hu Shih (1891–1962) One of the active promoters of language reform and the New Culture Movement (qv) in the 1920s. He was the descendant of Hu Wei, a noted scholar of the early Ch'ing and had himself received a classical education. He graduated from the Chinese Public Institute in 1909 and then studied at Cornell and Columbia Universities on a government scholarship, taking a B.A. and Ph.D. in philosophy in 1915 and 1917 respectively. He was deeply influenced by the pragmatist philosophy of John Dewey and others and on his return to China was an ardent supporter of the movement for writing in the vernacular. In 1921 he interpreted for Dewey on the latter's influential lecture tour of China and continued in his pragmatic approach by advocating evolutionary change and a rejection of ideology, in opposition to Marxists such as Li Ta-chao. He also wanted to see American technology and democracy introduced into China. From 1917 to 1949 he was associated with Peking National University and in his later years became preoccupied with educational administration and public affairs on Taiwan. His literary and philosophical ideas came under constant attack from commentators in the People's Republic.

Hua Kuo-feng (?1920–   ) Mao Tse-tung's successor as Chairman of the CCP. Hua was deputy governor of Hunan from 1958 to 1967 and from 1959 onwards served as secretary of the Hunan provincial party committee. He was a delegate to the National People's Congress in 1964 and Chairman of the Hunan provincial revolutionary committee that was formed in 1968. Hua was appointed Minister of

Public Security and on the death of Chou En-lai in January 1976 became acting premier. In April 1976 Hua was appointed premier and first vice-chairman of the CCP. After the death of Mao Tse-tung, Hua was responsible for the arrest and detention of Chiang Ch'ing and her supporters and took over as party Chairman.

Huai Army   Anti-Taiping force organised by Li Hung-chang (qv) in 1862 around a nucleus of 3,000 troops transferred from the Hunan (or Hsiang) army by Tseng Kuo-fan. Several thousand more men were recruited by Li, most of them from the Huai river region of Anhwei Province, hence the name. In 1862 the army saved Shanghai from an attack by the Taipings and in November 1863 attacked the rebel stronghold of Soochow aided by the Ever Victorious Army (qv) and pacified almost the whole of Kiangsu province. In 1867 the Huai army took over from the Hsiang Army the task of defeating the Nien rebels (qv), suppressed the eastern band in the same year, while the western band was being attacked by Tso Tsung-t'ang (qv), and helped bring about the downfall of the rebels in 1868. The army fought the Japanese in the war of 1894–95, but was defeated at Pyongyang in spite of years of training and preparation, partly because Li Hung-chang had only limited command authority. Like the Hsiang Army it was a forerunner of the private armies of the warlord period, and produced a new type of literate and well-trained military man.

Huai-Hai Campaign (October 1948–January 1949)   One of the decisive campaigns of the Civil War between the CCP and the KMT, fought in the region of Hsuchow. The name is derived from the Huai River and the Lung-Hai Railway between which most of the fighting took place. Communist forces under Ch'en Yi killed over 100,000 KMT troops. 200,000 KMT troops were captured, and two entire divisions defected to the CCP, depriving Chiang K'ai-shek of his best units. The success at the Huai-Hai enabled Mao to direct his forces on towards Nanking, the seat of the Nationalist government, which fell on April 21, 1949.

Huai River Region   In central Anhwei province at the boundary between north and south China.

Huai-nan   T'ang dynasty province in the area south (*nan*) of the River Huai.

Huang Ho   see *Yellow River*

Huang Hsing (1874–1916)   Founder of the China Revival Society

(*Hua-hsing hui*) in 1903 and an early republican revolutionary. In 1905 he, Sung Chiao-jen and Sun Yat-sen all merged their organisations to form the T'ung-meng hui (United League). Huang became head of the executive department and vice-chairman, under Sun. He rapidly became an important figure in the T'ung-meng hui and was asked to become a member of the Provisional Revolutionary Government after the 1911 revolution during which he led the Canton revolt. However when Yuan Shih-k'ai became president, Huang took the humble post of resident general in Nanking and later director-general of the Canton-Hankow and Szechwan railways, but resigned in 1913. Huang did not break completely with Yuan Shih-k'ai. This brought him into conflict with Sun Yat-sen and he spent most of the time before his death in America and Japan.

Huang-ti   see   *Five Emperors*

Huc, Abbé Régis Evariste   French Catholic missionary who travelled in China between 1839 and 1851. He learned Chinese in Hopei where his mission began, and Mongolian when he moved to the northern borderlands. Two books record his travels in the north and in Tibet from where he was eventually ejected by the Lhasa theocracy. He left China in 1851 and died in France in 1860, leaving behind a vivid description of the society and government of 19th century China.

Hui Chinese Moslems   see   *Islam*

Hui-chou Merchants   see   *Hsin-an Merchants*

Hülegü   Grandson of Chinggis Khan, who built up the Mongol Khanate of Persia. He captured Baghdad in 1258 and the Khanate lasted till 1335.

Hunan Army   see   *Hsiang Army*

Hunan Peasant Movement   Movement to develop peasant associations in Hunan province which greatly influenced Mao Tse-tung's thinking on the role of the peasantry in the Chinese revolution. Organisations of peasants in Hunan had begun in about 1925 and were stimulated by the May 30 incident in that year. Mao was involved in organising the militant peasants at this stage and wrote two articles: *Analysis of the Classes in Chinese Society* (March 1926) and *Report on an Investigation of the Peasant Movement in Hunan* (March 1927) in which he developed his analyses of social classes in rural China and the role and potential of peasants and their associations.

Hundred Days Reform (1898) Ill-fated reform movement at the end of the Ch'ing dynasty instigated principally by K'ang Yu-wei (qv). Through a series of memorials that began in 1888, K'ang and others had tried to persuade the emperor to adopt a constitutional form of monarchy on the European model, the modernisation of the examination system and the administrative structure and the establishment of a national assembly or parliament. However the implementation of K'ang's proposals was blocked by conservative elements in the government and court, notably the Empress Dowager. Worried that the proposals might undermine her hold on the government, she backed conservative countermeasures and many of the reforms of examinations, the press and government which were being put into effect were reversed. The movement failed because of the power of the Empress Dowager and the conservative opposition and the inexperience and poor strategy of the reformists. The very failure of the reform, however, was to precipitate the Boxer movement (qv) and develop the revolutionary republican movement that led to the revolution of 1911.

Hundred Flowers Period (1956–57) Period of political and intellectual debate initiated by Mao in 1956 after the Hungarian uprising and Krushchev's secret speech revealing the excesses of Stalin. On May 2 Mao suggested that 'a hundred flowers bloom, a hundred schools of thought contend'. At first, people were reluctant to come forward with criticism and suggestions, being wary of attack. Mao restated his policies, but it was not till about May 1957 that grievances about maladministration, employment, the press and bureaucracy began to be aired publicly for the first time. Many Communists and non-party members wrote articles which were published in the local and national press and some of the ideas put forward were so critical that the party authorities became worried by what they had let loose. An Anti-Rightist movement (qv) was quickly announced in which campaigns were launched against certain critics of the party judged to be rightists.

Hundred Schools of Thought Proliferation of philosophical ideas in the late Chou and Warring States period. As well as Confucian and Taoist ideas there were Naturalists who attempted to explain the workings of the cosmos by certain principles such as the *yin* and *yang*, Dialecticians concerned with meaning, logic and sophistry, Utilitarian disciples of Mo-tzu, followers of Mencius, Legalists, and many others.

Hung Hsiu-ch'uan (1814–64) Leader of the Taiping Rebellion (qv). Hung was born in Kwangtung of a Hakka family on January 1, 1814, went to school till the age of fourteen, supported by family financial sacrifices, and taught in a village school till 1843, attempting but failing the official examinations. In 1838 he suffered a prolonged illness during which he had visions. He later reinterpreted these in the light of a re-reading of a Protestant pamphlet he had acquired in 1837. He saw himself as the Son of God and younger brother of Jesus, specially chosen to establish the Kingdom of God on earth, and his ideas were reinforced when he studied with an American missionary in 1847. In that year he gathered around him a group of disciples, mostly poor Hakkas, who became known as the God-Worshippers. Their ranks were swelled by members of other anti-Manchu secret societies and in 1850 the open rebellion began in earnest. When the Heavenly Kingdom of Great Peace (*T'ai-p'ing T'ien-kuo*) was announced in 1851, Hung was proclaimed Heavenly King with five other kings under him. His forces captured Nanking in 1853 but the Heavenly Kingdom was disrupted by internal strife. This so dispirited Hung that he retired from the day-to-day leadership of the revolution. By 1864 the government forces under Tseng Kuo-fan and Li Hung-chang had defeated many rebel units and were surrounding Nanking. Knowing his cause to be lost, he committed suicide on June 1, 1864. He was succeeded by his son Hung Fu who was executed later in the year when the rebellion collapsed.

Hung-chih, Ming Emperor (reigned 1487–1505)   Ming emperor who succeeded at the age of seventeen and acquired a reputation for being a model ruler. He reigned humanely and uneventfully but was later criticised for having been too tolerant of eunuchs, although eunuchs behaved better under his reign than under most Ming emperors.

Hung-hsi, Ming Emperor (reigned 1425)   Ming emperor of maturity and experience who had served as regent but whose promise was cut short when he died within a year of acceding to the throne. He did, however, reign long enough to stop the voyages of Cheng Ho (qv), possibly considering them a waste of government money.

Hung-lou meng   see   *Dream of the Red Chamber*

Hung-wu, Ming Emperor (reigned 1368–98)   Born in the Huai River area north-west of Nanking, Chu Yuan-chang (1328–98) was orphaned and entered a Buddhist monastery as a novice, but in 1352 at the age of twenty-five he joined a rebel band. In 1356, having built up a large following, he seized Nanking. The power of the ruling Mongol house was declining and Chu was able to consolidate his control of the Yangtze valley, and parts of Hunan and Hopei, and by 1368 was able to seize Peking and proclaim the Ming dynasty (qv). He ruled as the Hung-wu Emperor till his death in 1398 and most of his reign was occupied with reorganising defences, particularly against the defeated Mongols, suppressing rebel bands that had rivalled his own, and organising a new legal code to consolidate his rule. His capital was at Nanking, the centre of his own power-base and the wealthiest part of the country, rather than in Peking which he had wrested from the Mongols.

Huns   see   *Hsiung-nu*

Hupei — Honan — Anhwei Base   see   *O-yu-wan*

Hwai — Hai Campaign   see   *Huai — Hai*

Hwang Ho   see   *Yellow River*

I

Ibn Battuta Arab traveller born in Tangier in 1304 who crossed Asia between 1325 and 1355 and left a record of visits to Mecca, the Caucasus, India and China. Although his report contains improbable travellers' tales, there are also vivid factual descriptions of the port of Ch'üan-chou (Zaytun) and other parts of China.

I-ching see *Book of Changes*

I-ho-t'uan see *Boxer Rebellion*

Ili River and valley in north-west China important in China's relationships with its central Asian neighbours. Yüeh-chih (qv) peoples settled there in the 2nd century BC. In the 13th and 14th century it was one route by which European travellers reached China. In the late 18th century it was captured by the Ch'ing government after the defeat of the Dzungars who lived there. It was occupied by the Russians between 1871 and 1881 because of its mineral riches and strategic importance but returned to China by the Treaty of St Petersburg (qv).

Ili, Treaty of (1851) Agreement by which Russia was granted a foothold in north Sinkiang and the right to trade, build warehouses and establish consulates in Ili and Tarbagatou. Subsequently the Russians occupied the region, holding it from 1871–1881.

Imperial Maritime Customs Foreign-dominated service that replaced the Chinese customs collectorate in 1854 when Western consuls in Shanghai took over the collection of duty during the Small Sword Rising, and remained to a large extent independent of the Chinese government till the nationalist upsurge of the 1920s. It was presided over by the Inspectors General, the most notable of whom was Robert Hart (qv) who served as Inspector General from 1863 to 1908 and created most of the organisational structure and procedures of the service. The maritime customs was responsible principally for preventing smuggling, examining cargoes and assessing the payment of tariffs, which were agreed on by the treaty powers between 1842, when the Treaty of Nanking was signed, and 1928–30, when China's tariffs became autonomous. As well as the Central Revenue Department that dealt with payment, there was a Marine Department which surveyed the coast and inland waterways and policed the harbours, and a Works Department which built and repaired Customs buildings. After Hart's departure for England in 1908, Robert E. Bredon and then Francis A. Aglen succeeded as acting and then substantive Inspectors General, Aglen serving till his dismissal in 1927.

Indusco Gung Ho (kung-ho) or Industrial Co-operative movement set up by Rewi Alley, Edgar Snow and others in 1938 to aid the war of resistance against the Japanese by organising industrial production and training among refugees from the Japanese. The movement was nominally under the control of the Nationalist Executive Yuan, and co-operatives were organised on three levels: portable units capable of operating even behind Japanese lines; semi-mobile but more substantial industries in intermediate areas; mining and machine-tool units in the area furthest from the front. By 1940 over 300,000 people were employed in over 3,000 small co-operative factories. Nationalist attitudes to the movement had always been ambivalent and it collapsed after Rewi Alley was dismissed in 1942 for trying to extend co-operatives to the communist-controlled areas. However the experiment proved a stimulus to post-1949 industrial co-operation.

Inner Asian Frontiers Owen Lattimore's term for the border regions beyond the Great Wall in which a mixed economy of pastoralism and agriculture had been the background for complex political relationships between nomads and Chinese officials throughout history. The cycle of dynastic rise and decline within China interacted with the cycle of unification and dispersal among steppe nomads and the results might be nomad invasion, Chinese domination of the steppe or an uneasy equilibrium.

Inner Mongolia That part of Mongolia nearest to China (cf. Outer Mongolia — now the Mongolian People's Republic) and now part of China as the Inner Mongolian Autonomous Region. It is bounded to the south by a series of mountain ranges on the rim of the Gobi and is a dry desert plain, sparsely populated by oasis people, caravan dwellers and semi-nomadic pastoralists. The pastoralists are today organised into over 2,000 herdsman co-operatives within more than 150 communes, and some agriculture has been developed.

Intrigues of the Warring States (*Chan-kuo ts'e*) Collection of historical romances, biographies and rhetorical exercises of unknown authorship but possibly dating back to the 2nd century BC. The content is mainly concerned with relationships between the Warring States and advocates pragmatic rather than Confucian morality. It is considered to be a work of fiction in a magnificent prose style rather than a historical record.

Iron Age   The Iron age in China is usually considered as being coeval with the Warring States and early Ch'in period. Iron was introduced into China in the 6th century and by the end of the Eastern Chou iron weapons had replaced bronze and an iron-tipped plough drawn by oxen had revolutionised agriculture in north China. See also *Periodisation*.

Irrigation   see   *Water Control*

Islam   By the 9th century Islam had spread to Central Asia where it rapidly supplanted Buddhism. It grew steadily and by modern times was embraced by many millions in north-west and south-west China. In the T'ang and Sung dynasties Islamic traders built up a commercial network that linked China with western Asia by both land and sea. Many Arab traders (qv) and Persians settled in Chinese ports. Islam, like other religions, was tolerated by the Mongol rulers and during the Yuan dynasty was able to consolidate its influence on the western borders. During the late 19th century Moslems in Yunnan, Sinkiang and the north west of China were involved in rebellions against Chinese imperial rule. Under the People's Republic Moslems were organised into the Chinese Islamic Religious Association which was founded in 1952, and is similar to organisations representing Taoists, Buddhists and Christians. It has been estimated that there are about ten million Moslems in China. Most are Kazakhs, Uighurs or Hui people (Dungans) from north-west China.

J

Jade Jade was used as a medium of exchange as early as the Shang dynasty and played a large part in the Han dynasty caravan trade across Central Asia. Jade-carving subsequently became one of the highest achievements of the craftsman. Jade was much revered and used for ritual objects notably for Buddhist figurines in mediaeval China, but later its interest was mainly for its antiquarian associations and as jewellery and ornaments for the banquet and the scholar's study.

Jade Burial Suits see *Manch'eng Tombs*

Jade Emperor One of the gods in the pantheon of popular Taoist deities, the supreme being who presided over all the gods in a hierarchy. The kitchen god in every household reported to the Jade emperor on the activities of the house each New Year.

January Storm (1967) or January Tempest or January Revolution. Critical stage in the Cultural Revolution in Shanghai after support for the old party committee and the new radical Workers' Headquarters had hardened. A radical group of journalists took over the *Wen-hui pao* newspaper on January 2, and on the 4th put out an appeal to the people of Shanghai denouncing the Municipal Committee and their supporters the Scarlet Guards. The appeal was supported by Mao and after a series of strikes and occupations, radical groups came to power in the city. See also *Shanghai Commune, Economism*.

Jao Shu-shih (born 1901) Chairman of the East China Military and Administrative Committee and director of the Central Committee's Organisation Department. In 1953–4, he and Kao Kang came out in support of the Soviet model of economic and industrial management and the separation of party officials and managers. Both Jao and Kao were purged and Jao was imprisoned because of the threat he posed to the positions of Liu Shao-ch'i and Chou En-lai.

Japanese Pirates Pirates were the scourge of China's east coast ports, particularly during the 16th century. The Ming emperor Hung-wu sent three missions to Japan in the period 1369–72 in an attempt to persuade the Japanese rulers to curb pirate activities. Like the privateers of Elizabethan England these were maritime adventurers who turned to trade or looting, whichever was the more profitable. Although known in Chinese records as Japanese Pirates (or more precisely 'dwarf pirates', *wo-k'u*, 'dwarf' being a pejorative epithet applied to the Japanese) the raiders included many Chinese — possibly a majority by the end of the Ming. The response of the Ming government was to prohibit maritime trade, since the dividing-line between legitimate traders and raiders was blurred, but this had the effect of forcing more crews into smuggling and piracy. In the 1550s pirate raids intensified and in some areas became actual invasions. Coastal areas were ravaged. Hangchow was attacked in 1555 and Nanking threatened. The pirates were driven off the mainland and established a base on Taiwan where they remained till suppressed by the armies of the Dutch and the Ch'ing in the mid-17th century.

Jardine Mathieson   Most prominent trading firm in early 20th century China with its head office in Hong Kong and branches in every major port. It had interests in banking, silk manufacture and steam navigation as well as in import and export. It had its origins in the opium trade of the early 19th century; in 1829–30 the firm handled 5,000 chests of opium, one third of the total import.

Jehol   One of the provinces of north-east China during the Republic 1911–1949. Its territory is now divided between the Inner Mongolian Autonomous Region and Liaoning province. The town of Jehol after which the province was named was the refuge of the Hsien-feng emperor and his court during the Arrow War and the rebellions of the 1850s. The region was the centre of the Liao or Khitan empire in the 10th to the 12th century.

Jenghiz Khan   see   **Chinggis Khan**

Jesuits   The first Jesuit in China was Matteo Ricci (1522–1610) (qv) who arrived in Macao in 1582 and became established in Peking in 1600, towards the end of the Ming dynasty. For nearly two hundred years Jesuits remained attached to the Imperial court, converting some Chinese to Christianity and serving as a channel for the exchange of knowledge between China and Europe. The period of their greatest influence was under the K'ang-hsi emperor (qv) of the Ch'ing dynasty, for whom they performed many services as astronomers, cartographers, mathematicians and translators. However their influence only extended to a small group of scholars and officials and never succeeded in affecting the political, economic and social structure of China. The influence of the Jesuits declined after the Rites Controversy (qv) in which they were forced to abandon their practice of allowing Christian converts to perform traditional Confucian rites such as ancestor worship, by which means they had won acceptability in the Chinese court.

Jews The earliest Jewish communities in China were composed of traders who came from the Mediterranean area along with Moslems and Christians and settled in Ch'ang-an. Small communities later appeared elsewhere, notably in Kaifeng, where one group persisted into the Yuan dynasty.

Jirgalang Nephew of Nurhachi (qv) and regent to the first Ch'ing emperor Shun-chih, jointly at first with Dorgon (qv) but reduced to assistant in 1644 and dismissed in 1647. On the death of Dorgon in 1650 Jirgalang returned to power.

Joffe, Adolph Comintern agent sent to China in 1922 to work out the basis of Soviet-KMT-CCP co-operation. Conversations with Sun Yat-sen (qv) led to the joint manifesto of January 26, 1923 which effectively accepted that communism on the Soviet model would not be imported into China and that the USSR renounced its extra-territorial rights and privileges. Following the manifesto and further discussions, Borodin was sent to China to reorganise the KMT.

John of Montecorvino Italian Franciscan Friar sent to Khubilai Khan by Pope Nicholas IV in 1289. He reached Peking in 1295, was appointed Archbishop of Cambaluc (Khanbaligh) in 1307 and died in 1332.

Journey to the West Picaresque novel (translated by Arthur Waley as *Monkey*) written in the Ming dynasty by Wu Ch'eng-en (c1500–1580). It is very loosely based on the historical travels to India of the Buddhist monk-pilgrim Hsüan-tsang (qv) in the 7th century in search of the scriptures, but weaves into the narrative the supernatural and often hilarious exploits of a monkey-spirit who escorts him, and his companions Sandy and Pigsy. As well as being an adventure story, popular in the Ming dynasty and ever since, it contains a strong element of satire, poking fun at the traditional bureacracy of imperial China which is paralleled by the highly stratified heavenly pantheon encountered by Monkey.

Jung-lu (died 1903) Manchu general and confidant of the Empress Dowager Tz'u-hsi. Jung-lu commanded the army in Peking and in 1895 became President of the Board of War. In 1898 with other conservatives he was appointed to the Grand Council after the failure of the Hundred Days reform. He commanded the Peking troops during the Boxer Rising and took part in the peace negotiations that followed its suppression.

Jurched or Jurchen (Ju-chen)   Tungusic-speaking tribesmen of the north-east and ancestors of the Manchus (qv). The Jurched rose to power under the leadership of a man known in Chinese as A-ku-ta, a vassal of the Liao against whom he revolted after uniting Jurched tribes. He founded the Chin dynasty which governed north China from 1122 to 1234 after the Liao dynasty had been destroyed. The Jurched language, an ancestor of Manchu, was written in characters similar in appearance to Chinese but is still largely undeciphered. The name Jurched fell into disuse in the 17th century when it was banned by Abahai because of its vassal associations and replaced by the term Manchu.

K

Kaifeng   In present-day Honan province, capital of the Northern Sung dynasty as well as some smaller ephemeral kingdoms before the Sung reunification. Although its position out on the north China plain made it difficult to defend, it was at the head of the Grand Canal, where it joined the Yellow River, and so was within easy access of the rice bowl of the lower Yangtze. Kaifeng was captured in 1126 by the Chin and made their capital when the Sung were forced south to Hangchow, and it was taken from the Chin by the Mongols in 1245.

Kaiping Mine   Officially-sponsored mine opened north of Tientsin in 1878 under the instructions of Li Hung-chang. Production did not begin till 1881 and coal was supplied to the China Merchants' Steam Navigation Company and the Tientsin Arsenal. Poor working conditions and low wages caused strikes in the following year. It fell into debt to foreign interests, was bought out by a British consortium in 1900, and merged in 1912 into the Kailin Mining Administration.

K'ang Sheng (1899–1975)   Senior communist politician. K'ang Sheng was a trade union organiser in Shanghai in the 1920s and Director of Security in the CCP in the 1930s and 1940s. During 1949–55 he was governor of Shantung and also concerned with higher education and liaison with foreign Communist Parties. In 1956 K'ang Sheng became an alternate member of the Politburo, in 1966 an adviser to the Cultural Revolution Group and after the Cultural Revolution a member of the Politburo's Standing Committee, a vice-chairman of the CCP and of the National People's Congress.

K'ang Yu-wei (1858–1927)   Radical reformer of the late 19th century. A highly educated Confucian scholar from a well-to-do family in Kwangtung, K'ang was impressed by the administration of the British-dominated cities of Shanghai and Hong Kong which he visited. In 1883, he abandoned a civil service career to devote himself to studying the West and spent the rest of his life teaching and writing about reform and submitting memorials on reforms to the emperor. He portrayed Confucius as a great reformer and had a utopian faith in equality which was expressed in his *Ta-t'ung shu* (Book of the Great Togetherness). He supported the Modern Text movement and the Society for the Study of National Strengthening and was most influential during the Hundred Days Reform of 1898 (qv) when his ideas on a constitutional monarchy interested the emperor but attracted the opposition of conservative elements at court. When the Empress Dowager Tz'u-hsi (qv) took over control in 1898 she ordered K'ang's arrest but he fled to Shanghai and then Hong Kong and Japan. After the establishment of the Republic in 1912 his monarchist ideas had lost their attraction and he lived mainly in retirement. He had many followers of whom the best known was Liang Ch'i-ch'ao (qv).

K'ang-hsi, Ch'ing Emperor (reigned 1662–1722) Hsüan-yeh, third son of the Shun-chih emperor, succeeded his father at the age of eight. In 1669 at the age of sixteen he took over personally from his regents with the help of Songgotu, an uncle. He was an energetic ruler working long hours in audiences, considering memorials and studying, and a keen traveller and huntsman. His reign was noted for concerted attempts to suppress corruption and reduce taxation and for his patronage of learning. In military matters, he completed the consolidation of the empire and put down the revolt of the Three Feudatories (qv). Wars with Mongol tribes and Russia followed, the latter being ended by the Treaty of Nerchinsk (qv) in 1689. K'ang-hsi is perhaps best known in the West for his spirit of inquiry and open-mindedness. He accepted Jesuit scholars in China and learned much about the West and Western science from them.

Kao Kang (1902–1954) Born into a Shensi landlord family, Kao Kang joined the CCP in 1926 and served in the Red Army and the Shen-Kan-Ning base area (qv) which he helped create in 1935. After holding important posts in Yenan, he was party secretary of the north-east (Manchuria). In 1953–54 he was criticised for anti-party activities, principally for having tried to make Manchuria more independent of the CCP government in Peking. He committed suicide in 1954.

Kao-tsu, Han Emperor (reigned 206–195 BC) Posthumous title of the first Han emperor, Liu Pang. Liu had been an officer in the army of Hsiang Yü who had rebelled against the Ch'in dynasty, but he defeated his former master in 202 BC and set up a new dynasty at Ch'ang-an (qv). He called his house the Han after the Han River and back-dated his accession as emperor to 206 BC when he had been named King of Han by Hsiang Yü. His reign was devoted to consolidating his control and liquidating vassal kings of his own creation who had become too powerful. He was succeeded in name by a son but in reality by the Empress Lü, one of his consorts. On her death in 180 BC Wen-ti, a son of Kao-tsu, succeeded.

Kao-tsu, T'ang Emperor (reigned 618–628)   Li Yuan was a prominent official of the Sui dynasty who captured Ch'ang-an in 617, spurred on by his ambitious son Li Shih-min, and became the first emperor of the T'ang, known to history by his posthumous title of Kao-tsu. In 628 he abdicated in favour of his son who was later known as T'ai-tsung.

Kao-tsung, T'ang Emperor (reigned 649–683)   Succeeded his father the T'ai-tsung emperor and made the Empress Wu (qv), a former concubine of his father's, his empress. In 683 she succeeded him and declared herself empress in 690. During Kao-tsung's reign, a costly military campaign brought Korea under Chinese rule.

Kara Khitai   Empire also known as the Western Liao established by the Khitan (qv) in East Turkestan from 1124–1211 after they had been driven west by the Jurched (qv). In 1211 it was overrun by the Mongols under Chinggis Khan.

Karakorum   Capital of the Mongol empire, built by Ögödei Khan. Khubilai Khan built a new capital, Khanbalik, near present-day Peking and Karakorum fell into ruin.

Kazakhs   Pastoral nomads, nominally Moslem, living on both sides of the Russo-Chinese border in the Sinkiang or Turkestan region. There was much dispute as to whether a great movement of Kazakhs across the border into Russia in 1962 was due to political pressure or merely part of their traditional migration pattern.

Key Economic Areas   Regions isolated by Chi Ch'ao-ting as having been important in particular periods of Chinese history. These were usually key areas of grain production which when controlled by a strong political power permitted that power to dominate the rest of the country and generally led to periods of stability.

Khanbaligh   Mongol capital built by Khubilai Khan outside present-day Peking. Khanbaligh, also called Tai-tu, Great Capital, by the Mongols and transcribed as Cambaluc by Marco Polo, means 'city of the Khan' in Turkish.

Khitan   Mongolian-speaking tribes who founded the Liao dynasty and later the Kara Khitai dynasty in north and north-west China. A semi-agricultural, semi-nomadic people with shamanistic religious beliefs, they came to power in southern Manchuria in the 10th century and gradually came to control much of Mongolia. They destroyed the Later Chin dynasty in 946, claimed the Chinese throne as the Liao dynasty, but were able to rule only the northern part of China. Each Khitan tribe was led by a military chieftain and supported itself in peacetime by growing millet and pasturing sheep and horses. Clans were in a hierarchy with the Yeh-lü clan at the head. Their military power was based on the combination of mounted archery and siege techniques.

Khubilai Khan (1215–94)   Grandson of Chinggis Khan (qv) who became Great Khan in 1260 and ruled for thirty-four years. After defeating a brother who claimed the throne at Karakorum, Khubilai established his winter capital at Peking from where his armies conquered south China. Hangchow, capital of the Southern Sung, was taken in 1276 and in 1279 Canton and the Sung fleet were destroyed. In spite of expeditions in 1274 and 1281 he never succeeded in conquering Japan. In 1271 Khubilai had taken the Chinese dynastic name Yuan (qv) for his rule and he became for history a Chinese-style emperor. He protected Confucian temples and scholars but discriminated against southerners in his administration. Marco Polo (qv) served Khubilai for seventeen years between 1275 and 1292.

Kiakhta, Treaty of (1727)   Treaty signed between Russia and China on October 21, 1727 after thirty meetings in six months to discuss frontier delimitation, trade and religious missions. A French Jesuit liaised between the two delegations. China lost a great deal of territory to Russia on the Mongolia-Siberia frontier and Russia gained considerable trading concessions and the right to station a religious mission in Peking.

Kiangnan   see   *Chiang-nan*

Kiangnan Arsenal   Major accomplishment of the early phase of the Self-Strengthening Movement (qv). The Kiangnan Arsenal under the sponsorship of Tseng Kuo-fan (qv) was set up in 1865 at Shanghai with machines brought from the United States by Yale's first Chinese graduate, Yung Wing. It manufactured guns and cannon, built ships and ran a translation bureau. Five ships were built but shipbuilding declined in favour of munitions after 1875. Many Western works on science, military affairs and technology were translated and read eagerly by, among others, K'ang Yu-wei (qv). By 1890 the arsenal employed over two thousand workers.

Kiangsi Soviet   Independent area governed by the CCP from 1931–34 with its headquarters and capital at Juichin in south Kiangsi. After Chiang K'ai-shek's massacre of communists and trade unionists

H

in Shanghai in April 1927 and the subsequent purge of government and mass organisations, the CCP retreated to the countryside, regrouped at Chingkangshan (qv) and then extended their control over south Kiangsi. As the area expanded, from the Central Soviet base around Juichin, other soviets were added in north-east Kiangsi, on the Honan-Hopei-Anhwei border, in west Hupei and in south Kwangsi. The Central Soviet Government was formally constituted in late 1931 with Mao Tse-tung as Chairman, after the failure of CCP forces, under the influence of the Li Li-san line (qv), to capture major urban centres. The Soviet Republic was established as a democratic dictatorship of workers and peasants, led in practice by the local Communist Party and Red Army. The support of the majority of peasants in the region was won by land reform (qv) policies which involved radical redistribution of land to the less wealthy farmers and new marriage and labour legislation was enacted. The Kiangsi Soviet finally collapsed after a series of five encirclement campaigns (qv) from 1930 to 1934 mounted by Nationalist forces. In mid-1934 the CCP decided to abandon the Soviet base and so began the legendary Long March (qv). In spite of this evacuation and the short period that the area was controlled by the CCP it was a time of extremely important experiments in revolutionary social and economic policies the results of which profoundly affected policies during the Yenan period and after 1949.

Kiaochow   Bay in Shantung province used as a winter harbour by Russia and seized by Germany 1897. The Chinese government was forced to grant a 99-year lease and concessions to build 285 miles of railway-track in Shantung between Tsingtao, the main port, and Tsinan. This precipitated a scramble for other concessions by European powers. In Shantung the occupation of Kiaochow caused many conflicts over railways, mines and churches and the Big Sword Society of that province, who called for patriotic Chinese to rise and kill the foreigners, were precursors of the Boxers. During the First World War Japan joined the allies, ousted Germany from the naval base and took over most of Shantung. When the port was not returned to China after the Versailles settlement, nationalist feeling was outraged. Japan returned Kiaochow to China in 1922 after the Washington Conference (qv) but re-occupied it between January 1938 and 1945.

Kingtechen   see   *Ching-te chen*

KMT   see   *Kuomintang* (Nationalist Party)

Ko Lao Hui   see   *Elder Brother Society*

Korea Came under Chinese suzerainty as early as the T'ang dynasty and was a tributary state of the Ch'ing empire. It was opened to trade with Japan in 1876 and after the Sino-Japanese War (qv) of 1894–5 came more and more under Japanese influence. After the Russo-Japanese War of 1904–5 (qv) Japan effectively controlled Korea, annexing it formally in 1910. After the Japanese defeat in 1945 Korea was partitioned, the North supported by the Soviet Union and the South by the United States.

Korean War The Korean War broke out in June 1950, and when United Nations forces moved into North Korea and on towards the frontier with China, the Chinese government perceived a threat to its crucial industrial complexes in Manchuria and committed large numbers of troops to the defence of the North. These Chinese People's Volunteers bore the brunt of the fighting between November 1950 and July 1951 when preparatory talks began that led to the armistice eventually signed in 1953. All China was mobilised in a Resist America and Aid Korea campaign, and the war had a profound effect on the economy and society of the new People's Republic. The demobilisation of the civil war armies which would have released more workers for agricultural and industrial production was held up just as the Agrarian Reform Law was announced. The mass *su-fan* (qv) campaigns against counter-revolutionaries and the Three-Anti, Five-Anti and thought reform campaigns (qqv) were part of the discipline and repression of the new war-time atmosphere.

Kowtow or Kotow The 'three kneelings and nine prostrations' required of those presenting tribute to the emperor. Although it was accepted by other Asian peoples as part of the conditions of trade, the kowtow (literally 'knocking the head') was unacceptable to Western diplomats and traders, notably Lord Macartney (qv) in his 1793 embassy.

Koxinga (1624–1662) Cheng Ch'eng-kung, a Ming loyalist and the son of a supporter of Prince T'ang who had been proclaimed emperor by supporters of the Ming in Canton in 1646, two years after the fall of the dynasty. The name Koxinga is a Dutch corruption of Kuo-hsing-yeh, Lord of the Imperial Surname, as Cheng was popularly known after being granted the Ming imperial surname of Chu by Prince T'ang in 1645. After further honours from the Prince, Koxinga embarked on a military career after his father's defection to the Manchu Ch'ing dynasty. He made Amoy and Quemoy his bases, raided the south-east coast of China and set up a military and civil organisation there. In 1658–9 he raided Chekiang and Kiangsu provinces and advanced on Nanking where he was defeated in September 1659. He retreated, taking Taiwan from its Dutch occupiers in 1661 and used it as a base for his operations against the Ch'ing. The government executed his father and brother and sealed off supplies to the island and although his son Cheng Ching carried on the resistance when Koxinga died in 1662 the spirit of the movement had gone; Taiwan fell to the Ch'ing forces in 1683 and in 1684 became a prefecture of Fukien province, completing the Ch'ing conquest of China.

Ku Yen-wu (1613–1682)   Early Ch'ing scholar who travelled widely and advocated the study of practical problems rather than the esoteric speculation practised by Wang Yang-ming (qv) and his followers. His systematic methods of study assisted in the liberation of Chinese thought from Ming metaphysics.

Kuang-hsu, Ch'ing Emperor (reigned 1875–1908)   Last but one of the Ch'ing emperors. Born Tsai-t'un, he was the son of Prince Chün and the Empress Dowager's sister. He was chosen by the Empress Dowager, Tz'u-hsi to succeed the T'ung-chih emperor, who died without issue, and acceded to the throne on January 12, 1875 at the age of four with dowagers Tz'u-hsi and Tz'u-an as co-regents. Emperor Kuang-hsu reached his majority in 1887 but was not able to rule personally till 1889 when Tz'u-hsi retired to the summer palace from where she continued to exercise considerable influence. Kuang-hsu's reign saw the defeat of the Chinese navy in the 1894–95 Sino-Japanese War, the failure of the Hundred Days reform (qv) in 1898 and the Boxer rebellion of 1900 (qv).

Kuang-wu, Han Emperor (25–57 AD)   Posthumous imperial title of Liu Hsiu who consolidated the power of the later or Eastern Han after the Wang Mang (qv) interregnum. He suppressed the Red Eyebrow (qv) rebellion, re-created the strong central administration of the earlier Han and subdued the Southern Hsiung-nu on the northern frontiers.

Kuan-tu shang-pan   Officially-supervised commercially-run businesses. The most common form of semi-official business enterprises in the late Ch'ing period. The system was intended to provide protection for the establishment of new industries in the face of Western competition but government control may have inhibited investment.

Kuantung Army   see   *Kwantung Army*

Kuantung Leased Territory   see   *Kwantung Leased Territory*

Kuan-tzu (Kuan Chung)   Administrative expert who advised Duke Huan of Ch'i state in the 7th century BC. The book known as the *Kuan-tzu* is attributed to him. The date and authorship of the book are in doubt but it is part of the Legalist (qv) tradition in Chinese philosophy. Kuan-tzu is also believed to have been responsible for the centralised government in Ch'i which was a model for later rulers and for the first state monopoly (qv) of salt and iron.

Kubilai Khan   see   *Khubilai Khan*

Kung, H. H. (1881–1967)   Financier and politician married to the elder sister of Soong Ching-ling and Soong Mei-ling (qqv), the wives of Sun Yat-sen and Chiang K'ai-shek respectively. H. H. Kung was a supporter of Sun in the 1911 Revolution and served Chiang K'ai-shek as Minister of Industry in 1928 and Minister of Finance from 1933 to 1944. After the war he retired from political life and lived mainly in the United States.

Kung, Prince   Younger brother of the Ch'ing emperor Hsien-feng (qv). Prince Kung was left in Peking to supervise the peace settlement in 1860 after the Arrow War (qv) and the Convention of Peking (qv) was dictated to him on October 24 by Lord Elgin. Since he had remained in Peking while the emperor and court had fled to Jehol, Prince Kung's power and influence grew, but on the death of the Hsien-feng emperor in 1861 he was pushed into the background, although he eventually emerged as co-regent with the Empress Dowager Tz'u-hsi. He was very much aware of the importance of foreign relations, and was responsible for the establishment of the Tsungli Yamen (qv) in Peking on March 11, 1861 and also for the creation of new superintendencies of trade at Tientsin and Shanghai. He appointed Horatio N. Lay as Inspector-General of customs thus institutionalising the foreign inspectorate of customs. As a keen supporter of the Self-Strengthening movement (qv) the prince commissioned the purchase of the first steamships for the Chinese navy, which he created. He was bitterly opposed by conservative elements in court and after quarrels with Tz'u-hsi in 1869 over his position and after manoeuvring against a eunuch favourite of the Empress Dowager, he lost all influence in the court.

Kuo Mo-jo (1892–1978)   Poet, novelist, playwright, literary critic, translator and historian. Kuo Mo-jo was born in Szechwan and studied medicine in Japan where he qualified as a doctor and began writing. He never practised medicine but devoted himself to literary and political activities. He became a Marxist in 1924–5 and was a leading member of the Creation Society, took part in the Northern Expedition in 1926–7 as deputy director of the National Revolutionary Army's Political Department, joined the Nanchang rising in 1927 and then fled to Japan after its failure, and studied ancient history and palaeography. His writing, which includes poetry, autobiography and short stories based on historical characters, was overshadowed in the 1950s and 1960s by his involvement in literary and political administration.

Kuomintang (Nationalist Party)   Political party formed by Sun Yat-sen and his lieutenant Sung Ch'iao-jen at the end of 1911 out of the T'ung-meng hui (qv) and other political splinter-groups. In the parliamentary elections of 1912 the Nationalists took 269 out of 596 seats in the lower house and 123 out of 274 in the upper house, giving them a clear majority over all the other parties, but their opposition to Yuan Shih-k'ai caused them to be outlawed in 1913. Sun fled to Japan and reorganised the Nationalists into the Chinese Revolutionary Party, a tighter, more centralised organisation. After the death of Yuan and the upsurge of the May 4 Movement (qv) the party was renamed the Chinese Nationalist Party (Kuomintang) and formed a republican administration in Canton in 1921. Sun received support and advice from the Soviet Union, began to reorganise the KMT on the democratic centralist lines of a communist party and admitted individual CCP members to the KMT in the first alliance between the two parties. When Sun died in 1925 the KMT, now led by Chiang K'ai-shek, spearheaded the Northern Expedition (qv) which re-unified most of China under the Nanking government (qv). In 1927 Chiang isolated and then expelled the CCP and tried to build an independent and centralised party organisation. The party remained in opposition to the CCP apart from the brief Second United Front (qv) after the Sian incident (qv) of 1936, its government moving to Chungking after the Japanese invasion of China. After the defeat of the Japanese the Nationalists moved back to Nanking, but after a costly civil war were forced to retreat to Taiwan by the Communists. The Nationalists now form the government of the Chinese Republic on Taiwan.

Kwantung Army   Army command established by the Japanese in about 1906 to control the Kwantung Leased Territory (see below). In 1928 the command moved with the railway to Mukden in the heart of Manchuria, and, almost free from Tokyo's control, became the main force attempting to wrest Manchuria from China. The Japanese officers who controlled the army saw it as a bulwark against the southward advance of the USSR. Clashes between Chinese and

Japanese in Manchuria led to the Mukden incident (qv) in 1931 after which the Kwantung Army occupied Mukden. Kwantung officers were instrumental in advocating the Japanese invasion of China in 1937.

Kwantung Leased Territory Name for the southern part of the Liaotung peninsula including Port Arthur (qv) and Dairen under its Japanese administration after 1906. Until 1919 it was administered by a governor-general who was concurrently the commander of the Kwantung Army. In 1919 the army command and civilian administration were separated, but the jurisdiction of both was extended to include the railway zone up to Manchuria. In the 1920s Kwantung was the springboard for Japanese expansion into Manchuria.

L

Labour Service Levies   see   *Corvée*

Lama Buddhism or Lamaism   Shamanistic version of Buddhism practised in Tibet and Mongolia and characterised by the spiritual authority of vast numbers of lamas ('superior ones'). Buddhism was introduced into Tibet in about the 8th century in a late and somewhat debased form which fused with the native popular cult known as Bon. Lamaism spread among the Mongols in the 13th century, partly because of its resemblance to traditional Mongol shamanism. During the 16th century a reforming sect of Lamaism, the Yellow or Yellow Hat sect, grew up in opposition to the established Red Sect, whose lack of monastic discipline they criticised. The Yellow Sect, whose head later received the title of Dalai Lama (qv), became established as the official religion in Mongolia, and by the skilful use of Manchu and Mongol support, eventually achieved spiritual and temporal power in Tibet.

Land Reform   Confiscation and redistribution of land, particularly with reference to the CCP from the 1930s onwards. Inequalities in the ownership of farm land have always posed problems in China; they limited agricultural productivity and were a major cause of rural poverty and famines. Proposals for reform appear early in Chinese history. In 9 AD Wang Mang (qv) attempted to break up large private estates, and the programmes of many post-Han peasant rebellions included the redistribution of land. See also *Equal Field System, Manorial System.* The best known pre-Communist proposals for reform were those of the Taiping rebels (qv) and Sun Yat-sen. The Taipings wanted to bring all land under common ownership and allocate it according to the size of families, with all grain produced surplus to subsistence requirements to be handed in to a public granary. Sun Yat-sen, deeply influenced by the Taiping programme, advocated 'land to the tiller' and although neither the Taiping policy nor his own was ever implemented, the ideas provided a stimulus to the agrarian policies of the CCP which were put into practice. The Communists introduced land reform in the areas they controlled from the 1930s, when stringent policies of confiscating land from landlords and redistribution were carried out, while the Kiangsi Soviet (qv) was being defended against the Nationalists. In Yenan, during the United Front (qv) period (1937–45) more moderate policies of lowering rents and interest rates were implemented but in the civil war period (1947–50) policies became harsher, much land was confiscated and many landlords were killed. In June 1950 when the CCP was firmly in control of China it was possible to promulgate an Agrarian Reform Law which laid down the precise criteria for confiscation and redistribution and tried to ensure that the policy was carried out uniformly throughout the country. As a result of this law, well over 100,000,000 acres of land were redistributed by the end of 1952. Since ownership of land was the basis of the rural power structure, the power of landlords was broken and the growth of Communist-led peasant associations (qv) in the reform movement enabled the new government to consolidate its control of the country-side. 'Land to the tiller' was not however meant as an end in itself; it was a prelude to the programme of collectivisation (qv) which it greatly facilitated by removing the economic and political basis of resistance.

Land Tax   Taxation based on land ownership and paid in kind. Land Tax formed the basis of state revenue from the Han dynasty onwards when the rate was fixed at 1/15th and later at 1/30th part of the produce. Rationalisation of tax payments in the T'ang dynasty produced the Double Tax system (qv) which was also adopted by the Ming although the latter further consolidated land taxes with other obligations in the single-whip (qv) system, which moved towards the collection of the greater part of the dues in silver. Part of the tax collected went to the various levels of local government and in some provinces part was also delivered direct to the capital as grain tribute (qv).

Landsmannschaften   Regional guilds or native place associations (*t'ung-hsiang hui*) organised by merchants from a particular area. They established guild halls in major commercial centres such as Peking and the great ports which offered mutual aid and mutual guarantees.

Lan-t'ien Man (*Sinanthropus Lantienensis*)   Palaeolithic man whose remains, some 600,000 years old, were discovered in 1963 in Lan-t'ien county in Shensi province. Lan-t'ien man is considered to be earlier than Peking man.

Lao She (1899–1966)   Writer and dramatist, real name Shu Ch'ing-ch'un, who taught Chinese in London and lectured in China and America. He wrote humorous stories and novels in the 1920s and 1930s but later became concerned with social issues and then patriotic themes during the war. He is best known for *Rickshaw Boy* and *Cat County*. He died during the Cultural Revolution in circumstances which are still not clear.

Lao Tzu   Author, probably mythical, of the most important work in the Taoist canon, the *Tao Te Ching* (qv). Lao Tzu, the Old Master, is traditionally supposed to have lived some time before Confucius, between about 570 and 490 BC.

Latifundia   Large estates owned by Han dynasty officials or merchants and worked by tenants or slaves. They spread in the Han period because of heavy taxation levied on independent peasants.

Laws of the Great Ming or Ming Code (*Ta Ming Lü*)   Penal and administrative code of the Ming compiled in 1373–4 and based on the T'ang code. It was revised completely for its third edition in 1397.

Lay, Horatio N.   Lord Elgin's assistant during the negotiations preparatory to the Treaty of Tientsin in 1858. In 1861 he was appointed Inspector-General of the Imperial Maritime Customs after having previously served as British vice-consul in Shanghai and Inspector of Customs after the resignation of Thomas Wade in 1855. On his appointment in 1861 however he went home to England pleading poor health. He was eventually succeeded by Robert Hart.

League of Left-Wing Writers   Radical organisation founded under the auspices of the CCP in February 1930. It was led by Ch'ü Ch'iu-pai but when Lu Hsun (qv) joined he became its best-known spokesman. With his prestige the League became the dominant group in literary circles. It published many journals advocating literature for the masses and influenced a whole generation of writers.

Left Kuomintang   Group of dissident Nationalists led by Wang Ching-wei (qv) which maintained an alliance with the CCP after its expulsion from the main KMT party organisation in April 1927 and which operated for a time as the Wuhan government. Through the influence of the warlord Feng Yu-hsiang, Wang and the Wuhan government moved towards the Nanking government of Chiang K'ai-shek and broke off their alliance with the CCP in July 1927. By 1928 the KMT had been reunified.

Legalists   Pragmatic authoritarian school of philosophy derived from Hsün-tzu (qv) that grew up in the Warring States period with Han Fei Tzu (qv) as its leading thinker. The Legalists felt that man's nature was essentially selfish and that harsh laws and strict rule were necessary to avoid conflict. In this they opposed the Confucian idea of the essential goodness of man and advocated states governed by absolute rulers with a comprehensive system of laws. The Ch'in statesmen Li Ssu and Shang Yang were closely associated with Legalist ideas and their application was considered to be one of the reasons why Ch'in was able to overcome the other Warring States and establish the first Chinese empire. However Legalist philosophers were later banned by the Han emperor Wu-ti and although the Chinese state became Legalist in terms of practical administration, its philosophy was Confucian and the opposing philosophies found some kind of equilibrium in the balance between practice and theory.

Legge, James (1815–1897)   Missionary in Malacca and Hong Kong, first professor of Chinese at Oxford University and author of an edition and translation of the Confucian classics.

Lei Feng (1939–1962)   Model communist whose diary was used as the central text in the emulation of heroes campaigns of the Socialist Education Movement (qv) in the early 1960s. He was born into a Hunan peasant family who had suffered at the hands of the KMT and the Japanese, and was orphaned as a young child. He was a member of the Young Pioneers and took an active part in the co-operativisation drive, and was admitted to the Communist Youth League in 1957 and the CCP in 1960. He drove a bulldozer in the iron and steel town of Anshan before joining the People's Liberation Army in 1959. Lei Feng was killed by a falling telegraph-pole while on duty, and his diary was read by hundreds of thousands who were urged to model themselves on his devotion to duty and close study of Mao Tse-tung's writings.

Li — Fournier Agreement (1884)   Agreement between Li Hung-chang (qv) and the French naval captain F. E. Fournier which called for Chinese recognition of French treaties with Annam (Vietnam), withdrawal of Chinese troops from Tongking and no French invasion or demand for indemnity from China. The French parliament refused to ratify the agreement because it recognised Chinese suzerainty over Annam. Final agreement on the French position in Annam was not reached till after the Franco-Chinese War (qv).

Li Fu-ch'un (1899–1975)   Senior Communist economic administrator. Li Fu-ch'un was deputy director of the central committee's Finance and Economic Committee and held various economic and industrial posts in the party and government. He became vice-premier and chairman of the State Planning Commission in 1954 and joined the Politburo in 1956 and its Standing Committee in 1966. He remained as vice-premier throughout the Cultural Revolution.

Li Hsien-nien (c1907–   ) Communist economic specialist and minister of finance and vice-premier in 1954. Li Hsien-nien joined the Politburo in 1956, became vice-premier in 1975 and served as party vice-chairman under Hua Kuo-feng.

Li Hung-chang (1823–1901) Modernising leader of the Self-Strengthening movement (qv). Li was one of the first to recognise that foreigners were beginning to dominate China because their military technology and science were superior to that of China. He was the founder of the Huai Army which played a major part in the defeat of the Taiping and Nien rebellions and learned about the superiority of Western armaments from his association with foreign units like the Ever-Victorious Army in these campaigns. From 1870 he was governor-general of Chihli and High Commissioner of the Northern Ports, positions which enabled him to put into practice his self-strengthening ideas and build up a substantial military and industrial empire, mainly in North China. He was responsible for initiating major projects such as the Nanking Arsenal in 1867, the China Merchants' Steam Navigation Company in 1872, naval and military academies in Tientsin in 1880 and 1885 respectively and the Peiyang fleet in 1888. In spite of his reform attempts, his Huai Army and Peiyang Fleet were defeated in the war of 1894–5 between China and Japan. In 1900 Li Hung-chang took the responsibility for negotiating the Boxer Protocol with the Western powers. He died in the following year.

Li Li-san Line   Advocacy of a new revolutionary upsurge in 1929–1930 by Li Li-san who dominated the CCP at that time. Li, like Mao Tse-tung was born in Hunan and after education at the Hunan Teachers' Training College went to France in 1919 on the Work-Study scheme. He went on to Moscow and on his return to China in 1923 was active as a trade union organiser in Canton before revisiting Moscow in 1926. After the Sixth Congress of the CCP in 1928 he became the effective leader of the party and concentrated on organising and arming the urban workers. Under his influence, massive offensives were launched on the cities of Changsha, Wuhan, Nanchang and other centres in the summer of 1930 to join up with risings of workers that were expected. The insurrections did not materialise and the military adventure was a failure. Li Li-san was subsequently condemned for his policies and lost all authority in the party until 1946 when he rejoined the Central Committee. In 1958 he became vice-chairman of the National Trade Union Federation and was for a time Minister of Labour. During the Cultural Revolution he was attacked by Red Guards and it was rumoured that he committed suicide in 1967.

Li Po (701–762)   Also known as Li T'ai-po. One of the two great poets of the T'ang dynasty and friend of the other, Tu Fu (qv). Probably born in Central Asia outside the boundaries of present-day China and possibly with Turkish connections, Li Po's family settled in Szechwan when he was five. He travelled constantly, drank heavily and in spite of his poetic talent refused to take examinations for the imperial civil service. He was a devoted follower of Taoism with an interest in the natural world and alchemy. The thousand or so poems that he wrote were in traditional free metres with a lush vocabulary and combined in their content a Chinese tradition with exotic echoes from his Inner Asian background.

Li Shih-chen (1518–1593)   Author of an illustrated materia medica the *Pen-tsao kang-mu* which was completed in 1578 after 26 years' work. It described more than two thousand drugs from animal, vegetable and mineral preparations and gave over eight thousand prescriptions.

Li Ssu (died 208 BC)   Leading Ch'in statesman and disciple of Hsün-tzu and the Legalists. Although a native of Ch'u he entered the service of the King of Ch'in in 247 BC and played an important part in the consolidation of Ch'in rule and the triumph of the first empire. He was instrumental in the standardisation of weights and measures, axle lengths, coinage and the writing system. In 213 he organised a literary inquisition of undesirable books which were destroyed in keeping with the legalist philosophy of pragmatic authoritarianism. The 'burning of the books' spared only the historical records of Ch'in, utilitarian works such as agricultural and medical treatises and certain official collections. On the death of the First Emperor, Shih Huang-ti, in 210 BC, he and the chief eunuch Chao Kao (qv) put a weak Second Emperor on the throne. Li Ssu was later however put to death by Chao Kao.

Li Ta-chao (1888–1927)   One of the founding fathers of Chinese Marxism. Born of humble origins in Hopei, Li studied in Peking and Japan where like many other Chinese students he became a keen nationalist. On returning to China he worked as a journalist in Peking. In 1918 he was appointed Director of the Peking University Library and then Professor of History. In collaboration with Ch'en Tu-hsiu (qv) he founded the journals *Weekly Critic* and *New Tide* as well as being involved in *New Youth*. He was probably the first Chinese to become fully aware of the importance of the Russian Revolution and his eventual conversion to Marxism can be dated from an article of his in the May 1919 issue of *New Youth*. He was executed by the police of Chang Tso-lin (qv) in the Soviet embassy in Peking in April 1927.

Li Teh   see   *Braun, Otto*

Li Tsung-jen   Leader of the Kwangsi warlord clique in the 1920s who remained independent in south-west China till the 1930s when his forces joined in the Nanking Government's resistance against Japan. In 1948 he was elected vice-president of the Chinese Republic under Chiang K'ai-shek's presidency and took over the government in 1949 when Chiang resigned temporarily. Li Tsung-jen entered into negotiations with the Communists in vain and yielded the presidency to Chiang on Taiwan in 1950.

Li Tzu-ch'eng (c1605–1645)   Leader of one of the many rebellions that preceded the downfall of the Ming dynasty. His forces advanced on Peking in April 1644 and took the town on 25 April, the Ming emperor hanging himself when the city fell. The rebels captured the father of Wu San-kuei (qv), commander of the forces at Shanhaikuan, in an attempt to force his son to surrender. Wu retreated to his garrison and invited the Manchus to join him against the rebels. The combined Ch'ing armies forced Li back to Peking where he killed Wu's father and proclaimed himself emperor. As the Ch'ing forces advanced he burned part of the city, and escaped to the West when they entered Peking on June 6. He was killed in June or July 1645 when fleeing from the Ch'ing armies, reputedly by villagers whom he was raiding for food.

Li Yuan   see   *Kao-tsu, T'ang Emperor*

Liang   Various states and minor dynasties bore the name Liang in the period of division after the fall of the Han. An Earlier Liang dynasty controlled the Kansu corridor from 313 to 376 and the Later Liang was established there by a Tibetan general in 386. The Southern Liang, 397–414, and Northern Liang, 397–439, which were Hsien-pei and Hsiung-nu states respectively, and the Western Liang, 401–421, which was possibly Chinese, were all in the same area. One of the Six Dynasties (qv) was known as Liang and ruled from Nanking between 502 and 557. After the collapse of the T'ang dynasty, a Later Liang which was established in 907 controlled north China for sixteen years.

Liang Ch'i-ch'ao (1873–1921)   Disciple of K'ang Yu-wei (qv) and a leader of the late 19th century reform movement. After travelling in the West he fled to Japan in 1898 after the failure of the reform movement and published a journal, *New Citizen* in Yokohama in which he wrote many articles on the major figures in the Western liberal tradition and attempted to reinterpret the traditional Confucian ethic in the light of these studies. He advocated national and provincial assemblies and a constitutional monarchy, ideas which were swept aside in the republican turmoil of the 20th century, in the same way that his own ideas had superseded those of his teacher K'ang Yu-wei. He had long arguments with the revolutionaries and in 1913 he founded the Democratic Party to oppose the Kuomintang, but also opposed Yuan Shih-k'ai's monarchical adventure of 1915. Liang became finance minister in the northern warlord government in Peking in 1917, but he later withdrew from political life in disillusion after travelling through Europe and seeing the devastation of the First World War which contrasted sharply with his image of Western civilisation.

Liang-che Province   Sung name for the region now included in South Kiangsu and Chekiang. In the 8th to the 12th centuries it was the chief centre of agricultural development originating techniques that spread throughout the rice-growing region.

Liang-shan-po   Great marsh near the confluence of the Yellow River and the Grand Canal in west Shantung province. Around 1121 in the Sung dynasty it was the lair of the legendary bandit Sung Chiang and his companions. Stories based on their exploits were told by marketplace storytellers in the Sung dynasty, found their way into Yuan dramas and were eventually collected and woven into a narrative in *Water Margin* (*Shui-hu Chuan*) (qv) by Shih Nai-an. Liang-shan-po has since come to have the same symbolic associations as the Greenwood in the Robin Hood legend.

Liao Dynasty (907–1125)   Dynasty of the Khitan (qv) who controlled most of north China after the fall of the T'ang Empire. The Liao was a barbarian dynasty which relied heavily on the advice of Chinese supporters. It had five capitals, each ruling a circuit, dual prime ministers (Chinese and Khitan) and cabinets for the northern and southern regions, the southern retaining the six ministries inherited from the T'ang. The Liao monarchy grew into a Chinese-style institution as later conquest dynasties were to do, using Chinese titles, ceremonies and written language, but the Khitan identity was maintained in speech, tribal organisation and food and clothing. The Liao empire was small in comparison with the Southern Sung which ruled most of China proper and which made silk and silver gifts to the Khitan rulers to keep the peace. The Chin empire of the Jurched forced the Liao west in the 12th century and the empire continued as the Kara Khitai (qv).

Liao Mo-sha (1907–　　) Director of the United Front Department of the Peking Municipal Committee who collaborated with Teng T'o and Wu Han (qv) in a series of articles criticising the party leadership through historical analogies or satire, published in the Peking party's theoretical journal *Frontline* under the pseudonym Wu Nan-hsing (derived from their three individual pseudonyms) between October 10, 1961 and July 1964.

Liberated Areas Regions controlled by the Communist-led bases during the Sino-Japanese War, either in the Shen-Kan-Ning region based on Yenan or behind the Japanese lines. From 1937 the other main bases were Shansi-Chahar-Hopei (Chin-Ch'a-Chi), Shansi-Hopei-Shantung-Honan (Chin-Chi-Lu-Yu), Shansi-Suiyuan (Chin-Sui), Shantung, O-Yu-Wan (Hupei-Honan-Anhwei) (qqv), Hainan and the Canton delta. They were all administered autonomously, partly out of necessity since communications were so difficult, and were characterised by moderate economic policies because of the United Front with the KMT, and varying levels of democracy involving many non-party mass organisations.

Liberation (*Chieh-fang*) The final victory of the CCP over the Nationalists after the 1946–49 Civil War and the establishment of the People's Republic. Liberation came to different areas at different times and conditions are often described as before and after liberation.

Liberation Army Daily Paper which was controlled by the General Political Department of the People's Liberation Army General Staff and which supported many of the ideas of the Cultural Revolution in its early stages.

Li-chia System devised by the Ming government to enforce local tax collections and organise labour for public work. 110 neighbouring households formed a tax unit (*li*) and ten of the wealthier families supplied a unit head in rotation. The remaining 100 families were divided into ten *chia* which undertook compulsory labour services in rotation. It was the responsibility of the unit head (*li-chang*) to supervise the *chia* and ensure that taxes were paid. The system led to bribery and corruption with the burden falling on the poorest people. It was inherited by the Ch'ing dynasty but discontinued in the 18th century. See also *pao-chia*.

Likin Tax levied in the second half of the 19th century on commodities transported over customs barriers. It was first introduced in 1854, initially to meet the increase in long-term expenditure necessary to finance the suppression of the Taiping, Nien and other rebellions (qqv) when the traditional revenue systems such as the Land Tax were incapable of meeting these demands. The system of collection varied throughout the country. Provincial authorities applied *likin* to suit local conditions, or themselves, but rates were about 2%–3% of the value of the goods at each collectorate or up to 10% where the tax was consolidated in one levy for the whole province. The tax put a heavy burden on handicraft producers and traders and put prices up for the population as a whole. It was a severe restraint on trade in the late 19th and early 20th century and put local products at a disadvantage in comparison with imported products which usually had to pay only one entry tax. *Likin* was not abolished when the rebellions were put down, but was levied until 1931 and even when it was abolished was replaced by other taxes on manufacturing and trade.

Lin Piao (1907–71) Commander-in-Chief of the Chinese armed forces and Mao Tse-tung's 'close comrade-in-arms' and designated successor during the Cultural Revolution. He was born into a peasant family in Hupeh and graduated in 1926 from Whampoa Military Academy. He joined the CCP in 1927 and served with Chu Teh in Kiangsi before commanding the First Army Corps on the Long March during which time he developed a strong personal loyalty to Mao. In 1945 he led CCP troops in Manchuria and in 1947–8 commanded the Fourth or North-East Field Army in the crucial Peking-Tientsin campaign against the Nationalists. In 1954 he became a vice-premier, in 1955 one of ten marshals of the People's Liberation Army and in 1958 a member of the Politburo Standing Committee. In 1959 he replaced the disgraced P'eng Teh-huai (qv) as Minister of Defence and during the 1960s he popularised *Quotations* from Mao Tse-tung in the Army and, through the Socialist Education Movement (qv), throughout China. When the Cultural Revolution began in 1966 he threw the army firmly behind it and Mao, although the

J

CCP was under the control of Liu Shao-ch'i. After the radical supporters of Mao came to power during the Cultural Revolution Lin was elected vice-chairman of the party Central Committee at the Ninth Party Congress in April 1969. The new party constitution adopted by the conference reaffirmed Mao Tse-tung Thought as the guiding principle of the state and party and designated Lin as Mao's successor. His rapid rise to power was followed by an even swifter and more dramatic downfall. The details are not entirely clear but Mao and Lin began to differ after the Lushan Conference (qv) of the Central Committee in August 1970 and Lin, afraid of being ousted in the same way as Ch'en Po-ta, planned a military coup. He was betrayed by a senior air force officer and apparently fled towards the USSR in a Trident jet which crashed while attempting to refuel in Mongolia, killing all aboard. Lin Piao wrote one important pamphlet: *Long Live the Victory of People's War* (qv).

Lin Tse-hsu (1785–1850)   Commissioner Lin, Governor-General of Hu-Kwang (Hupeh and Hunan) charged by the emperor with the suppression of the opium trade at Canton in 1838. Lin Tse-hsu was a Fukien man who had proceeded to his governor-generalship through the imperial degree examinations and successive official posts. He arrived in Canton in March 1839 and began dealing severely with Chinese opium traders and firmly with foreign dealers. On March 18, he ordered the Europeans to surrender all their opium and demanded that they promise to cease dealing. When this was refused the British warehouse was put under siege. The opium was then handed over on May 18 to Lin who had it destroyed with salt and lime and flushed into the sea, an act which was followed by other incidents and led to the Opium War (qv) between Britain and China in 1840. Lin Tse-hsu organised the Chinese forces in the war but was dismissed and exiled to Ili in Sinkiang after British complaints that he had treated them unfairly, and he died in 1850 en route to take up a new appointment after a proposal to rehabilitate him.

Lineage   see   *Clan*

Li-shih yen-chiu (Historical Studies)   Most important historical journal in the People's Republic. It was published continuously from 1954 to 1966 and resumed in 1973 after a break during the Cultural Revolution. It tends to be weighted towards pre-1911 Chinese history.

Literary Inquisition of Ch'ien-lung   While the Ch'ien-lung emperor's scholars were finding and reviewing all the major written sources for the compilation known as the *Four Treasuries* (qv) in the 1770s, the opportunity was taken to weed out and suppress works considered to be objectionable because of seditious or abusive language or anti-Manchu content. About 2,300 writings were listed for total suppression and another 350 for partial suppression, and many were lost for good, including Ming loyalist works and some books that were simply not orthodox or literary enough for the taste of the censors. The Ch'ien-lung censorship was the most thorough of a series of literary inquisitions carried out by the Manchus. See also *Burning of the Books*.

Literary Research Society see *Society for Literary Studies*

Literati Conventional translation of the Chinese *ju,* Confucian scholars, intended to convey the importance attached to study and written excellence in men who were to rule. The term is usually restricted to scholars who had proved themselves excellent and orthodox by their attainment of one of the three degrees awarded in the examination system (qv). Possession of a degree conferred the privileges of exemption from labour service, freedom from corporal punishment and the possibility of entering public service as a local or central government official.

Little Red Book see *Quotations from Chairman Mao Tse-tung*

Liu Pang see *Kao-tsu, Han Emperor*

Liu Po-ch'eng (1892–   ) Born in Szechwan, Liu had a military education and joined the CCP in 1926. He became one of the most outstanding commanders of the Red Army, led some of the vanguard units on the Long March and became a Marshal of the People's Liberation Army in 1955. He was later a member of the Politburo and a vice-chairman of the National People's Congress.

Liu Shao-ch'i (1898–?) Communist leader and Chairman of the People's Republic from 1959–1969. Liu was born in Hunan where he attended the same college as Mao, and studied in Moscow in 1920. After joining the Socialist Youth League in 1921 he concentrated on trades union work and joined the Central Committee of the CCP in 1927. From 1927 to 1932 he was involved in underground labour organisations during the repressive Nanking Government, but in 1932 joined the Kiangsi Soviet as a trade union organiser. Between 1936 and 1942 he was active in building CCP cells in the Japanese-occupied cities of Peking, Tientsin and Shanghai. In 1948 he became chairman of the All China Federation of Labour and from 1954 to 1959 he was chairman of the Standing Committee of the National

People's Congress. In 1959 he was appointed Chairman of the People's Republic of China, that is head of state, and from then onwards was in conflict over policy trends with Mao Tse-tung who was chairman of the CCP. The conflict broke dramatically in the Cultural Revolution during which Liu Shao-ch'i was criticised as a revisionist, as China's Khrushchev and as the 'leading party person in authority taking the capitalist road'. In 1968 he lost all his public posts except that of Chairman of the People's Republic from which he was formally removed in 1969. Unconfirmed reports have stated that he died in the early 1970s.

Liu Tombs   see   *Manch'eng Tombs*

Liuhsia Chih   Robber Chih from Liuhsia in present-day Honan who is thought to have lived towards the end of the Spring and Autumn period (770–476 BC) and to have led a rising of slaves. His case was resurrected during the 1975 Anti-Confucian campaign to demonstrate the hatred of the slaves for Confucius' ideas.

Livadia, Treaty of (1879)   Agreement between Russia and China in which the Chinese possibly through ignorance or incompetence ceded large areas of disputed territory in Central Asia to the Russians.

Lo Jui-ch'ing (1906–1978)   Chief-of-Staff of the People's Liberation Army who was attacked during the Cultural Revolution. Lo was born in Szechwan, attended the Whampoa Military Academy and joined the CCP while fighting in the 1926 Northern Expedition (qv). After training in 1932–34 in security and intelligence work in the USSR he spent the years up to 1949 in political and security work in the army and after 1949 became Minister of Public Security and subsequently a member of the Central Committee. In 1959 he became Chief-of-Staff of the People's Liberation Army and Vice Minister of Defence under Lin Piao and in 1965 Vice Chairman of the National Defence Council. As an advocate of political and military expertise he soon came into conflict with Lin Piao and during the Cultural Revolution was criticised and attacked by Red Guards. He disappeared from public affairs but re-emerged on Army Day 1975 and was later named as Deputy Director of the National Defence Scientific and Technological Commission.

Local Histories   see   *Gazetteers*

Loess Region   Region between the Ordos desert and Great Wall in the north and the Huai River in the south, lying mainly in the basin of the Yellow River and covered with thick deposits of fine fertile soil which has also been deposited by the Yellow River as alluvium over a large part of the North China Plain. The soil, thought to have been formed from fine dust blown in from Mongolia and Central Asia was very easily worked so the agricultural and irrigation techniques associated with the Neolithic revolution in the pre-Shang period probably originated in this region. It is therefore often considered to have been the cradle area of Chinese civilisation.

Long Live the Victory of People's War Pamphlet written by Lin Piao (qv) and published in 1965 in which he extended Mao's thesis of the peasant countryside against the urban bourgeoisie and advanced the thesis that the Third World as the 'countryside' would surround and defeat the 'city' areas of the industrialised capitalist states. The booklet made Lin into the leading interpreter of Mao Tse-tung Thought.

Long March Six-thousand-mile epic journey embarked upon by the CCP in 1934 when the fifth encirclement campaign (qv) of the KMT armies had succeeded in dislodging them from their Kiangsi Soviet bases (qv). The Long March began officially on October 15, 1934 when about 100,000 soldiers, officials and others left Kiangsi. In January 1935 the March reached northern Kweichow where the Tsunyi Conference (qv) installed Mao as chairman of the ruling Revolutionary Military Council in place of Chou En-lai and Yeh Chien-ying (qqv). Mao led the march through the western marches of China, defeated a proposal by Chang Kuo-t'ao at Maoerhkai (qv) in January 1935 to establish a base in the far west and arrived in north Shensi with only 8,000 people in October 1935. His forces were swelled by the later arrival of units under Ho Lung, Chang Kuo-t'ao and Chu Teh and by the local Red Fifteenth Army Corps. In December 1936 the CCP moved its headquarters to Yenan and began the task of reconstruction. The Long March has since gone down in CCP history as a great turning point and innumerable legends have sprung up around it.

Lo-yang Capital of the Eastern Chou period, of the Eastern or Later Han when it restored its authority in 25 AD and moved east from Ch'ang-an, and of several subsequent ruling houses, including the Northern Wei (380–534). Lo-yang is in the Yellow River valley in present-day Honan province. It was the eastern capital or second city of the T'ang.

Lü, Empress One of the consorts of the Han emperor Kao-tsu who became empress dowager on the accession of her infant son when

Kao-tsu died. She ruled through members of her own family till her death in 180 BC after which the family were massacred by old followers of Kao-tsu to prevent them from usurping the throne. The problem of the powerful dowager empress recurs throughout Chinese history, notably in the case of Tz'u-hsi (qv).

Lu Hsun (Chou Shu-jen) (1881–1936)   The one outstanding 20th century Chinese writer, often compared with Maxim Gorky. His particular forte was the sharp, satirical short story or the pointed *tsa-wen*, an essay form which he made his own. He was best known for *Diary of a Madman*, an ironical treatment of a man whose persecution complex illuminated the violence and hypocrisy of Chinese society at that time and *The True Story of Ah Q* (qv), but he wrote many essays, poems and some uncharacteristically romantic reminiscences. After a classical education he graduated from the Nanking Mining Academy in 1902 and went on to study Japanese and medicine in Japan. On returning to China he taught and took part in the New Culture Movement after May 4, 1919. He was a founder-member of the League of Left-Wing Writers (qv) and a radical democrat who later declared himself a Marxist although he never joined the CCP. He abandoned medicine in favour of writing which he saw as a cure for China's national sickness.

Lukouch'iao Incident   see   *Marco Polo Bridge Incident*

Lung-ch'ing, Ming Emperor (reigned 1567–73)   Succeeded his father the Chia-ching emperor in 1567 and his short reign was noted for the relaxation of tension on the northern borders, made possible by the agreements he came to with the Mongol leader Altan Khan (qv).

Lung-shan Culture   see   *Black Pottery Culture*

Lushan Conference or Lushan Plenum 1959   Conference of the CCP Central Committee at which the Defence Minister P'eng Teh-huai (qv) criticised Mao's Great Leap Forward policies and advocated an 'expert', that is professional, army, as opposed to one that stressed 'redness' or ideological correctness.

Lushan Conference or Lushan Plenum 1970   First open split between Mao and Lin Piao after the Cultural Revolution. This meeting of the Second Plenum of the CCP Central Committee discussed the question of the state chairmanship, left vacant since the dismissal of Liu Shao-ch'i, to which Lin aspired. Lin was supported by several senior Chiefs-of-Staff but lost ground when Ch'en Po-ta, another supporter, was purged. His failure led to his desperate attempt at a coup.

M

Macao Portuguese colony to the west of the Canton delta, one of only three areas of geographical China (the others being Hong Kong and Taiwan (qqv)) not ruled today from Peking. Macao was settled in the 1520s by Portuguese traders who gained legal rights to land their cargoes there in 1535 and in 1557 appointed officials to rule it as a colony. From this base they were able to monopolise the Canton trade, blocking the Dutch who attacked the colony unsuccessfully in 1622. In the early 17th century Macao was the usual way into China for Jesuits (qv) and other foreign travellers, and when trade built up in the 18th century traders bound for Canton had to call in at Macao for a pilot, a linguist and a compradore (qv), and it was at Macao that they had to lodge if they wished to stay in the area after their business in Canton was done. Commercial rivalry for the Canton trade led to Macao being occupied by the British in 1802 and 1808 to prevent its seizure by the French. Portugal claimed sovereignty over Macao in 1849 and this was ratified by a treaty signed in 1887.

Macartney, Lord (1737–1806) Former member of Parliament and governor of Grenada and Madras, chosen to lead the first British embassy to China in 1793. He left London on September 26, 1792 having been designated Ambassador Extraordinary and Plenipotentiary from the King of Great Britain to the Emperor of China, and with Sir George Staunton as his secretary and deputy. His main tasks were to collect all available information about China and to negotiate commercial and diplomatic relations. The three ships of the mission arrived off Canton on June 19, 1793, proceeded north to Tientsin and then overland to Peking in the form of a tributary mission to the 83-year-old Ch'ien-lung emperor. Macartney's audience with the emperor, celebrated for his unwillingness to perform the *kowtow* (qv), took place at the emperor's summer retreat of Jehol outside the Great Wall on September 14, 1793. However attempts to open negotiations about trade or diplomacy met with no success and Macartney and his entourage returned home disappointed, reaching London on September 4, 1794. Ch'ien-lung issued two edicts to King George III as a result of the mission, both of which rejected claims to establish relations, but further attempts were made to open negotiations by the Amherst Mission (qv) in 1816.

Magistrate (*chih-hsien*) Most important single official in the local governmental system of imperial China. The magistrate was responsible for order and revenue collection in a county, *hsien* (qv). He collected taxes, conscripted men to labour gangs, presided over straightforward court cases, and was responsible for promoting the knowledge of Confucian orthodoxy among the local people.

Manch'eng Tombs Two large tombs dating from the Han dynasty discovered in 1968 in Lingshan Mountain in the western suburb of Manch'eng in Hopei province. The tombs were of Liu Sheng, a prince of the Western Han period and his wife Tou Wan and were divided into central, north and south auxiliary and rear chambers. The south chamber of Liu Sheng's tomb contained several chariots and a dozen horses and the north contained several hundred pieces of earthenware. The coffin and more precious furniture and vessels were in the rear chamber. Among the funerary objects unearthed were articles of gold, silver, jade and bronze, and lacquerware and silk providing clear examples of the best of Han craftsmanship, but the most remarkable finds were the shrouds of the corpses which were made of small jade wafers sewn through the corners with gold thread. The suits were exhibited throughout the world as part of the great exhibition of Chinese art and archaeology.

Manchus Tungusic people of the same stock as the Jurcheds (qv) of the 12th–13th century. The Manchus rose to power in the 16th century on the periphery of the state and culture of China. During the Ming dynasty they had been incorporated uneasily into the Chinese state by the commandery system which divided up the Jurched tribes. The tribes became united and powerful under the leadership of Nurhachi who created Banners to which all tribesmen came to owe their loyalty. Other administrative reforms were carried out, and a Manchu written alphabet was created by modifying the existing Mongolian script. The name Manchu was decreed by Abahai in 1635 to supersede Jurched, which still bore the stigma of Chinese suzerainty. Two capable leaders, Abahai and Dorgon, followed Nurhachi (qqv) and built on his successes. They extended the power of the Manchus through Mongolia, Korea and parts of north China and made raids on the cities of the declining Ming dynasty, proclaiming themselves the Ch'ing dynasty at Mukden in 1636. In 1644 the Manchu armies were invited to enter China through the pass at Shanhaikuan by Wu San-kuei (qv), a general of the Ming, to help put down the rebellion of Li Tzu-ch'eng. They took control of Peking and the Ch'ing dynasty was extended gradually to include the whole of China which was ruled by a Manchu-Chinese dyarchy.

Manchukuo   The 'Manchu State', a puppet regime established by the Japanese on March 9, 1932 to justify their intervention in Manchuria; P'u-i (qv), the last Ch'ing emporer, who had been deposed in 1911 and brought up in Japan, was made chief executive, but the legality of the state was not, as had been hoped, recognised by the League of Nations. Japan continued to try and unite Manchukuo and National- ist China against the Communists, but the only Chinese leader to accept the state was Wang Ching-wei, who set up his own puppet government in Nanking. Manchukuo finally collapsed in 1945 with the defeat of Japan and P'u-yi was captured by the Russians and handed over to the Chinese government. Under Japanese control a great deal of effort was put into developing the local economy to provide a sound basis for a state independent of China. Mineral resources and agriculture were developed and a number of industries established and the South Manchurian Railway Company provided military and civilian transport and a comprehensive research service.

Manchuria   Originally the homeland of the Manchus, the name is often given to the north-east provinces of China — Heilungkiang, Liaoning and Kirin — properly called the North-East. Manchuria was part of the Ch'ing empire till 1911 and was controlled by the warlord Chang Tso-lin during the 1920s. It was occupied by the Japanese in 1931 and the state of Manchukuo (qv) created in 1932. Although the 1943 Cairo Declaration accepted that Manchuria was part of China the USSR wished to retain its influence there and Soviet troops were not withdrawn until 1955. The North-East is China's industrial heartland and provides most of the People's Republic's oil, coal and iron.

Manchurian Incident   see   *Mukden Incident*

Mandarin   General Western term for Chinese officials, usually of provincial or lower rank, deriving from the Portuguese word *mandare* to order. By extension the name was applied to the standard Chinese spoken by these officials, often from different dialect areas, to communicate with each other, and known in Chinese as *Kuan-hua*, 'official speech'. Since this standard was based on the speech of north China and particularly Peking, Mandarin came to mean northern standard Chinese, as distinct from the southern dialects. Although still commonly used, the term Mandarin is obsolete, as 'official speech' has been superseded firstly by *Kuo-yu*, 'national language' and now by *P'u-t'ung-hua*, 'common speech', both based on the current Peking standard.

Mandate of Heaven   Traditional spiritual authority to rule of the emperors of China and the equivalent of the Divine Right of Kings in the English tradition. It was in fact a piece of political rhetoric to show that power had been transferred from one emperor or dynasty to another, and was always applied after the event to justify the transfer. A fallen dynasty was said to have forfeited heaven's mandate to rule by whatever crimes or inadequacies it could be accused of, and the mandate was then conferred on the victorious new emperor.

Manorial System (*chuang*)   After the failure of the Equal Field system (qv) to control the growth of landholdings in the T'ang period, many smallholdings were sold off and large private estates or manors grew rapidly, farmed by tenant-serfs who were bound to the manor, as distinct from free tenants. The power of the manors was quite considerable during the T'ang and particularly the Sung dynasty and extended to various facets of local administration till the manor became the dominant institution in the countryside. Although manors varied in size and organisation most undertook irrigation and other projects as well as cultivation of grains.

Mao Tse-tung (1893–1976)   Founder-member and eventually Chairman of the CCP, Marxist philosopher, poet and military strategist. Mao was born on December 6, 1893 in the village of Shaoshan in Hunan province. Early in his life he clashed with his father who had orginally been a poor peasant but was then more comfortably off, and was forced to leave his primary school at thirteen, after five years of traditional classical education. At sixteen he managed to enrol in a local higher primary school, where he gradually became aware of the social problems of rural China and particularly of China's subjugation by foreigners. In 1911 he transferred to a school in Changsha and became involved with the ideas of the Republican Revolution of that year, spending some six months in a unit of one of the new armies. From 1913–1918 he studied at the Normal School (Teacher Training College) in Changsha where he imbibed the ideas of the *New Youth* journal that was then moving towards Marxism. He took an active part in student politics during the May 4th Movement of 1919, became a part-time labour organiser in 1920–21 while head of a primary school, and in July 1921 attended the founding congress of the CCP in Shanghai. He held a number of posts in the party and in the KMT with which it collaborated until 1927, but the crucial period for his political development was his involvement in peasant associations (qv) in Hunan from 1925–27 during which he came to understand the revolutionary power of the peasantry. After the Shanghai Coup (qv) by the KMT against the CCP in 1927, Mao fled to Chingkangshan (qv) to set up a rural base which grew into the Kiangsi Soviet (qv). Because of his unorthodox peasant-based attitudes, Mao took a back seat while more traditionally-minded communists played leading roles. He did not consolidate his power till the Tsunyi Conference (qv) in 1935 during the Long March, which he then led to Yenan. In Yenan he set up a Soviet administration that firmly established his personal power and provided the springboard for victory over the KMT in the 1946–49 civil war. From the establishment of the People's Republic in 1949 he held the office of Party Chairman, but was by no means able to have his own way politically. After the controversy over the Great Leap Forward (qv) in 1958, he yielded the state chairmanship to Liu Shao-ch'i and the policies of the first half of the 1960s were more Liu's than Mao's. In the Cultural Revolution (qv) the more radical or idealistic policies of Mao made a comeback, but by the 1970s it was difficult to see whether any of these would be permanent. The Cultural Revolution cost Mao many of his political allies, including Ch'en Po-ta and Lin Piao. Mao died in September 1976 leaving two major factions, one led by Hua Kuo-feng and the other by Mao's widow, Chiang Ch'ing, to squabble for his mantle and argue over his political will. He now lies in a mausoleum in T'ien-an men square. The official edition of Mao's collected works runs to five volumes, but he wrote much more. The most important aspect of his writing was his ability to incorporate the apparently alien philosophy of Marxism into the Chinese experience. He tackled this on all levels, from dialectical philosophy to tactical, political and economic problems. He was also a poet whose verse in the classical tradition is admired by many non-Marxist Chinese.

Mao Tun (1896–   ) Novelist, critic and Minister of Culture up to the Cultural Revolution. Mao Tun, whose real name is Shen Yen-ping, took an active part in the May 4th Movement and was a founder of the Society for Literary Studies (qv). He became interested in Marxism and Soviet literature and served as Mao Tse-tung's secretary for a time in the 1920s. He became a member of the League of Left-Wing Writers in 1930 and wrote many short stories and novels, perhaps the most famous of which is *Twilight* (*Tzu-yeh*) in which he successfully portrays the complexities of Chinese society in the 1930s.

Maoerhkai Meeting Incident on the Long March when one of the marching columns, the First Front Army under Chu Teh and Mao Tse-tung, met Chang Kuo-t'ao's Fourth Front Army. On July 10,

1935 the columns met at Maoerhkai in Szechwan, a meeting of the Politburo of the CCP was convened there and differing views of the goal of the Long March were discussed. Chang favoured settling in west Szechwan but agreed to go along with Mao to Shensi, only to change his mind a few days later and break away from the main column. His troops eventually joined Mao in north Shensi in 1936, but the Maoerhkai meeting marked an irreparable breach between the two leaders.

Marco Polo Bridge Incident Incident manufactured by Japanese officers of the Kwantung Army (qv) on July 7, 1937 which provided the excuse for an attack on the local Chinese garrison and subsequently the invasion of North China. The Japanese garrison, permitted to be stationed in north China by the 1901 Boxer Protocol (qv), had been holding manoeuvres near the Marco Polo Bridge (Lu-k'ou ch'iao) some ten miles west of Peking. On the pretext that a soldier was missing they demanded to search Wanping, a nearby town, and when refused by the Chinese garrison commander, bombarded and occupied the town. The Nationalist Government at Nanking was committed to resist, but Japanese reinforcements from Manchuria and Japan poured into north China in a blitzkrieg attack which soon overran the region.

Margary Affair (1875) On February 21, 1875 Augustus Margary, a British vice-consul, was ambushed and killed on the China-Burma frontier while travelling to meet an expedition which was attempting to establish the possibility of a trade and railway route from Burma to Yunnan. Against the precedents of international law, the British government held the Chinese responsible for the murder and demanded redress including the trial of the acting governor-general of Yunnan and Kweichow. When Peking agreed to only some of the demands the British threatened to break off diplomatic relations. The affair was settled by the Chefoo convention of 1876 which agreed that an indemnity be paid to the bereaved family, that trade be increased and that an apology mission be sent to London. This eventually became the first Chinese resident legation abroad.

Maring, H. (Sneevliet) Dutch agent of the Comintern who was sent to China to meet Sun Yat-sen in 1921. He became convinced that the CCP should work within the KMT which he saw as a coalition rather than a bourgeois party, and he made sure that his policies were put into effect. Maring, who had attended the First Congress of the CCP, was a former Comintern worker in the Dutch East Indies who later abandoned Communism and disappeared during the Second World War.

Marriage Law 1950   One of the first major social reforms carried out by the CCP after it came to power. The Law codified many of the policies that had been carried out in the liberated areas before 1949: women were given full legal equality in matters of marriage, divorce and the ownership of property, and forced arranged marriages were forbidden. The law was a conscious attempt to free women from the constraints of the traditional family and clan network and a recognition of the part women had played in making the CCP's victory possible.

Marshall Mission   In November 1945 President Truman appointed General George C. Marshall, a distinguished Second-World-War Commander, to succeed Patrick Hurley as his representative in China. Marshall's task was to aid the KMT in re-establishing its authority over China without direct US military intervention. He arrived in China in mid-December with proposals for a cease-fire in the Civil War, a consultative conference to discuss a coalition government and the integration of KMT and CCP forces into a national army. His mediation made political negotiations possible for a time and large US loans were arranged for the Nationalists, but fundamental differences between the CCP and KMT made long-term agreement impossible and fighting soon broke out again, both parties feeling that Marshall stood in the way of their victory. He was recalled by President Truman on January 6, 1947.

Mass Line   One of the basic principles of political leadership in the People's Republic. It was designed to reconcile central policy decisions with popular wishes and was evolved before 1949 in the Yenan base area. According to this theory cadres should take the lead by systematising ideas drawn from the masses and presenting them to the masses as concrete policies. It is intended to be an ongoing process with policies being modified according to mass criticism.

Mass Organisations   Non-party organisations used by the CCP to mobilise opinion in favour of their policies both before and after 1949. The most important mass organisations before liberation were the Peasant Associations, National Salvation Association and the All China Federation of Democratic Women. Since 1949 the most significant have been the All China Federation of Trade Unions and the Communist Youth League.

Matsu   see   *Quemoy and Matsu*

Ma-wan-t'ui Han dynasty tomb site near Changsha excavated since 1972. Three aristocratic tombs have yields lacquered vessels, clothes and other textiles, and wall paintings.

May 4th Movement On May 4, 1919 a demonstration of some 5,000 Peking students called for a rejection of the Versailles Peace Conference decision that Japan have rights over Shantung. The demonstration grew into a powerful and vociferous mass movement against the warlord government in Peking who were regarded as traitors because of their acceptance of the Japanese demands. Nationalist feeling which had hitherto been limited to a few intellectuals now spread through all levels of society. When demonstrators were arrested, a student strike in Peking rapidly spread not only to colleges in other centres but also to factory, office and shop workers, and a massive boycott of Japanese goods was organised. This May 4th Movement spilled over into an intellectual revolution, the New Culture Movement (qv), as China grappled with new ideas to try and explain her situation.

May 7th Cadre Schools Organisations set up during the Cultural Revolution to re-educate cadres, party and government officials and intellectuals who had fallen foul of the radical realignments. Life in the schools, which were generally situated in rural areas, consisted partly of farm or other manual labour and partly of the study of Mao Tse-tung's writings.

May 16th Circular Circular distributed by the Central Committee of the CCP on May 16, 1966. It repudiated the report of P'eng Chen's Group of Five which had been considering the nature of art and literature in socialist society after the criticism of Wu Han (qv), and announced the formation of a new Cultural Revolution Group (qv), thus marking the beginning of the academic stage of the Cultural Revolution.

May 16th Group Radical Peking Cultural Revolution group that criticised Chou En-lai's role in the Cultural Revolution in a Notification issued on May 16, 1967. It had its origins in the Department of Philosophy and Social Science of the Academy of Sciences and was joined by important members of the Cultural Revolution Group, including, allegedly, Ch'en Po-ta. It was branded as ultra-leftist in the later stages of the movement and blamed for many of the excesses that had been carried out in the name of Mao and the Cultural Revolution.

May 30th Incident (1925)   When Shanghai students were arrested at a public memorial service for Chinese workers shot during a strike at a Japanese owned cotton-mill, a 3,000-strong demonstration was held on May 30 to protest at the atrocities. A British police lieutenant ordered his men to open fire on the crowd: eleven Chinese were killed, dozens injured and fifty more students arrested. Public anger at this incident led to strikes, boycotts and protests throughout China and did not subside until the lieutenant and his superior were sacked and an indemnity paid to the wounded and bereaved. The incident sparked off other incidences of nationalist agitation which provided some of the impetus for the Northern Expedition (qv) of 1926.

Memorials   Suggestions for policy changes made to the emperor by his governors or other officials. The imperial response, if any, was in the form of an edict (qv).

Mencius (c372–c288 BC)   Meng-tzu (Mencius) was a native of Tsou, a small principality near Confucius' home state of Lu, and a philosopher who championed Confucianism. He held high office in the state of Ch'i but also wandered as a consultant philosopher round the courts of several states just as Confucius had done. His assertion, that man is by nature good, became one of the central tenets of Confucianism. For Mencius, even more than for Confucius, government was an exercise in ethics and applied morality. In the Sung dynasty his writings, collected in the *Mencius*, were included among the Four Books (qv) of the Confucian canon.

Merchant Colonisation   Opening-up of frontier land in the Ming dynasty by merchants engaged in supplying border garrisons. As the garrisons could not be self-sufficient grain had to be supplied from the interior. One important method was the Salt Exchange (qv) system in which merchants supplying grain received in exchange a certificate which entitled them to obtain salt, a government monopoly, and trade in it, a lucrative business. At first traders bought grain and shipped it to the borders, but many later used their finances to open up new agricultural land near the garrison so that grain could be supplied locally. The system declined later in the dynasty when dealing in government salt became less profitable.

Mexican Dollars   see   *Silver Trade*

Miao Rebellion (1855–1872)   When taxes were increased substantially to pay for the suppression of the Taiping rebellion (qv) the Miao minority peoples of Hunan, Kwangsi, Yunnan and Szechwan border areas who had been engaged in sporadic revolts for decades rose in rebellion. The Miao co-operated with rebellious secret societies in Kweichow and some of the Taiping bands which operated in the same province. The rebellion was not put down till May 1872 when a large contingent of the Hunan Army (qv) commanded by Hsi Pao-t'ien, a Hunanese officer under Tseng Kuo-fan, finally captured and executed the main Miao leaders.

Middle Ages   see   *Periodisation*

Mif, Pavel   Comintern representative sent to China in the 1930s. He brought with him a group of his former students from the Sun Yat-sen University in Moscow led by Wang Ming (qv) who were later known ironically as the Twenty-eight Bolsheviks (qv).

Military Affairs Commission   Highest military policy-making body of the Central Committee of the CCP. It has existed in one form or another since the 1930s and controls the Ministry of Defence and all the armed services.

Military Colonies (*T'un-t'ien*)   Self-sufficient colonies of soldier-farmers garrisoned along the northern frontier and at other strategic points. This type of organisation was first developed in the Han period, became very important during the Six Dynasties and remained a feature of frontier garrisons during the Ming and early Ch'ing period.

Military Households   Families which had to provide specified numbers of men for military duty. The policy was begun under the Mongol Yuan dynasty and continued by the Ming but inherited occupations gradually disappeared in the 16th century.

Ming Dynasty (1368–1644)   Name, meaning 'bright', given to the dynasty founded by Chu Yuan-chang who led one of a number of rebel bands towards the end of the Mongol Yuan dynasty. His capture of Nanking in 1356 marked his road to power and by 1382 he had unified all China proper and ruled as the Hung-wu emperor. While Hung-wu's reign was characterised by consolidation and pacification, that of his successor Yung-lo marked the beginning of the rebuilding of the empire: the capital was moved to Peking, the voyages of Cheng Ho (qv) began and scholars began to compile the great encyclopaedias. Great progress was made in the development of organs of central and local government and the traditional examinations for the Civil Service were revived and remodelled, to last in this form till the early 20th century. This created an elite group, the gentry (qv), who came to be very powerful in the countryside, providing a link between the autocratic government and the populace. The middle years of the Ming, particularly the reigns of Chia-ching and Wan-li, were a period of great economic growth. Industry and commerce grew in spite of the court's anti-commercial bias and there were a number of fiscal reforms, notably the Single-Whip system (qv). A number of problems such as the growth of eunuch power (qv), the pressure of the Mongols on the northern borders and the increasing burden of taxes which had been with the dynasty since its early years, eventually became so serious that they brought about its collapse. The last twenty years of the dynasty were marred by corruption, court factionalism and eventually rebellion. Li Tzu-ch'eng rose against the government in the 1630s and by 1644 held much of north China. In April of that year he descended on Peking, the last Ming emperor hanged himself and General Wu San-kuei (qv) invited the Manchu armies in to suppress the rebellion. They did so, and then declared themselves the Ch'ing dynasty and rulers of all China. In spite of its problems the Ming dynasty is thought of as a glorious period in Chinese history. Art, literature and scholarship flourished; the famous blue-and-white porcelains from Ching-te chen were a product of the mid-Ming; the great novels such as *Water Margin, Journey to the West* and the *Golden Lotus* (qqv) were written, and monumental works of scholarship such as the multivolume local histories, the technological encyclopaedia *Creations of Nature and Man*, and Li Shih-chen's great materia medica (qqv) were produced during the Ming dynasty.

Ming Loyalist Scholars   Scholars who upheld the traditions and supremacy of the Ming rule after its collapse and refused to serve the Ch'ing dynasty which they considered alien and barbarian. Many of them spent the rest of their lives analysing the causes of the Ming downfall but their influence in China was small since the anti-Manchu nature of their work made it unpublishable. While some Ming loyalists secluded themselves in China others fled to Japan where they exerted some influence on Japanese historical writing.

Ming Precious Ships   Capital ships of the early Ming dynasty navy that sailed in Cheng Ho's expeditions.

Ming Tombs   Tombs of thirteen of the sixteen Ming emperors just to the north of Peking. The main tomb is that of the third Ming

K

emperor Yung-lo who was the first to adopt Peking as his capital, and the other tombs are arranged around his.

Mining Tax   All mining was a monopoly (qv) of the government in the early years of the Ming dynasty. When the iron monopoly was abolished in 1395 private production was taxed. Tax from the mining of iron, copper and silver was an important source of government revenue in the 16th century.

Ministries, Six or Six Boards   The six ministries (*liu-pu*) which dated from the T'ang dynasty were the main agencies for implementing governmental policy. They were:
Civil Appointments or Personnel, responsible for staffing and posting in the civil service and the conduct of examinations.
Finance or Revenue: collection of taxation and supervision of resources.
Rites: Religious ceremonies and the reception of foreign visitors.
War: Military officers and operations, equipment and supplies.
Punishments or Justice.
Works: State buildings and projects, conscription of manpower, communications.

The T'ang model was copied almost exactly by the Ming government although the tasks of some of the boards varied and the organisation was modified. It had also been adopted by the southern section of the Liao dynasty, by the Chin dynasty of the Jurched, and later by the Mongols of the Yuan dynasty. The Manchus set up the Six Ministries in Mukden in 1631 even before their conquest of China and retained them throughout the dynasty till 1906 when as part of the constitutional reforms a reorganisation turned them into eleven ministries.

Minorities, National   That part of the population of China not considered to be Han Chinese and known to the ancient Chinese as barbarians (qv). Today they comprise roughly 6% of the population and can be considered in two groups. The first group, in the north and north-west, consists largely of nomadic peoples such as Tibetans, Mongols and Uighurs who find themselves in China because of the way China's inner Asian frontier has moved westward over the centuries. The Tibetans live in Szechwan, Yunnan and Ch'inghai provinces as well as Tibet and neighbouring countries across the Himalayas. Mongols live in the Inner Mongolian Autonomous region of China as well as the People's Republic of Mongolia which is an independent state and the Buriat Mongol Autonomous Republic which is a constituent republic of the USSR. Uighurs live in Sinkiang as do Kazakhs who are also found in the USSR. The second group of non-Han peoples is found mainly in the south-west of China. They are related to peoples living in northern Vietnam, Laos, north Burma and north Thailand and are survivors of centuries of Han expansion from the central China area to the tropics. Unlike the Tibetans, Mongols and Uighurs who have long histories and highly developed cultures, many of these tribes were very primitive and some had no written language until the Chinese developed one for them. Chinese history records many conflicts between Han and non-Han, particularly on the northern frontier when strong nomadic tribal confederations of Mongols and Manchus came to power. Today the People's Republic is faced with the problem of integrating more than fifty different nationalities of various languages and stages of development into a modernising state dominated by Han Chinese. The Peking government often seems to be treading a tightrope between great Han chauvinism and allowing the growth of minority nationalist movements.

Min-pao see *People's Tribune*

Missionaries China has long been the object of missionary ventures. Buddhist missionaries appeared in China as early as the 2nd century AD and were active during the T'ang and Six Dynasties period when they competed with Nestorian Christians (qv). Jesuit priests (qv) first came to China in the later part of the Ming dynasty after Matteo Ricci (qv) and were important members of K'ang-hsi's court. The greatest missionary effort however was in the 19th and 20th century when thousands of Christians of all denominations went to China. Although missionaries never converted more than 1% of the Chinese population they left their mark in the introduction of Western ideas, particularly in education. Inevitably they were caught up in the nationalist upsurge that began in the mid-19th century, being easily identifiable with Western military and commercial might, and risings were often marked by attacks on missionaries — as in the Boxer rising (qv). Missions continued till the middle of the 20th century when the establishment of the People's Republic brought them to an end.

Mo Tzu or **Mo Ti** (c470–c391 BC) Philosopher born at about the time of Confucius' death and the founder of the Mohist school. He argued a utilitarian but altruistic philosophy. He was particularly critical of wealth and luxury, of elaborate rituals and the waste involved in warfare and preached the idea of universal love or neighbourliness as the only guarantee of peace and order.

Modern Text Movement (*Chin-wen*)   One side of a historical controversy over the authenticity of classical Chinese texts. After the destruction of the classics by the Ch'in emperor Shih Huang-ti (see *Burning of the Books*), Modern Text scholars of the Han period accepted current editions of classic texts as the authentic and unchangeable teachings of the Master, but this was questioned by Ancient Text (qv) scholars who supported the view that texts written in an older script which were discovered were genuine. The Ancient Text school was generally accepted after the Han but the controversy was renewed in the Ch'ing dynasty when antiquarian studies were revived and several scholars promoted the Modern Texts. The controversy became important because K'ang Yu-wei (qv) used it to advance his reformist policies, reinterpreting the Modern Texts to suit his case.

Mohists   see   *Mo Tzu*

Mongols   One of a series of nomadic peoples who came to power in the Central Asian steppes, conquered all or part of China and set up Chinese-style dynasties such as the Northern Wei, Liao and Chin. Before the birth of Chinggis Khan (qv) the Mongols lived in a large number of disparate tribes, some hunting and fishing in the Siberian forests but most living a nomadic life on the steppe. It was Chinggis Khan's role to unite these tribes, forge a common identity for them and develop them into a powerful empire. This was done by religious and administrative organisation, but was due most of all to a terrible, efficient military organisation. Mongol warriors were highly disciplined troops who fought under hereditary leaders to whom they owed loyalty. They used mounted flying columns in battle and carried bows with armour-piercing arrows. Between 1205 and 1209 they subjugated the Hsi Hsia empire, then the Western Liao kingdom of the Kara Khitai, before overrunning the Turkish empire of Korezm. At the time of Chinggis' death in 1227 the Mongol empire was divided amongst his four sons. Ögödei became Great Khan of East Asia, Chagadai Khan of Turkestan, Hulegü Khan of Persia and Batu Khan of the Golden Horde of the Volga. The conquest of China began with the first attacks on the Chin empire in 1211–15 and by 1234 the Chin royal line had been extinguished. In 1251 the Mongol armies moved against the Southern Sung and the conquest was completed by Khubilai, grandson of Chinggis when he took the Sung capital at Hangchow in 1276. The Mongols adopted the Chinese dynastic title of Yuan in 1271 and ruled China till 1368. They were driven back to the steppes by the new Ming regime in the 14th century after internal dissention and rebellions caused by floods, famines and heavy taxation, but continued to harry the Chinese throughout the Ming. Their unity, however, which had been their greatest strength, had been lost. In 1634–35 the Inner Mongols were defeated by the Manchus who enrolled them in their forces as vassals and kept control by a divide-and-rule policy. They were subsequently absorbed into the Manchu empire to which they remained subordinate till the 20th century when part of the Mongol nation gained its independence in the Mongolian People's Republic. Today Mongols live in the USSR and the Inner Mongolian Autonomous Region of China as well as in the Mongolian People's Republic.

Monkey   see   *Journey to the West*

Monopolies, State   Rigid government control of the more important sectors of the economy, particularly salt and iron, was a consistent feature of imperial Chinese history. Monopolies of salt and iron go back as far as Kuan-tzu (qv) and the state of Ch'i in the Warring States period. The Ch'in also practised monopolies which were restored by the Han emperor Wu-ti who also controlled the minting of copper coins and the production of liquor. The T'ang state controlled the production of salt, tea and liquor but did not attempt to monopolise iron-working. The Sung, Ming and Ch'ing dynasties all operated a salt monopoly but permitted private trading under licence. The aim of the monopolies was to ensure reasonable supplies of vital goods and to extract tax from them for state revenues. None of the monopolies was fully effective all the time and smuggling and illicit dealing were quite common.

Morrison, George Ernest (1862–1920)   Resident correspondent of *The Times* in Peking from 1897 to 1912 and adviser to Yuan Shih-k'ai's government from 1912 on. An Australian educated in Edinburgh, Morrison became well acquainted with Chinese politics, though he never learned the language. He found his post as adviser highly frustrating as he never had the influence he thought proper to his position.

Moscow Conference (1960)   Conference of 81 Communist Parties held in November 1960 in Moscow to adjudicate in the growing dispute between the USSR and China over the leadership of the international Communist movement. The Chinese delegation ridiculed Khrushchev's policy of peaceful co-existence and argued that wars of liberation and national independence should be supported, and although China signed the December 6 communiqué on peaceful co-existence with only minor changes, the fact that they had challenged the USSR without being expelled from the conference was an indication of the strength of the Chinese position.

Moscow Declaration (1957)   Declaration presented for the acceptance of Communist Parties at the 1957 Moscow Conference. It was a militant, uncompromising declaration of ideological war on the capitalist world, signed and co-sponsored by the Chinese, thus presenting them for the first time as a great Communist power.

Moslems   see   *Islam*

Most Favoured Nation Clause   Clause inserted in the unequal treaties (qv) of the 19th century to ensure that any privilege extended to one European nation be enjoyed by all.

Mukden Incident   The explosion of a bomb on the South Manchurian Railway track outside Mukden on September 18, 1931 that sparked off the Japanese occupation of Manchuria. Although damage was so slight that railway services were not even disrupted, the incident developed into a large-scale clash between Chinese soldiers and Japanese troops of the Kwantung Army. The following morning Mukden was occupied by the Japanese and the Kwantung Army advanced, reinforced by troops of the Korean Command of the Japanese Army in defiance of the Japanese cabinet. Manchuria was overrun in five months and the puppet state of Manchukuo (qv) set up in 1932.

Mutual Aid Teams   Intermediate stage in the collectivisation (qv) of agriculture. After the success of land reform, a primitive form of co-operation was organised in the form of Mutual Aid Teams which pooled labour and equipment at first on a temporary basis but later permanently. Some of these teams which were organised in the mid-1950s were based on existing mutual aid groups in the villages as peasants had often combined to carry out heavy seasonal work. The Mutual Aid Teams formed the basis for Agricultural Producers Co-operatives (qv), each of which incorporated several teams.

N

Nanchang Rising Rising organised by a group of CCP members in Nanchang, the capital of Kiangsi province on August 1, 1927. Backed by a newly-formed army of peasants and workers they held the city for three full days before being besieged by Nationalist troops. On August 5 they broke out of the encirclement and fled to the border areas of Kwantung, Kiangsi and Fukien. The rising was carried out partly because it was expected by Stalin who in his dispute with Trotsky had been claiming that a new revolutionary high tide in China justified armed insurrections and the establishment of Soviets. The failure of the Nanchang rising and the subsequent Autumn Harvest Insurrection and Canton Commune (qqv) eventually convinced Mao of the need to work in the peasant movement.

Nanking City in Kiangsu province which became the capital of the Ming emperor Hung-wu. His son and successor Yung-lo transferred his capital to Peking (Northern Capital) and Nanking acquired its present name, which means Southern Capital. Much of the city's present shape dates from the Ming period when it was a busy town with shipyards and many other industries as well as a market and a cultural centre. It suffered during the Taiping rebellion (qv) when it was for a time the seat of the rebel kingdom and was severely damaged when retaken by the imperial armies. After the 1911 Revolution Sun Yat-sen (qv) was elected President of the Chinese Republic in Nanking but when Yuan Shih-k'ai succeeded him the capital was moved to Peking. After the success of the Northern Expedition in 1926 Nanking once again became the Chinese capital but in 1937 the KMT government was forced to flee to Chungking and Japanese armies occupied the town till the end of the Second World War. Today it is the capital of Kiangsu province.

Nanking Arsenal One of the monuments of the Self-Strengthening movement inspired by Li Hung-chang who founded it in 1865 and placed a former British army doctor, Halliday Macartney, in charge of it. It produced only armaments but of a higher quality than those from the Kiangnan Arsenal (qv).

Nanking Government (1928–1937) Nationalist government of China with its capital at Nanking, established after the success of the Northern Expedition (qv). Although the overriding aim of national unification had apparently been achieved with most of China owing nominal allegiance to the central government, the period from 1928 to the Anti-Japanese War, which broke out in 1937, was fraught with domestic crises as well as foreign aggression. Internally there was the question of the allegiance of the new warlords who had maintained their regional power-bases by supporting the KMT, the civil war in the Communist-controlled areas of Kiangsi and later Yenan, and severe economic and social problems. The main external problem was the growth of a Japanese power-base in Manchuria. After the Mukden Incident (qv) of 1931 the Japanese Kwantung Army took control of all of Manchuria in five months. The Nanking government came to an end in 1937 when Japanese forces invaded north China and then moved south to take the capital. Chiang K'ai-shek set up a temporary headquarters in Wuhan but moved his capital to Chungking in Szechwan where it remained till the end of the war.

Nanking, Treaty of (1842)   Peace treaty which formally concluded the Opium War (qv) between China and Britain. The terms were accepted by the Chinese on August 17, 1842 when the British after capturing Shanghai and Chinkiang on the Yangtze were poised for an attack on Nanking and the treaty was signed on August 29. In broad outline the Thirteen Articles of the Treaty included an indemnity of 21 million dollars to be paid to Britain, the abolition of the Cohong monopoly of trade in Canton, the opening of five ports — Canton, Amoy, Foochow, Ningpo and Shanghai — to trade with resident British consuls, merchants and their families, the cession of Hong Kong (qv) to Britain and fixed rates of customs tariffs. Supplementary treaties, such as the Treaty of the Bogue signed in 1843 and other agreements with France and America established fixed tariffs, and the principles of extraterritoriality and 'most favoured nation' (qqv). The Nanking Treaty was the first of the series of unequal treaties (qv) that reduced China in the eyes of many Chinese to a dependency of European powers.

Nan-yüeh   Semi-sinicised state, controlling the area now in Kwangtung, Kwangsi and North Vietnam, conquered by the Ch'in dynasty and re-conquered by the Han emperor Wu-ti in 111 BC, thus incorporating it in the Chinese empire as the commandery of Jihnan.

Napier Mission (1834)   Mission by Lord William John Napier to the governor-general of Canton when the East India Company's monopoly of Far Eastern trade was due to expire. His aim was similar to that of the previous Macartney and Amherst embassies, to establish friendly relations between Britain and China and to extend trade beyond Canton. Napier, however, violated Chinese regulations by not securing permission before he established himself in Canton in 1834 and was forced to leave for Macao when Chinese troops surrounded his place of residence. The mission failed, partly because of confusion over whether Napier was a commercial or official representative and partly because of his obstinacy. His attempt was the last to secure peaceful relations before the outbreak of the Opium War.

National People's Congress (NPC)   Supreme legislative organ of the Chinese state (as distinct from the CCP) under the constitution (qv). Plans for convening the NPC, including electoral machinery, were drawn up in 1953, and it eventually met for the first time in September 1954. It took over from the Central People's Government Council which had been acting as the highest organ of state from 1949, and adopted the first constitution of the People's Republic. Between 1954 and 1966 it met almost once a year, in three congresses elected respectively in 1953–4, 1959 and 1964. The Cultural Revolution delayed the convening of the fourth NPC until January 1975 when it met to approve a new constitution and to approve resolutions and appointments proposed by the party Central Committee. Although it is the highest legislative body in China on paper, critics have often considered the NPC to have been simply a rubber stamp for decisions made by the CCP and its Central Committee.

Nationalist Party   see   *Kuomintang*

Neo-Confucianism   Philosophical synthesis that developed mainly in the Sung dynasty and remained the dominant philosophy of China till the 20th century. It began in the late T'ang period when many intellectuals began to turn away from Buddhism because of its foreign origins. In 630 it was decreed that temples to Confucius be erected in every prefecture and all the old sacrifices to him were reinstituted. There was a revival of interest in the ideas of the Confucian philosophers and the beginnings of an attempt to build a new Confucian metaphysics, drawing on ideas and concepts from Taoism and Buddhism. The first to rediscover and reinterpret traditional Confucian classics was probably Han Yü (qv) of the T'ang period but the best known and the one who succeeded in unifying the new philosophy was Chu Hsi (qv). The Confucian orthodoxy that survived in China up to the 20th century was largely that laid down by Chu Hsi in the 12th century.

Neolithic Period   The heartland of Neolithic culture in China seems to have been the North China plain, where the remains of several primitive agricultural societies predating the Shang dynasty (qv) have been discovered. The best known of these are the Painted Pottery and Black Pottery cultures (qqv).

Nerchinsk, Treaty of (1689)   Treaty signed between Russia and China to settle the boundary dispute in the Amur region. Nerchinsk had been founded on a tributary of the Amur in 1658 by Russians expanding eastward, a move which threatened the northern borders of the newly established Ch'ing empire. The town was the site of protracted border negotiations between Russian and Chinese diplomats, through the mediation of two Jesuit priests. The official text of the treaty was in Latin, with translations into Chinese, Russian, Manchu and Mongolian; it fixed the boundaries so that Russia retained control of Nerchinsk. The treaty regularised Sino-Russian relations and unlike the unequal treaties (qv) of the 19th century was not imposed on China. It resulted in the exchange of trade and diplomatic missions.

Nestorians   Nestorian Christians travelled to China from Persia during the T'ang dynasty and a stone stele erected in the capital, Ch'ang-an in 781 suggests that the church was flourishing around that time, though probably only among foreigners. In common with Zoroastrianism and Manichaeanism it was virtually wiped out in the 841–45 religious persecution. It was revived by the Khitan and Jurched peoples and survived among some of the western border peoples of China. Many of the Uighurs (qv) of the Turfan area who served Chinggis Khan in the 13th century were Nestorians and the Great Khan Guyug (reigned 1246–48) was probably a convert. The church was strong enough in China in 1275 for the patriarch of Baghdad to create an archbishopric at Peking. See also *Prester John*.

New Culture Movement   Intellectual ferment in China that followed the May 4th Movement (qv) of 1919. It was characterised initially by an interest in the West, modernisation and democracy, but later on divided into supporters of Marxism around the journal *New Youth* and those who favoured gradual change. Foreign thinkers invited to China in this period, notably John Dewey in 1919–21 and Bertrand Russell in 1920–21 stimulated debates on politics and philosophy and there was a flood of translations of the works of the early German philosophers, of Marx and Engels, and of the revolutionary writings of Lenin, Bukharin and Plekhanov that were beginning to emerge in Russia. Ch'en Tu-hsiu and Li Ta-chao were among the best-known advocates of Marxist ideas, and they were opposed by the pragmatist Hu Shih who favoured the gradual evolution of society.

New Democracy   Theory and practice of government adopted by the Communists before and immediately after the founding of the People's Republic in 1949, as distinct from the old democratic ideas of the Nationalist period. Mao's essay *On New Democracy* published in 1940 crystallised the theory of the transition of China from a semi-colonial, semi-feudal society to a socialist society. The plan was for a three-level economy consisting of a state sector which would assume the leading position and attempt to out-produce the private sector, an agricultural sector in which individual farms would be collectivised, and a private sector in which middle and small capitalists would operate. The guiding principle of the political structure was to be democratic centralism with some elected bodies and the co-existence of the Four-class alliance (qv) under the leadership of the proletariat and its party, the CCP. The period of New Democracy came to an end in 1953 with the drive for the socialist transformation of the economy, and the private sector became absorbed into the state sector which co-operated with an increasingly collectivised agricultural economy. New Democracy was an essential period of transition which provided the basis on which the new order could be built.

New Democratic Revolution   Revolutionary movement since 1919 in current Communist terminology, characterised by the developing leadership of the CCP.

New Fourth Army Incident   Final breach in the strained Second United Front (qv) between the CCP and the KMT that had begun in 1937 with the Japanese invasion of China. On October 19, 1939 the Communist New Fourth Army, based in west Shantung and Kiangsu, refused to obey a government order to transfer north of the Yellow River and extended its operations in Kiangsu. This led to a series of incidents culminating in a major clash between the New Fourth Army and the KMT 40th Division on January 5, 1941. On January 17 the Nationalists disbanded the New Fourth Army and arrested its commander but the CCP appointed Ch'en Yi to command and increased the Army's strength, after which the United Front was effectively at an end.

New Life Movement   Nationalist campaign launched in 1934 to try and revitalise ideas and life in China in the face of Japanese aggression. The movement stressed hygiene, promptness, truthfulness and courtesy, and the four traditional values of politeness (*li*), righteousness (*i*), integrity (*lien*) and self-respect (*ch'ih*). Generally the younger generation did not take to these old virtues, but the military instruction and training that went with the movement gave them some sort of psychological uplift.

New Territories see *Hong Kong*

New Year Most important festival of the Chinese year, falling between January 21 and February 19. The festival marks the beginning of spring; presents are exchanged, fireworks let off and houses and streets are decorated with lanterns and paper dragons. Traditionally, a few days before the New Year, an image of the Kitchen God is burnt to symbolise his journey to heaven to report on the conduct of the family during the year.

New Youth (*Hsin ch'ing-nien*) Subtitled *La Jeunesse*. Monthly radical journal founded by Ch'en Tu-hsiu in 1915 on his return from Japan, known at first as *Youth Magazine* and later renamed. It attacked all traditional Confucian literature, ethics and customs, monarchism and warlordism and demanded a new culture. The initial aim was to introduce science and democracy into China but *New Youth* soon became a platform for Marxist writers and the driving force of the cultural revolution that followed the May 4th movement. In January 1917 it published Hu Shih's advocacy of literature in the vernacular. Lu Hsun's *Diary of A Madman* appeared in *New Youth* in 1918. The original editorial group split in 1920 when Hu Shih left and the journal became a Marxist publication.

Nieh Jung-chen (1899–   ) Communist military commander born in Szechwan. Nieh studied in France and Russia and joined the CCP in 1923. He was at the Whampoa Military Academy and became political commissar of the First Army Corps in 1932. In the Anti-Japanese War he was deputy commander of Lin Piao's 115th Division. Nieh was deputy chief-of-staff in 1949–54, vice-premier in 1956, a member of the Politburo in 1967 and vice-chairman of the National People's Congress in 1975.

Nieh Yüan-tzu Leading signatory of the first big character poster or wall-newspaper of the Cultural Revolution. It was put up on May 25, 1965 and criticised the President of Peking University and the Secretary of the University Party Committee. Nieh Yüan-tzu, then 45, was a lecturer in philosophy at the University and she came to the attention of the public when Mao personally defended her views and had the criticisms broadcast and subsequently published in the press. She later became a vice-chairman of the Peking Revolutionary Committee as a representative of the mass organisations and an alternate member of the Central Committee of the CCP in April 1968.

Nien Rebellion   One of a series of risings that almost brought down the Ch'ing dynasty in the late 19th century. It lasted from 1851 to 1868 and spread over eight provinces in roughly the same period as the Taiping Rebellion (qv) and the Moslem rebellions (qv) of Yunnan and the north-west. Nien, meaning band, was the name given to the rising of secret society members and bandits in the East Central area. They had been proscribed in the early 19th century but rose in support of the Taiping rebels in 1853, frequently co-operating with them in military operations. They specialised in mounted guerrilla tactics and the construction of widespread defensive earthworks. Their most powerful leader Chang Lo-hsing was killed in 1863 by troops under the Mongolian general Seng-ko-lin-ch'in. When he in turn was killed in action in 1865 the operations against the Nien were taken over by Tseng Kuo-fan (qv) and then by Li Hung-chang (qv) who suppressed the eastern band of the Nien in late 1867. The western band which had split off and developed contacts with the Moslem rebels in the north-west was finally defeated by armies under Li and Tso Tsung-t'ang in August 1868.

Nine Field System   see   *Wellfield System*

Nine Mansions Sect or Nine Palaces   Religious sect which rebelled in 1786–88 and was still active in the 1890s.

Nirchinsk, Treaty of   see   *Nerchinsk, Treaty of*

Nixon Visit (1972)   After secret visits to Peking in 1971 by President Richard Nixon's Foreign Affairs adviser, Dr Henry Kissinger, and 'Ping-pong Diplomacy' (qv), the president accepted an invitation to visit China. It was a diplomatic breakthrough in the history of Sino-American relations since 1949 and welcomed by the Chinese in the light of their dispute with the Soviet Union. Nixon met Chou En-lai at the airport in Peking, was received by Mao in his study for an hour-long meeting and spent some time touring China. Negotiations on relations between China and the USA were difficult enough to require six days of talks after which the Shanghai communiqué of February 28 was issued. This reaffirmed hopes that the Taiwan question would be settled peacefully, endorsed the Five Principles (qv) of peaceful co-existence put forward at Bandung (qv) in 1955 and agreed to reduce the danger of military conflict, to make cultural and scientific exchanges possible and to seek further normalisation of relations.

North-East Kiangsi Soviet Communist base area formally established in June 1928 by Fang Chih-min (qv) and Shao Shih-p'ing and modelled on the Chingkangshan base of Mao and Chu Teh. Fang and Shao had begun organising peasant associations in north-east Kiangsi in 1924 and returned there after the failure of the Nanchang rising. The base expanded between 1928 and 1934 as one of the satellites of the main Kiangsi Soviet (qv) but was abandoned in 1934 under pressure from the encirclement campaigns of the Nationalists.

Northern and Southern Dynasties (420–589) States that ruled China in the later part of the Six Dynasties (qv) period between the Han and the Sui empires when the country was divided between the north and the south. Among the more important dynasties were the Northern Wei (qv) in the north and the Southern Ch'i, Liang and Ch'en in the south.

Northern Expedition Military campaign to unify China mounted in 1926 by the Nationalist Armies of the Canton KMT government under Chiang K'ai-shek. The expedition, against the northern warlords, had been planned long before but was delayed and began on July 28, 1926 after a series of pacification campaigns in Kwangtung and Kwangsi which removed all local opposition to the Canton government. The National Revolutionary Army of 85,000 troops and 6,000 cadets from the Whampoa Military Academy was pitted against Wu P'ei-fu the Chihli warlord, Sun Ch'uan-fang who was based in Nanking and Chang Tso-lin the Manchurian warlord. The forces of two other warlords, Feng Yu-hsiang in the north-west and Yen Hsi-shan in Shansi were officially neutral but were sympathetic to the Nationalists. The National Revolutionary Army marched north from Canton into central China, backed by Soviet supplies and helped considerably by CCP activists who mobilised peasant and worker organisations and organised strikes and demonstrations in support of the Nationalist armies. Wuhan was taken in September 1926, Nanchang in November, Foochow in December and Shanghai and Nanking in March 1927, by which time most of south China was under the control of the KMT government. The progress of the Northern Expedition was delayed by the split between the CCP and the KMT and was not completed till 1928 (the Second Northern Expedition) when Chiang-K'ai-shek having consolidated his position marched on Peking, which was controlled by Chang Tso-lin, took it with the help of Feng Yü-hsiang and Yen Hsi-shan and renamed it Peiping (Northern Peace). Chang's son, Chang Hsueh-liang, then pledged loyalty to the Nationalist Nanking Government (qv).

Northern Sung   Sung dynasty (qv) prior to the capture of its capital Kaifeng in 1126.

Northern Wei Dynasty (386–534)   Barbarian state founded in north China by a group of Hsien-pei (qv) peoples known as the T'o-pa (qv), after their state of Tai (338–376) had been subsumed by the Earlier Ch'in. It formed a buffer between the nomads of the north and the Chinese states further south and extended westwards into central Asia. After the incorporation of the north China plain agricultural land into its empire, the Northern Wei, already semi-sinicised, began a conscious policy of sinification. The capital was moved from north Shansi to Lo-yang which had been the capital of the Chinese dynasties of the Eastern Chou and Later Han, Chinese became the official language of the court and T'o-pa aristocrats were ordered to adopt Chinese dress, customs and names. The revolt of tribal military forces against the sinification led to the collapse of the Northern Wei and the eventual reunification of China under the Sui dynasty. Apart from its synthesis of tribal and Chinese cultures the Northern Wei is best remembered for the patronage given to Buddhism and for the Buddhist cave temples at Yun-kang near their north Shansi capital and Lung-men near their Lo-yang capital.

Nurhachi (1559–1626)   Founder of the Manchu state who rose to power during the Ming dynasty and was accorded great honours by the Ming court. After securing the loyalty of smaller chieftains living near him, he embarked on negotiations, arranged marriages and alliances, and within thirty years had united the main Jurched tribes of the north. He fortified his home area in north-east Liaotung (qv) and constructed a solid power-base there with the aid of Chinese advisers. He organised the newly united tribesmen into banners (qv) with appointed officers rather than hereditary chiefs, so that they were less divided, and in 1599 ordered Chinese works to be written down in Manchu, using a modified form of the Mongolian alphabet, the beginning of written Manchu. In 1616 he took the title of Emperor of the Later Chin, to continue the Chin dynasty of 1122–1234, and in 1618 attacked China and captured part of Liaotung. In 1625 he moved his capital to Mukden and after his death was succeeded by his eighth son Abahai (qv) and then his fourteenth son Dorgon who continued his work of unifying the Manchus until the seizure of Peking from the Ming and the establishment of the Manchu Ch'ing dynasty in 1644. See also *Manchus* and *Ch'ing Dynasty*.

O

Officials see *Civil Service*

Ögödei Khan Third son of Chinggis Khan. Ögödei ruled as Great Khan from 1229 and his reign was noted for administrative reforms carried out by Yeh-lü Ch'u-ts'ai (qv) and for the construction of the capital city of Karakorum.

Oirats Group of warrior tribesmen from the mountainous country south-west of Lake Baikal in western Mongolia who had become separated from the eastern Mongols or Tartars (qv). After the collapse of the Yuan dynasty they became powerful in the Altai region, and spreading eastward vied with the Tartars for power and made many raids into north China. Chinese strategy was to play the two groups off against each other and commercial relations were established between the Ming court and the Oirats often in the guise of tribute missions which were a way of keeping the Oirats pacified till they later declined in power.

Old Democratic Revolution Current term in the People's Republic for the pre-Communist revolutionary movement up to about 1919. The period since 1919 is known as the New Democratic Revolution.

Open Door Policy Policy for a commercial open door, or equal opportunity in trade in China advanced by Britain in the closing years of the 19th century and co-sponsored by the USA in a note delivered to Britain, Germany, Russia, France, Italy and Japan in September 1899. The burden of the note was that none of the Western powers or Japan should interfere with the interests of or discriminate against the other powers. A second declaration on July 3, 1900 pledged support for the territorial and administrative integrity and peace and safety of China. The effect of this agreement was to prevent the dismemberment of China into separate colonies, although Japan's activities in Manchuria showed that she paid only lip service to the declaration.

Opium Wars Wars between China and Britain in the mid-19th century which were precipitated by China's attempts to prevent the import of opium, although a deeper cause was Britain's desire to increase trade with China and Chinese concern about an adverse balance of silver payments. Opium had been introduced into China by Arab and Turkish traders in the 7th or 8th centuries and demand for it grew, leading to its cultivation in south China and then to imports from abroad. Portuguese traders dealt in opium but the import was taken over by Britain and in 1773 the East India Company was granted a monopoly of opium cultivation in Bengal. The opium was shipped to China in ships under licence from the company, which remained, however, legally and officially apart from the trade. Opium imports rose rapidly: two hundred chests a year were imported in 1729, 1,000 in 1767, 4,500 by 1820, 10,000 by 1830, reaching a peak of 40,000 chests in 1838 after the abolition of the company's monopoly had led to an increase in private trade. The opium entered China through a variety of illicit organisations and the rate of addiction rose sharply, resulting in growing demand, social problems and a massive outflow of silver from China to pay for the imports. Chinese government policy was to oppose the import and use of opium, but this was ineffective till 1839 when Li Tse-hsü (qv) was ordered to stamp out the traffic. He demanded the surrender of all British opium, and destroyed over 20,000 chests of it, precipitating the despatch of a British Expeditionary Force in 1840. The British blockaded ports, besieged Canton and in the spring of 1842 occupied Shanghai and cut off north-south traffic along the Grand Canal. Faced with superior firepower, the Ch'ing government was forced to yield to British demands for huge indemnities and the extension of trade to the treaty ports as agreed in the Treaty of Nanking (qv) that year. A second clash between China on the one hand and Britain and France on the other in 1856 is referred to as the Second Opium War or the Arrow War (qv). The defeat of the Chinese in the clashes with the western powers led to the unequal treaties (qv) of which the Nanking Treaty was the first, and to the establishment of a powerful European presence in China. The defeat also provoked a reaction in many Chinese who became concerned with self-strengthening (qv) and contributed to the growth of revolutionary nationalist feeling.

Oracle Bones or Dragon Bones   Scapulae or shoulder bones of cattle, other flat bones and the under-shells of tortoises dating from the Shang period. Questions were inscribed on the bones and the answers were divined by carving a groove and applying heat. Cracks appeared from which the diviner apparently derived yes or no answers. This method is known as scapulimancy. The bones which were noticed first in 1899 began to appear on the Peking market as 'dragon bones' which were to be ground up for medicinal purposes. They were traced to Anyang in Honan province, the site of the Shang capital, and systematic excavation revealed thousands of bones, many

L

of them inscribed with the questions asked of the diviner and some with the answers. The inscriptions included the names of practically all the Shang rulers known to the Chinese historical tradition and dispelled the doubts and scepticism that a Shang dynasty had really existed. From the inscriptions, a great deal has been learned about the earliest form of written Chinese, and much about the society of the Shang period. The authority of the traditional account in the *Historical Records* is vindicated. Many of the questions concerned sacrifices, relations with the spirits, crops, weather, war, hunting, fishing, travel, illness and luck.

Ordos   Dry region of Inner Mongolia, bounded by the bend of the Yellow River in the west and north and by the Great Wall in the east and south. It is populated by nomadic Mongolians, but with some arable farming at oases.

Oriental Despotism   Analytical construct proposed by Karl Wittfogel for describing early Chinese society and based on Marx's concept of the Asiatic mode of production. In this analysis, the key feature is the necessity for large-scale water-conservancy and irrigation projects to service agriculture. These projects required the employment and thus the direction of large numbers of people, a requirement which tended to produce a despotic monarchy supported by a bureaucratic elite who ruled over a peasant mass. This kind of society, also called hydraulic, is thought to have existed early in Chinese history and also in the other ancient river valley civilisations of Egypt and Mesopotamia.

Ortaq   Merchant corporations authorised to trade abroad by the Mongol emperors. The name is Turkish and indicates that foreign trade in Yuan dynasty China was carried out mainly by Moslem merchants from Central Asia. As well as being trading associations the ortaqs also developed tax-farming roles which complemented their commercial activities.

Ou-yang Hsiu (1007–1072)   Sung dynasty statesman, poet and scholar noted for his historical writing which revived interest in ancient texts and contributed to the development of Neo-Confucian thought.

Overseas Chinese   Chinese living outside the People's Republic or Taiwan, mainly in south-east Asia where there are over twelve million, but also in Europe, America and Australia. They are included in the official population figures for the country and they remain important to China partly because they are a useful channel of communication with the outside world and partly because of their role in the revolutionary movements in south-east Asia. The large-scale emigration of Chinese began in the 19th century with the economic difficulties, rebellion and persecution that accompanied the decline of the Ch'ing dynasty. Many began as sailors, but settlements were rapidly established throughout south-east Asia. In the late 19th and early 20th century these overseas communities gave much financial and moral support to the nationalist and republican cause in China.

O-yu-wan Base Area   Communist base area, second in size only to the main Kiangsi Soviet base (qv). The O-yu-wan soviet government on the borders of Honan, Hupei and Anhwei was created in January 1931. Chang Kuo-t'ao became head of the party branch and chairman of the government in the soviet and under his leadership it retained a great deal of independence from the Kiangsi Soviet.

P

Pa Chin (1904–   )   Pen-name of the novelist, short story writer and translator Li Fei-kan. He was influenced by anarchist ideas and his novels, such as *Family*, are preoccupied with attacks on the traditional family system and the decadence of the old gentry class. He wrote little after 1949 but was criticised during the Cultural Revolution.

Pacify the East, West, North, South   Administrative protectorates set up by the T'ang rulers in the border regions they conquered. Pacify the West (An-hsi) was in the Tarim basin in present-day Sinkiang. Pacify the North (An-pei) was in Mongolia and Pacify the East (An-tung) in southern Manchuria, while in North Vietnam the administration of An-nan (Pacify the South) later gave its name to the whole region of Annam.

Pai Lang Rebellion   Revolt in north-west China against Yuan Skih-k'ai's conservative presidency of the Chinese Republic. The guerrilla bands of Pai Lang, known inaccurately as White Wolf because of the similarity in pronunciation between the name of the leader and the words for white and wolf, occupied large areas of Shansi, Shensi and Kansu and were not suppressed till 1914.

Painted Pootery Culture   One of the distinctive Neolithic cultures also known as the Red Pottery or Yang-shao culture which appeared in north China towards the end of the Neolithic period, some time before 2000 BC. The other was the Black Pottery culture (qv). Painted Pottery sites were first excavated at Yang-shao in western Honan by the Swedish geologist Andersson in 1921 and are found mainly along the Yellow River in north-west Honan province, but also stretch from Sinkiang to Manchuria. They are named after the typical large red pots painted in bold geometric designs. See also *Pan-p'o*.

Pan Ch'ao (32–102 AD)   Han dynasty official, and brother of the historian Pan Ku, Pan Ch'ao was largely responsible for the reconquest of Central Asia. His first attempt in 73 AD was unsuccessful and he was recalled but in 91 AD he was made Protector-General of the Western Regions. From his headquarters at Kucha on the northern edge of the Tarim Basin he led an army across the Pamirs, conquered the whole area as far as the Caspian sea and defeated the Kushan Empire of the Yüeh-chih (qv). Pan Ch'ao retired and died in 102 AD and his sons maintained some Chinese control in the region but with the decline of the Later Han, the influence of the Chinese empire declined in Central Asia.

Pan Ku (32–92 AD)   Foremost historian of the Han dynasty and the author of the *History of the (Earlier) Han (Han Shu)*. The work was in fact started by Pan Ku's father Pan Piao although most of it was written by the son. It was completed by Pan Ku's sister Pan Chao. The *History* followed the pattern established by Ssu-ma Ch'ien's *Historical Records* (qv) but added sections on law, science, geography and literature. It became the prototype for the subsequent series of histories that became known as the Dynastic (Standard) Histories (qv).

P'an Ku   Creator of the universe in the mythological history of early China.

Pan-p'o   Neolithic village site of the Painted Pottery culture in Sian city in south Shensi excavated in the early 1960s. It has been opened to the public as a museum and the remains of the village can be seen from specially built galleries. The picture of Painted Pottery (qv) civilisation afforded by the dwelling sites, defences and implements for farming, hunting and fishing is much fuller than that given by the type-site at Yang-shao.

Pao-chia System   System of control by means of mutual surveillance and responsibility. Its origins lie at least as far back as the Northern Wei period, but the name *pao-chia* stems from the revival of the system by Wang An-shih (qv) in the 11th century. The tradition was continued by the Ming and then the Ch'ing who perfected it. In its ideal form 100 households formed a *chia* and 10 *chia* a *pao*. Each *pao* had a headman, selected by the villagers, who was responsible for the registration of the population, for keeping order and for ensuring that outside each household hung an official placard bearing the names of those residing there. As all villagers were supposed to report crimes or sedition to the headmen, the fear and suspicion engendered by the system inhibited crime and plots to some extent. The *pao-chia* system was an unofficial control mechanism under the official local government organisation and the head of each *pao* had to make monthly reports to the district magistrate. It has often been compared with the present-day system of street committees (qv). See also *Li-chia*.

Paper   Paper was invented by the Chinese during the Han dynasty and pure rag paper dating from about 100 AD has been found in the remains of Han outposts in Central Asia. It very quickly replaced wooden and bamboo slips and silk cloth which had been used till then. Books, however, did not become common until the 7th or 8th century.

Parkes, Harry   British consul at Canton during the Arrow War (qv) who protested against the boarding of the Arrow by Chinese troops and insisted on its rights to British protection. When Canton was taken by force on December 28, 1857, Parkes presided over the Allied Commission that took over the running of the city. In 1860 he was detained in Peking but was released when Elgin entered Peking. He later became the British minister in Japan.

Party Congress   see   *Congresses of the Chinese Communist Party*

Pax Mongolica   Name given to the Mongol rule in Asia after the consolidation of the conquests because of the possibility of safe travel between widely separated parts of the empire.

Peasant Association Movement   Radical village groups organised in the mid-1920s, some spontaneously, some under CCP leadership, particularly in Hunan province. Their growth was an indication of the revolutionary forces set in motion by the Northern Expedition (qv). In November 1926 over a million peasants belonged to the associations and by January 1927 this had risen to almost two million. In some areas the associations replaced the existing local administrations as the *de facto* power while in others they negotiated for the reduction of land rents. From 1925–26 Mao Tse-tung had been in charge of the KMT's National Peasant Movement Institute in Canton and he later took over responsibility for peasant work within the CCP. During this time he carried out detailed investigations into the associations and developed his ideas of the importance of the peasantry in China's revolution. The result of his study, *Report on an Investigation of the Peasant Movement in Hunan*, was written in 1927. Peasant Associations continued to play a vital part in CCP agricultural policies throughout the 1930s and 1940s, most notably during the Land Reform Movement (qv) in the late 1940s and early 1950s when they provided essential grass-roots support.

Peasant Nationalism   Theory that the Communist revolution in China succeeded mainly because of nationalist sentiments engendered in the peasantry by the Japanese invasion and the subsequent war of resistance, rather than depending mainly on the social conditions in rural China. In this interpretation the war is seen as having created a mass peasant nationalism. The CCP, as the most efficient and staunchest resistance to the Japanese, became identified with patriotism and nationalism and thus gained the support of large numbers of country people. Critics of this interpretation have argued that it greatly underestimates the appeal of the more revolutionary aspects of communist policy, such as Land Reform (qv), to the peasants.

Peasant Rebellions Peasant rebellions were a constant feature of Chinese history. As dynasties came to a close, peasants tended to suffer heavily from debt and high taxation, and forced labour and famine were always present. These problems produced many minor revolts and several large-scale uprisings that often hastened the end of an imperial house. The rebellions were not always purely peasant: many were led by dissident scholars or were connected with millen-arian religious beliefs or secret societies, but almost all had egalitarian aims. Among the most important rebellions in Chinese history are that of Ch'en Sheng (qv) and Wu Kuang at the end of the Ch'in dynasty, the Yellow Turbans (qv) in the Late Han, the Red Turbans towards the end of the Mongol Yuan dynasty and Li Tzu-ch'eng's (qv) rising which brought about the downfall of the Ming and caused the Manchu invasion. In more modern times, the Taiping, Nien (qqv) and Moslem risings and the Boxer rebellion (qv) speeded the collapse of the Ch'ing dynasty, and in the 20th century the tradition of peasant rebellions merged with the revolutionary policies of the CCP in the Peasant Associations and Soviets of the 1920s and 1930s. Modern Chinese historians lay great stress on this tradition of rebellion as a corrective to the view of Chinese history handed down through the histories written by officials and the gentry.

Peiping see *Peking*

Peiyang Army Forces controlled by the Peiyang (Northern Ocean) clique of warlords and commanded by Jung-lu, the governor-general of Chihli and henchman of the Dowager Empress Tz'u-hsi. The army was involved in the attack on the foreign legations in Peking during the Boxer Rising.

Peiyang Fleet Navy created by Li Hung-chang (qv) and formally established in 1888 with 25 foreign-made ships. It was the only fleet to take part in the Sino-Japanese war of 1894–5 as the other provincial squadrons remained neutral. Although the fleet was larger than the Japanese navy, the ships were old and slow and were soon defeated.

Peking   Present capital of China and the capital for most of the period since the Yuan dynasty. Peking first became a capital city under the Khitan who made it their southern headquarters in the 10th century and in 1153 the Chin dynasty who were in the process of conquering China moved their capital from Manchuria to Peking (then known as Yen-ching). Under the Mongol Yuan dynasty it became the winter capital of Khubilai Khan (qv) and then his main capital, known to the Mongols as the Great Capital (Daidu, Tai-tu) or Khanbaligh — City of the Khan. The Mongols in the 13th century built a new city outside present-day Peking and excavations in the 1960s revealed a rectangular plan with thick rammed-earth walls, and eleven gates, with a complex of streets and rivers and lakes, and sophisticated drainage and water supply systems. Nanking was the first capital of the Ming dynasty because it was the power base of the founding emperor, but in 1421 the Yung-lo emperor moved his court to Peking, leaving Nanking as a subsidiary capital, because Peking was more convenient for the defence against the Mongol threat. Peking was rebuilt on a more extensive plan with the Imperial City in the centre, and within that the Forbidden City, the Imperial Palace itself. The Ch'ing dynasty retained Peking as a capital but from the establishment of the Republic in 1911 the seat of government was moved to Canton, Nanking and then Chungking. After the city was taken by the second Northern Expedition in 1928 it was renamed Peiping (Northern Peace) and is still known as Peiping by the Nationalist government on Taiwan although it became the capital of the People's Republic of China as Peking in 1949.

Peking Man   Homo Erectus Pekinensis or Sinanthropus Pekinensis, palaeolithic man whose remains were discovered in a cave near Chou k'ou-tien some thirty miles south of Peking in 1926–27. On the evolutionary scale, Peking Man, who lived about 400,000 BC, is later than Java man or Lan-t'ien man (qv) but earlier than Neanderthal man. Evidence from the site indicates that he could use fire and crude stone tools and was probably a carnivore.

Peking, Convention of (1860)   Final peace settlement between Britain and France on the one hand and China on the other, after the Arrow War (qv). The war was officially concluded by the treaty of Tientsin (qv) in 1858, but the Chinese attempted to go back on the agreements — for more European trade and representation — by diplomatic manoeuvring. Allied forces were sent to Peking to support a mission by Lord Elgin (qv) to enforce ratification of the terms of the treaty. The Convention of Peking, dictated by Elgin to Prince Kung (qv) under duress established finally the rights of the British to diplomatic representation in the Chinese capital. In addition, both Britain and France had their indemnity increased to eight million taels each, Tientsin was opened to foreign trade and residence, Britain acquired Kowloon opposite Hong Kong, and France gained the right for Catholic missionaries to own properties in the interior of China.

Peking, Siege of   During the Boxer Rebellion (qv) of 1899–1900 foreign legations in Peking and Tientsin were put under siege by Boxer forces which stormed into the city on June 13, 1900. Since the Chinese government ignored the foreigners' demands for protection an allied expeditionary force was mounted. The Western troops finally broke through to relieve the siege of Tientsin on July 14 and Peking fell to the allies on August 14 as Boxer resistance crumbled. The relief of the siege was accompanied by much looting and brutality on the part of Western troops.

P'eng Chen (1902–   )   Influential Mayor of Peking from 1951 to 1966. He was instrumental in the expulsion from the CCP of Kao Kang and Jao Shu-shih (qqv) in 1954. In the late 1950s and early 1960s he opposed the attempt by Chiang Ch'ing to revolutionise Peking opera and by the mid-1960s it was clear that he was backing the criticisms of Mao Tse-tung's policies being voiced by Teng T'o and others in the Peking press. P'eng's deputy, Wu Han (qv), who was also involved in these critical articles was attacked and on March 26, 1966 P'eng Chen, who had been heading a group investigating the question of art and literature in the light of the criticism of Wu Han, himself disappeared. At the time of his purge, as well as being Mayor of Peking, he was a vice-premier of the state and the eighth senior member of the CCP Politburo.

P'eng Teh-huai (1898–   )   Minister of Defence from 1954 to 1959. P'eng had been opposed to the Great Leap Forward (qv) because of the threat he saw in it to China's long-term economic development, and as a professionally orientated military man with much experience in the Red Army, he was also unhappy about the role of the army and Mao Tse-tung's foreign policy, and was in favour of close co-operation with the USSR. The conflict between P'eng and Mao came to a head in 1959. After a seven-week tour of the Soviet Union and Eastern Europe, P'eng wrote a circular letter criticising the errors and excesses of the Great Leap. The Lushan Plenum of the Central Committee of the CCP in August 1959 resolved the conflict by dismissing P'eng and replacing him with Lin Piao. He unsuccessfully demanded his own rehabilitation in 1962.

People's Daily (*Jen-min jih-pao*) Official newspaper of the Central Committee of the CCP, the nearest Chinese equivalent to *Pravda* and the most important daily paper in Peking and indeed the whole of China. It contains a high proportion of policy statements and includes news reports of political and economic developments in China and abroad, notably from south-east Asia and other Third World countries.

People's Democratic Dictatorship or Dictatorship of People's Democracy Title of an essay written by Mao Tse-tung and published on June 30, 1949, shortly before liberation, to commemorate the 28th anniversary of the CCP. In this work, which marked an important turning-point in his thinking, Mao clearly ruled out the possibility of any real co-operation with the United States or any imperialist country after his experience of American mediation in the civil war. Because the military situation was now more favourable to the CCP he felt able to abandon the compromises made with the KMT and reject its leading role which he had acknowledged in *New Democracy* and *On Coalition Government*. The new article laid down quite specific plans for the future. Wide sections of the population, including the bourgeoisie, were to enjoy democratic rights and participate in a 'people's democratic dictatorship directed against the reactionaries'. These ideas were implemented during the period known as New Democracy from 1949 until 1953 when the transition to socialism began.

People's Liberation Army (PLA) Name given to the armed forces of the CCP previously known as the Red Army and created in July 1946 out of the Eighth Route Army, remnants of the New Fourth Army and new units formed in Manchuria. It includes army units engaged in border defence and garrison works, the Navy and the Air Force. After the PLA's outstanding successes in the 1946–49 civil war against the Nationalists, its prestige in the People's Republic was very high. Although its main tasks were military it became increasingly involved in internal politics. In the late 1950s, after a mixed performance in Korea, controversy over whether the PLA should emphasise professional expertise in the Soviet manner or 'redness' — ideological soundness — led to the dismissal of the Defence Minister P'eng Teh-huai (qv) and his replacement by Lin Piao. Under Lin the army became a much more important political force than ever before. High priority was given to the education of soldiers in Mao Tse-tung Thought and the army was held up to the rest of the population as a model to emulate. By the time of the Cultural Revolution in 1966, this emphasis on ideological training had created an army that could be mobilised behind Mao and the policies of the Cultural Revolution Group. During the Cultural Revolution the PLA was moved into many trouble-spots to resolve political conflicts in favour of the radicals. By the end of the Cultural Revolution, military intervention was so deep and widespread that local administration in large parts of the country was completely under military control. High-ranking PLA commanders occupied many seats in the rebuilt party Central Committee and Politburo after the Cultural Revolution and retained a great deal of influence in the selection of leading party personalities.

People's Militia   Part-time territorial-style military units that are part of the Commune (qv) organisation. Military training is given to all so that these units can function as local self-defence forces and support the regular People's Liberation Army whenever necessary.

People's Political Consultative Committee   Interim body summoned by Mao Tse-tung on September 12, 1949 to prepare for the formation of the new government. It was a national assembly made up of a coalition of different political forces but dominated by the Communists. The conference met for twelve days and adopted an Organic Law which set up the Central People's Government and a Common Programme of national aims. It became obsolete in 1954 when a new constitution was accepted and the National People's Congress (qv) became the highest organ of state.

People's Republic of China   State formally established on October 1, 1949 after the victory of the CCP.

People's Tribune (*Min-pao*)   Newspaper of the T'ung-meng hui (qv) between 1905 and its closure in 1908.

Periodisation   The division of historical time into periods is notoriously difficult and particularly so in China where historians must attempt to reconcile the facts of Chinese history with the Marxist scheme of historical development. According to modern Communist historiography Chinese society in the Shang dynasty and most of the Chou dynasty was a Slave Society. Feudalism developed in the late Chou period and continued right up to the mid-19th century. Western encroachment produced a semi-feudal, semi-colonial society in the late 19th and early 20th century. The revolution against this was in two phases, the Old Democratic up to 1919 and the New Democratic under CCP leadership from the 1920s onwards.

Non-Marxist historians often use the term Ancient China to refer to the period from the beginnings of written history up to the Han dynasty. Mediaeval China probably ends in the late T'ang or Sung dynasty when the Early Modern period is said to begin. Chinese history becomes Modern in the 1840s and Contemporary after the May 4th Movement of 1919. Prehistoric China is the period before the Chou, evidence for which is primarily archaeological and the Ancient period can be subdivided into Palaeolithic (before c3000 BC), Neolithic (c3000–c1750 BC), Bronze Age (Shang, Chou and Warring States periods to c500 BC) and Iron Age (up to the Han dynasty).

Pigtail see *Queue*

P'inghsingkuan, Battle of At the end of September 1937, Japanese troops moving southwards on their invasion of China were the victims of a surprise attack at P'inghsingkuan by the Communist 115th Division under Lin Piao and other 8th Route Army and Government units. The 115th Division captured 1,000 weapons and 100 vehicles from the Japanese, but the success was an isolated one and Japan occupied most of eastern China until 1945.

Ping-pong Diplomacy Visit of an American table tennis team to China early in 1971 and Chou En-lai's warm welcome. This opened the negotiations that led to the Kissinger mission to Peking on July 9–11 and the subsequent visit of President Nixon to China in February 1972.

Pirates see *Japanese Pirates*

Po Chü-i (772–846) One of the great poets of the T'ang dynasty who became governor of Hangchow. He wrote in a simple, almost vernacular style, unlike most poets of the period, and achieved great popularity in his own time.

Po I-po (1907–) Former auxiliary of the warlord Yen Hsi-shan who became one of the earliest organisers of the Shansi-Hopei-Shantung-Honan Communist base area in 1938. Po became vice-chairman of the provincial assembly for the base area and after 1949 became a vice-premier, Chairman of the State Economic Commission and one of the leading figures in Chinese economics and finance.

Po Ku (1907–1946) Pseudonym of Ch'in Pang-hsien, a leader of the Twenty-Eight Bolsheviks (qv) group of students who controlled the CCP in the early 1930s. During 1931–5 he was general secretary of the CCP and after Mao's rise to power Po Ku played an important part in Communist affairs as a Politburo member and in information and propaganda work. He was killed in an air crash while on his way back to Yenan from negotiations in Chungking in 1946.

Politburo (Political Bureau)   Top decision-making body of the CCP. It is elected by the Central Committee (qv) and fixes the policy lines that the Central Committee discusses when it meets. Day-to-day policy decisions are in the hands of a Standing Committee of six or seven which constitutes the real power in China at any given time.

Polo, Marco   Marco Polo set out for central Asia with his father Niccolo and his uncle Maffio, both Venetian merchants, in 1271. Marco and Niccolo had already travelled across Asia to China and back between 1260 and 1269. This second expedition reached Khubilai Khan's summer residence at Shang-tu (Xanadu) and also the capital Peking (Cambaluc) and Marco Polo spent seventeen years from 1275 to 1292 in the service of Khubilai. He acquired languages easily and though he knew Persian better than Chinese, he was able to observe far more of East Asia than any other traveller of his time. The Polos reached Venice in 1295 after returning via Sumatra and the Persian Gulf. Marco Polo's *Description of the World* was dictated to a professional scribe in a Genoese prison where Marco had been thrown as a prisoner of war in the fighting between Venice and Genoa. The book, known to English readers as *The Travels of Marco Polo*, does not survive in an original manuscript but variations in about 120 manuscripts and several languages have been found. Marco Polo's description of the grandeur and power of the Mongol empire in China and its superior culture and technology was considered incredible by the merchant communities who considered their Mediterranean area to be the centre of civilisation.

Poor and Lower Middle Peasant Associations   Organisations set up throughout the Chinese countryside from 1964 onwards to widen the basis of positive popular support for the government. The name and form of the organisations harked back to the Peasant Associations (qv) which had begun in the 1920s and were the backbone of the Land Reform movement in the late 1940s and early 1950s. Membership of the new Associations was limited to the poorest rural groups and they were linked to county and provincial Associations. Among many functions the Association served as a check on lower level cadres and as a means for transmitting policy directives to the people and the response of the people to the leadership. However since the chairmen of the provincial Associations were also usually provincial party secretaries the main task was to ensure that the less well off country people were fully integrated into the party and state apparatus.

Porcelain Porcelain, a high-temperature fired translucent pottery, is a Chinese invention, as suggested by its alternative name, China-ware. By the Han dynasty, pottery firing and glazing techniques had reached a very high level indeed and fine pottery-ware, known sometimes as proto-porcelain, was beginning to appear. The dating of the first true porcelain is difficult to establish, but large quantities were certainly being produced during the T'ang period, possibly as early as the 7th century. Many T'ang dynasty kilns have been excavated but Sung ware, which had more pleasing colours and shapes, is better known. Even better known are the polychrome and blue-and-white bowls, jugs and vases of the Ming dynasty, many of them manufactured in the town of Ching-te chen (qv), which found their way to Europe from the 17th century onwards and can now be seen in many large English collections. The Ch'ing period also produced fine wares, many of them like armorial porcelain, *famille rose*, and *famille verte* specially designed for the European taste. The quality of production declined during the Republican period and never attained its former peak. The porcelain industry still forms an important part of China's export production although it is mechanised now rather than being a handicraft industry, and is aimed at a mass market rather than at individual wealthy collectors.

Port Arthur Naval port and shipyard on the end of the Liaotung peninsula in north China, built after 1882 as part of Li Hung-chang's self-strengthening efforts (qv). It was occupied by the Japanese in November 1894 during the Sino-Japanese War as was the port of Dairen. As ice-free Asiatic ports, both were attractive to the Russians who in December 1897 imposed a twenty-five year lease on the ports and the adjacent areas and obtained permission to extend a branch of the Trans-Siberian Railway to Port Arthur. After Japan's defeat of Russia in 1905 the Japanese took over all the Russian rights in the area and renamed the southern part of Liaotung, including the two ports, the Kwantung Leased Territory (qv). In 1928 the Kwantung Army, until then based in Port Arthur, moved its headquarters to Mukden as part of the advance into Manchuria. After the Second World War the USSR was allowed naval use of Port Arthur while Dairen was to become a free port. Stalin did not relinquish his rights to Port Arthur and it was not returned completely to China until 1955.

Portuguese Traders   The Portuguese were the first Europeans to play a significant part in the trade with China. They became involved in the China trade routes, until then controlled by Arab or Chinese merchants, in the late 15th century. In 1511 they captured Malacca which gave them an entrepôt and enabled them to take over from Moslems as the principal traders in the East Indies. In 1514 Alvarez became the first recorded Portuguese visitor to China when he came to trade tung oil. The first official Portuguese embassy arrived in Canton in 1517 but the ambassador Pires was not able to go to Peking till 1520 and he had still not seen the emperor when the latter died in 1521. The Chinese then banned trade with the Europeans because the Portuguese were said to have been selling children into slavery and committing other crimes. Pires and his companions were imprisoned and never released. Illegal trading continued along the coast and between 1520 and 1557 the Portuguese gradually established themselves at Macao (qv) which they retained as a colony from 1557 onwards. From this base they continued to monopolise foreign trade and were granted access to Canton in 1653. They were, however, strongly challenged by Dutch merchants who established themselves in Taiwan in 1624 and gradually took over an important part of the China trade from the Portuguese.

Post-station System   Elaborate communications network established by the T'ang dynasty administration to help bind the empire together. Post stations, providing hostels, dining facilities, horses and boats for official travellers were placed at 10-mile intervals along the main roads and waterways from the capital to the provinces. The system was to remain throughout all subsequent dynasties, and the Liao dynasty and particularly the Mongols extended it greatly. Mongol post stations stretched out across the deserts and plains of Central Asia, marking the routes and providing shelter, supply and some protection against banditry.

Poyang Lake, Battle of (1363)   Poyang Lake, the centre of the water communications network of north-east Kiangsi, was the scene of an important naval battle between rival rebel groups at the end of the Yuan dynasty. The forces of Ch'en Yu-liang were defeated by Chu Yuan-chang who then went on to found the Ming dynasty.

Prefect (*chih-fu*)   Local government official in imperial China in charge of a prefecture which was subdivided into *hsien* (districts or counties) each of which was supervised by a magistrate (qv). The prefect provided the link between the district magistrate and the provincial and central government authorities.

Prehistoric China see *Periodisation*

Prester John Subject of a legend circulating in mediaeval Europe, according to which Prester John was supposed to have been a descendant of one of the Three Wise Men, who founded a Christian kingdom in Central Asia. He was probably Khan of one of the Mongol tribes who was converted to Nestorian (qv) Christianity in the 13th century.

Primogeniture, Abolition of Inheritance of the father's property by his eldest son was practised in China before the 2nd century BC, but abolished by the Ch'in dynasty. All property, particularly land, was divided equally between the heirs, leaving only ceremonial duties and possibly a small extra share of land to the eldest son. The virtue of equal division of property was further extolled by the Neo-Confucian (qv) philosophers of the 11th and 12th century. The effect of this lack of primogeniture throughout the centuries was to inhibit the growth of large family estates and also the possibility of capital accumulation.

Printing, Invention of As early as Han times, inscribed versions of the classics on stone tablets were transferred to paper by a process of rubbing with lamp-black or India ink on soft, thin paper. By the 7th century, carved wooden seals had developed into wood-blocks of whole pictures or texts, so that a series of blocks would produce a complete text in scroll form. Because of the large number of characters, this block-printing persisted, but moveable type of individual characters in wood, porcelain and copper had been developed in China as early as 1030, 400 years or so before its appearance in Europe. This invention, combined with growing urbanism, aided the spread of literacy and the wider availability of literature and scholarship.

Production Brigades Subdivision of the Communes (qv) that were organised in rural China from 1958 onwards. The brigades, generally corresponding to the earlier Higher Producers' Co-operatives (qv), took responsibility for primary schools and health clinics and small projects like reservoirs, whereas the Commune would be responsible for secondary schools and larger projects. A Commune has somewhere between ten and twenty brigades, each of which is divided into Production Teams.

Production Teams Subdivision of the Production Brigades (qv) in the Communes and the most important level of organisation in the Commune. They usually coincide with a village of 100–200 inhabitants, organise their own accounting and share out the income to their members after paying a fixed amount to the state and to Brigade reserves.

Protector-General of the Western Frontiers   Title given to Pan Ch'ao (qv) in 91 AD when he began his expedition to bring Central Asia under Chinese control.

Province   Main territorial subdivision which has persisted throughout much of Chinese history. The Han dynasty divided China into commanderies (qv) but these were abolished by the Sui empire which created prefectures and districts. The first provinces were created during the T'ang period when they were known as *tao* or circuits. The modern name for a province, *sheng*, and their permanent position as an extension of the central government, originated during the Mongol rule of China. The Ming dynasty had fifteen provinces, and the Ch'ing later created three more out of further subdivisions, and these were under the control of a governor (*hsün-fu*). During the Ch'ing period there was also a governor-general (qv) or viceroy who ruled two or more provinces. Both the Republic and the People's Republic retained provincial administrations and today provincial party government organisations exercise considerable powers.

P'u-i, Henry (1905–67)   Last Manchu emperor of China. P'u-i, the grand-nephew of the Dowager Empress Tz'u-hsi, succeeded to the throne as the Hsuan-t'ung emperor on the death of the Kuang-hsu emperor in 1908, with his father acting as regent. He was deposed in 1911 after the Republican revolution but temporarily restored by leaders of the Peiyang warlord clique in 1917. In 1932 he was made Chief Executive of the Japanese puppet state of Manchukuo (qv) and enthroned by the Japanese in March 1934. He was captured by the Russians in 1945 and was later returned to China. In spite of his collaboration with the Japanese he was allowed to rehabilitate himself after 1949 and worked as a tropical plants specialist in the botanical gardens of Academia Sinica. His autobiography *From Emperor to Citizen* (published in New York as *The Last Manchu*) appeared in 1965. He died of cancer in Peking in 1967.

Pure Land Sect (*Ching-t'u*)   Sectarian Buddhist movement that appeared during the 5th century and stressed simple popular observances such as calling the name of Buddha. Its name derives from its claim to offer easy access to the Western paradise known as the Pure Land. See also *Ch'an Buddhism*.

M

Q

Quemoy and Matsu Islands off the south-east coast of China between Amoy and Taiwan. In the mid-17th century Quemoy (Ch'in-men) was one of the bases used by Koxinga (qv) for his raids on Ch'ing China till it was recaptured by the Imperial forces with the help of the Dutch in 1644. In more recent history both Quemoy and Matsu have been held by the Nationalists since they retreated to Taiwan in 1949. The islands have been heavily fortified and up to a third of Nationalist active forces are stationed on them. Shelling by Nationalists and Communists of each others' positions precipitated crises in 1954 and 1958 but the confrontation across the straits is today limited to propaganda by leaflet and radio.

Queue Long hair in a pigtail imposed on Chinese males by the Manchu conquerors in 1644 and compulsory until 1911. Cutting the queue was a symbolic act for 19th century revolutionaries.

Quinsai Early name for Hangchow (qv).

Quotations from Chairman Mao Tse-tung Aphorisms and short selections from Mao's political writings which were organised topically and printed in massive editions. The impetus for publication came from Lin Piao and the army at the beginning of the Cultural Revolution which coincided with the end of a concerted campaign to eulogise Mao and his works throughout the army. In 1967, 350 million copies were printed and during the Cultural Revolution it was the one book carried by and referred to by everyone in China. The settling of arguments by referring to quotations largely replaced the serious study of Mao's work. After the Cultural Revolution *Quotations* went gradually out of fashion.

R

Railway Protection Movement Campaign that began in Szechwan in the summer of 1911 and was a precursor of the Revolution of that year (qv). A projected railway from Hankow to Szechwan which had been underwritten mainly by Szechwanese merchants and landlords was due to be nationalised like all provincial railways by a decree issued by the Ch'ing government in May 1911. Opposition to a local enterprise being taken over by a corrupt government subservient to foreign interests coalesced with the rising tide of nationalism that culminated in the Wuchang rising and the birth of the Chinese Republic.

Rebellions see *Peasant Rebellions*

Record of Rituals (*Li chi*) Han dynasty work and one of the Five Classics. The book centres on the idea of *li*, propriety, and the importance of proper conduct in society. Two chapters of the *Record*, the *Doctrine of the Mean* and the *Great Learning*, are often considered separately.

Record of the Three Kingdoms (*San kuo chih*) One of the Dynastic Histories (qv) that deals with the period of the Three Kingdoms, Wei, Shu Han, and Wu, during the 3rd century AD. It is not to be confused with *Romance of the Three Kingdoms* (qv).

Records of the Grand Historian (*Shih Chi*) The *Records*, written by Ssu-ma T'an and Ssu-ma Ch'ien (qv) who were court astronomers and historians during the 2nd century and at the beginning of the 3rd century BC, were the first in a long series of what became known as the Standard or Dynastic Histories. The work is a history of China from the earliest times down to the Han dynasty, basically in an annalistic style, but with the addition of monographs on the historical development of certain selected institutions such as the calendar, rituals or fiscal management and biographies of important personalities in each age. Both the monographs and the biographies were innovations.

Rectification Campaign (*Cheng-feng*) (1942–44) In 1942, the Communist base area of Yenan was greatly expanded by the influx of discontented students and other intellectuals from the areas invaded by Japan or under Nationalist control. The result was that the CCP embraced many who had not experienced the Long March or the founding of the Yenan base. The Rectification Campaign, aimed mainly at these new recruits, was designed to correct unorthodox sectarian and deviationist policies and inculcate a thorough understanding of Marxism and Leninism as defined by Mao and his colleagues. Stereotyped political writing was also attacked, but the main result was to establish the primacy of Mao's ideas in the CCP once and for all.

Rectification Movement (1957)   Campaign launched by the Central Committee of the CCP on April 27, 1957 to mobilise all positive forces to rectify the evils of bureaucratism, sectarianism and subjectivism among party members and cadres. It followed Mao's famous Hundred Flowers speech made on May 2, 1956 and the realisation that there was considerable public dissatisfaction with the conduct of many party officials. The first phase of the campaign followed the open criticism of the CCP solicited by Mao's speech, but the second phase was a complete reversal. It took the form of an Anti-Rightist movement (qv) during which many of those who had accepted the invitation to criticise the CCP were themselves denounced as rightists.

Red Army   Armed forces of the CCP from the earliest times till its transformation into the People's Liberation Army. The nucleus of the first Red Army was made up of groups of revolutionaries under Mao, Chu Teh and P'eng Teh-huai that came together in the Chingkangshan base in 1927. Throughout the 1930s the Red Army defended the Kiangsi Soviet against the Nationalist encirclement campaigns (qv). It grew in size from about 10,000 poorly equipped men in 1927 to 80,000 in 1937 after the Long March. Following the agreement to form the Second, anti-Japanese, United Front with the KMT the name Red Army was dropped and the CCP forces were incorporated, in name at least, into the national army. The main north China Communist forces were known as the Eighth Route Army (qv) and the New Fourth Army was the most important unit outside north China. After the war of resistance against Japan the Communist units were formally organised into the People's Liberation Army (qv) on June 30, 1946 by which time they numbered some 900,000 men backed by a militia force of over two million.

Red Band or Red Gang   Another name for the Triad secret society (qv).

Red Bases   Areas controlled by the CCP before 1949. The first of these was Chingkangshan, but the Communists moved to Kiangsi in 1930. The Central Soviet Base was organised on the Kiangsi-Fukien border with its capital at Juichin. The north-east Kiangsi base area was on the borders of Kiangsi with Chekiang and Fukien, while the Honan-Hopei-Anhwei or O-yü-wan (qv) base lasted from 1930 to 1933 and there were others on the Hunan-Hupei border and in south Kwangsi. After the Long March the main Communist area was the Yenan base in north Shensi, but as the CCP expanded the territory under its control other northern bases or liberated areas were formed in the border areas of Shansi-Chahar-Hopei (Chin-Ch'a-Chi), Shansi-Hopei-Shantung-Honan (Chin-Chi-Lu-Yü), Shansi-Suiyuan (Chin-Sui) and in Shantung (qqv). There were also bases in central and south China, some of these, as with the northern bases, behind the Japanese lines. These regions were the basis for the CCP advance which brought them eventual victory in 1949.

Red Eyebrows   Leaders of a peasant uprising in Shantung in 18 AD during the rule of Wang Mang (qv). The rebellion, which rapidly spread throughout the empire, had its origins in a series of famines caused by bad harvests and the breakdown of the Wei valley irrigation system. The Red Eyebrows, so called because of the way they chose to distinguish themselves, were originally a secret society practising a popular form of Taoism. They were able to bring about the collapse of Wang Mang's power but had not the expertise to replace it. Wang Mang was succeeded by Liu Hsiu, a landlord and a descendant of the earlier Han rulers, who suppressed the Red Eyebrows and other rebel groups as he consolidated his imperial rule.

Red Flag (*Hung ch'i*)   Main theoretical journal of the CCP which contains major policy statements and political analyses.

Red Guards (*Hung wei-ping*)   Name given to the militant young supporters of the Cultural Revolution. Their creation was announced by the Central Committee of the CCP in August 1966 although a number of radical groups in schools and universities had already adopted the name, the first being in a school attached to Tsinghua University in Peking in May. The term Red Guards was probably borrowed from the Russian *Krasnaya Gvardia*. The official seal of approval for the new Red Guards was given in Peking on August 18, 1966 when Mao Tse-tung personally attended a mass rally of young people from all over the country and himself donned a Red Guard armband. After this, hundreds of new groups were formed and Red Guard activities spread all over China as Peking radicals took to the trains to liaise with units in other cities. Red Guards were active throughout the Cultural Revolution, in overthrowing the existing party authorities in their towns, clashing with rival organisations, marching, meeting and urgently propagandising. Many of their leaflets and pamphlets written at this time give valuable insights into conditions during the Cultural Revolution and Chinese politics in general. As the Cultural Revolution was brought to a close the divergent groups of Red Guards were forced to unify and eventually required to accept army control. Their influence declined rapidly after 1969. See also *Scarlet Guards*.

Red Hat Sect   The older established sect of Lama Buddhism as distinct from the Yellow Hat Sect (qv) which sought to reform the religion in the 15th century.

Red Spear Society   Secret society which appeared in Honan, west Shantung, and south Hopei in about 1920, possibly connected with the Boxers and the White Lotus society. Members of the society practised traditional sacred boxing and wore amulets which they claimed would give invulnerability, but on a more practical level they organised village self-defence groups to protect the peasants from bandits or warlord armies. In 1925–1927 the CCP and the Communist International took an interest in the Red Spears who had already acquired some rudimentary political ideas. Li Ta-chao in particular made a study of their history and organisation and proposed that the CCP try and win them over. Similar self-defence groups were used by the CCP in the peasant movement.

Red Turban Rising   Another name for a rebellion by members of the White Lotus society in 1351 towards the end of the Yuan dynasty.

Red Versus Expert   Controversy, running throughout contemporary Chinese politics, over whether priority should be given to correct political attitudes — 'redness' — or technical and professional expertise. Different groups have varied in their attitudes, but in general the 'red' side has been identified with Mao, Chiang Ch'ing and other radicals and with periods such as the Great Leap Forward and the Cultural Revolution. P'eng Teh-huai, Liu Shao-ch'i and Teng Hsiao-p'ing all seem to have stressed expertise which was given prominence in the mid-1950s and in the period between the Great Leap Forward and the Cultural Revolution. The two positions were not mutually exclusive but the less radical were often content to accept technical competence whether or not ideological attitudes were sound.

Reform Through Labour   Institution for dealing with criminals in the People's Republic. Convicted prisoners are sentenced to long terms of hard labour in prison camps and many commonly remain to work in the camps for wages after the expiry of their sentences. See also *Education Through Labour*.

Regional Commanders   T'ang dynasty officials made responsible by the emperor for military and civil affairs in the frontier regions of Central Asia, Szechwan and Canton. They eventually acquired a considerable amount of power in their own right and some eventually became effectively independent kings in their own areas as T'ang rule collapsed. See also *An Lu-shan*.

Regional Guilds   see   *Landsmannschaften*

Republic of China   State which replaced the Empire when the last emperor of the Ch'ing dynasty formally abdicated on February 12, 1912. Sun Yat-sen resigned as provisional president the following day in favour of Yuan Shih-k'ai. Yuan tried to restore the monarchy in 1916 but died in the same year, leaving China in a state of civil war as regionally-based warlords vied for power. Sun was unable to bring all China under a republican government before his death in 1925; this was left to Chiang K'ai-shek with the KMT who succeeded partially in the Northern Expedition in 1926. From 1928 to 1937 the Republic was governed from Nanking but torn by civil war with the CCP, famine, and poverty. The Japanese invasion of 1937 put an end to the possibility of a Republican government, although it staggered on through war and civil war till 1949 when the CCP took over. The Nationalists withdrew to Taiwan and their administration on the island, which has continued as the Republic of China, also lays claim to the mainland.

Returned Students   General name for Chinese who had studied abroad, in for example Japan, Europe or the United States, and returned to China. Returned students played an important part in the introduction of ideas and technology into China. The Twenty-Eight Bolsheviks (qv) were also known as the Returned Students Faction.

Revisionism   In general the revision of fundamental Marxist principles but in particular the accusation made by the Chinese in the 1960s that the Russians had gone back on a previously correct ideological position. The term was first used of Yugoslavia, then of the USSR during the Sino-Soviet dispute and it became the most common pejorative adjective used of political opponents during the 1960s.

Revive China Society (*Hsing-Chung hui*)   Secret organisation formed in 1894 by Sun Yat-sen. After an unsuccessful rebellion in Canton in 1895, Sun lived in exile and in 1905 merged the society with others to form the T'ung-meng hui (qv).

Revolution of 1911   Transference of power that took place when the Ch'ing dynasty collapsed. Republican pressure had been building up ever since the failure of the attempts to build a constitutional monarchy in the last years of the 19th century and the final straw for the imperial regime was the Wuchang Rising (qv) of army units in October 1911. The Revolution failed to transform Chinese society but it did bring to an end centralised imperial government. This was replaced by the growth of provincial assemblies in which a new urban bourgeoisie, gentry with a more modern outlook, warlords and the regional armies exercised most power with the assistance in some areas of the secret societies. The breakdown of central power and authority made the establishment of a central republican government more difficult and the first seventeen years after the revolution of 1911 were a period of division and warlordism (qv).

Revolutionary Civil Wars   Conventional Chinese subdivisions of the modern revolutionary period. The First Revolutionary Civil War from 1924–27 was fought by the KMT in co-operation with the CCP, against the Northern Warlords. The Second from 1927–37 was marked by the split between the Communists and Nationalists, the Kiangsi Soviet and the Long March. After a further period of co-operation in the Second United Front, the CCP fought and defeated the KMT in the Third and final Revolutionary Civil War from 1945-49.

Revolutionary Committee of the Kuomintang   One of the non-Communist political parties allowed to function in post-1949 China. The Revolutionary Committee was formed out of rebel elements of the KMT who came over to the Communist side in January 1948 in Hong Kong and declared their opposition to Chiang K'ai-shek. The most important people to go over were Li Chi-shen who had put down the Canton Commune (qv) and Soong Ch'ing-ling (Mme Sun Yat-sen) (qv). The Revolutionary Committee disappeared from public view during the Cultural Revolution.

Revolutionary Committees   New organs of local government that sprang up during the Cultural Revolution. After the radical power seizures of 1967 that dismantled the existing party organisations in the provinces and the failure of the Shanghai Commune experiment, Revolutionary Committees were formed with military support and often with a large proportion of People's Liberation Army members, although they included representatives of 'revolutionary cadres' and the 'revolutionary masses'. The model for the committees was the Heilungkiang Revolutionary Committee formed on January 31, 1967. Revolutionary Committees were formed in all other provinces and large cities and then in counties, towns, factories, schools and colleges. Some delegates to the committees were elected but there was a decisive element of control from above. As the Cultural Revolution drew to a close the Revolutionary Committees remained in name but lost much of their radical impetus and were transformed into local management bodies.

Ricci, Matteo (1552–1610)   Pioneer Jesuit missionary who became established in Peking in 1600, towards the end of the Ming dynasty. He had been in Macao since 1582 but had to wait to be given permission to settle in Peking. He sent back to Europe favourable reports of China, studied the language and immersed himself in Chinese scholarship, but made few converts. Ricci and his colleague Ruggieri impressed the Chinese with their knowledge of astronomy, mathematics, geography and mechanical devices such as clocks and established a place for the Jesuits in China. Ricci became something of a celebrity in Peking where he died after an illness in 1610. His work was continued by generations of dedicated Jesuits (qv).

Rites Controversy   The insistence in the 18th century that Jesuits choose between the primacy of the Pope and the Son of Heaven. Missionaries in China had permitted Christian converts to practise ancestral rituals but not specifically religious Confucian ceremonies. In 1704 the Pope banned the use of even ancestral rites, but the K'ang-hsi emperor regarded this as papal interference in Chinese religious matters. The papal stand was reaffirmed by a Papal Bull from Clement XI in 1715 and reiterated by Pope Benedict XIV in 1742. Jesuits were put in a position that was practically impossible and their work and influence declined.

Ritual of Chou (*Chou-li*)   Reconstruction in the Confucian tradition of the supposedly ideal governmental structure of early Chou China. It was used by both Wang Mang and Wang An-shih to justify reforms that they planned.

Romance of the Three Kingdoms (*San-kuo-chih yen-i*) Extremely popular historical novel of the Three Kingdoms period (qv) based on the exploits of Ts'ao Ts'ao and Chu-ko Liang. It evolved from a cycle of legends and reached its final form in the 14th century. It was written by Lo Kuan-chung from Hangchow who based his work on story-tellers' stories from the Sung period.

Roy, M. N. Comintern representative in China who replaced Borodin (qv) in 1927. He was an Indian communist who advocated continued collaboration with the Left KMT (qv) and left China when the alliance failed.

Russo-Japanese War (1904–5) Conflict over influence in Manchuria and Korea. Japan attacked the Russian navy at Port Arthur (qv) in 1904 and defeated Russian armies in Korea and Manchuria. Japanese victory led to the treaty signed in Portsmouth, New Hampshire in September 1905 after American mediation. Japan took over Russian concessions in Port Arthur and in what became the Kwantung Leased Territory (qv) and effectively controlled Korea which she annexed in 1910.

S

Sage Emperors   see   *Three Sovereigns* and *Five Emperors*

St Petersburg, Treaty of (1881)   Peace settlement reached between Russia and China after prolonged Russian encroachment in the Sinkiang region. China regained Ili which had been occupied by Russia but one of the most significant outcomes was that Sinkiang was fully integrated into China and became a province in 1885.

Salt and Iron, Discourses on (*Yen-t'ieh lun*)   Han dynasty work which originated in a set of notes taken during a court conference held to discuss government monopolies (qv) of salt and iron. The book reveals the conflicting approaches of the Confucians who argued that monopolies fostered greed and the Legalists who insisted that the revenues from them were vital for the upkeep of defences against the Hsiung-nu.

Salt Exchange   Arrangement made in the Ming dynasty following a Sung precedent for supplying grain to Chinese garrisons on the northern frontier. As the transport of supplies to the border was arduous, merchants were given salt certificates in exchange for the delivery. The certificates enabled them to trade in salt, which was still a government monopoly and a highly lucrative commodity. Salt exchange began in north Shansi in 1370 and spread over the whole border region by the early 15th century. Merchant colonisation (qv) which developed farming on the frontiers grew out of this system.

Salt Monopoly   Because it was such an essential part of the Chinese diet, the production and sale of salt were generally controlled by the government throughout most of Chinese history. The monopoly dates back to the Warring States period and is traditionally attributed to Kuan-tzu (qv) who was adviser to Duke Huan of the state of Ch'i in the 7th century BC. It was reintroduced by the Han emperor Wu Ti in 119 BC although not without opposition, (see *Salt and Iron, Discourses on*) and revived by the T'ang rulers after which it operated almost continuously. The Ming and Ch'ing governments allowed scope for private enterprises granting licences to private businessmen to engage in the salt trade (see *Salt Exchange*). Inevitably there was a considerable amount of smuggling and illicit trade.

San Min Chu I see *Three Peoples Principles*

San-fan see *Three-Anti-Movement*

Scapulimancy see *Oracle Bones*

Scarlet Guards (Chi-wei-tui) Conservative mass organisations which appeared in Shanghai during the Cultural Revolution in opposition to the more radical Red Guard Units. After the Shanghai party newspaper *Liberation Daily* had been seized by radical units in December 1966 the conservative local authorities relied heavily on the Scarlet Guards who were very influential in the factories, to push through their policies of economism (qv).

Schall, Adam see *Bell, Adam Schall von*

Scholar Gentry see *Gentry*

Scholars (*Ju-lin wai-shih*) *The Scholars,* literally the *Unofficial History of Confucian Scholars,* a novel written by Wu Ching-tzu (1701–54) in Nanking between about 1739 and 1750. It gives a detailed picture of life in 18th century China with portraits of the scholar-gentry among whom Wu lived, and is also a satire on the sterile learning produced by the state examinations and the incompetence and corruption of the official class.

Scissors and Paste Historiography Description of traditional Chinese historical writing in which books were compiled out of whole documents and extracts from earlier works, added together with little attempt at continuity or analysis. The Dynastic Histories and the major encyclopaedias from the T'ang period onwards are often criticised for being little more than scissors-and-paste compilations.

Seamen's Union Trade Union which developed out of the Seamen's Mutual Benefit Society that was formed in 1914. The Seamen's Union, founded in about 1919 in Hong Kong became more and more radical and eventually organised a strike of Chinese seamen employed in foreign shipping firms on January 12, 1922. The Hong Kong government tried to close down the union and arrested leading union members but was forced to rescind the closure, release the strikers and grant a 15%–30% wage increase. The success of the union greatly stimulated the development of the Chinese labour movement.

Second Emperor (Erh-shih Huang-ti)   Succeeded his father Shih Huang-ti as emperor of the first Chinese dynasty, the Ch'in in 209 BC. The Second Emperor, a minor, was manipulated by Chao Kao (qv), the chief eunuch, and was murdered at his instigation. His death in 207 BC led to the collapse of the dynasty.

Second Northern Expedition   see   *Northern Expedition*

Second Revolution   Unsuccessful rebellion of seven southern provinces against Yuan Shih-k'ai in 1913. The Second Revolution followed the Nationalist success in the parliamentary elections of 1912 and Yuan's attempt to crush them. Military weakness and internal dissension prevented Yuan's being overthrown and he went on to restore the monarchy.

Secret History of the Mongols   Chronicle of Mongol history, particularly during the lifetime of Chinggis Khan, that incorporated traditional material and was first written down in about 1240. It was secret as it was intended to be read only by Mongols and not by Chinese.

Secret Societies   Underground political and religious organisations usually opposed to the current government. Secret societies have existed throughout Chinese history. The White Lotus (qv) society for example can be traced back directly to the 12th century and can claim descent from groups existing in the 4th century. The societies drew on all classes of the population but mainly attracted the poor such as dispossessed farmers, boatmen and labourers. Although in existence continuously, they came to notice during periods of turmoil and rebellion. Secret societies were active during the years that led up to the collapse of the Yuan and the foundation of the Ming dynasty and particularly towards the end of the Ch'ing dynasty when they were fiercely anti-Manchu. They were involved in the White Lotus rebellion at the end of the 18th century, in the Taiping rising, the Boxer rebellion, the 1911 Revolution (qqv) and the political turbulence of the 1920s and 1930s and still exist today in Hong Kong and South-East Asia and Chinese communities elsewhere, although they have lost much of their political importance. Apart from the White Lotus, the most important societies were the Triads (qv) and the Elder Brother Society (qv).

Selected Works of Mao Tse-tung   Definitive official edition of Mao's collected writings. Volumes I–IV, which include articles and essays written up to 1949, were first published in 1965. Volume V, published in 1977, takes the collection up to 1957. All the most important writings of Mao are in these volumes, but they have been revised with Mao's approval and are often significantly different from the original texts. The originals are available in a Chinese ten-volume collection, but only selected items are available in English.

Self-Criticism One of the most important methods used by the CCP to try and enforce conformity. Party members and other citizens who have been criticised for some lapse or for holding unorthodox views are expected to follow this up with an analysis of their own mistakes. Only genuine whole-hearted self-criticisms are usually accepted and these have to be made in a standard form.

Self-Strengthening Movement (1861–95) Part of the Ch'ing dynastic revival that began in 1861 with the reign of the T'ung-chih emperor and lasted till 1895. Self-strengthening was concerned principally with military modernisation and with the development of an industrial base which made modernisation possible. It followed the defeats of the Chinese at the hands of the British in the Opium Wars and the humiliating treaties they were forced to sign. During the first decade of the movement, great emphasis was placed on the adoption of western military technology and scientific knowledge and the training of technical and diplomatic personnel. The Tsungli Yamen, the Kiangnan and Nanking Arsenals (qqv) and various schools and other munitions factories were started. During the second decade the emphasis moved to the establishment of a sound economic base with a number of government-sponsored industries in the Western style of profit-oriented concerns — the so-called Foreign Matters movement (qv) — although military matters were not neglected. The last decade continued these concerns but the idea of enriching the nation through light industries was also put forward and textile production was greatly encouraged. Although the reforms attempted were impressive their implementation was unco-ordinated and under-capitalised and Chinese industry never succeeded in breaking the stranglehold of technical backwardness and imperialism. The failure of self-strengthening under the empire gave added impetus to the growing republicanism of the late 19th century.

Semi-Colony Mao Tse-tung's description of the status of imperial China in the decades after the Opium War. Whereas Africa or other parts of Asia had been partitioned off into colonies of various European powers China had remained a political entity, never partitioned. Certain areas were under the influence of one or other foreign power which might enjoy considerable economic power in those regions, but they remained an integral part of China.

Seng-ko-lin-ch'in   Mongol prince who commanded imperial troops against the Taiping rebels. He was killed in action against the Nien in 1865.

Shang Dynasty or Yin (18th century–12th century BC)   The second, after the Hsia, of the traditional dynasties of prehistoric China. According to tradition, the Shang dynasty was formed after the people had revolted against the corrupt ruler of the Hsia. Sceptical modern historians had assumed that the Shang period was purely legendary but archaeological evidence that began to appear from the 1920s onwards has confirmed many of the ancient traditions. The Oracle bones (qv), the excavations at Anyang (qv) which revealed weapons, and elaborately decorated ritual vessels of bronze and other evidence indicate a stratified, sheep and cattle-rearing agricultural society based on a city-state ruled over by hereditary kings. Imposing palace buildings contrasted with crude pit dwellings for the common people, and the society seems to have been bound together by shamanistic beliefs. There is evidence of human sacrifice and many Chinese historians believe Shang to have been a slave-owning society. The alternative name, Yin, is the one given to the latter part of the Shang by its successors. After its fall in the 11th century it was followed by the Chou dynasty.

Shang Yang (390–338 BC)   Also known as Kung-sun Yang, a great statesman of the state of Ch'in who was executed in 338 BC after having been the leading official of the kingdom since 361 BC. He assisted in bringing all the feudal territories of the state under the control of the state administration and in 350 BC divided it into prefectures under a central government official known as a prefect. These reforms and other authoritarian policies along Legalist lines helped to set Ch'in on the road to becoming one of the major Warring States and it was eventually able to unify China under the first empire. The *Book of Lord Shang* (qv) has often been attributed to Shang Yang.

Shanghai Commune   Proposed new administration for Shanghai after the January Storm (qv) and power seizure of 1967 during the Cultural Revolution. Radical elements led by Chang Ch'un-ch'iao and Yao Wen-yuan wanted an organisation modelled on the Paris Commune of 1871 with delegates elected by popular assemblies and subject to immediate recall. This model was unacceptable to Mao and others in the central leadership and was superseded by revolutionary committees (qv) throughout China.

Shanghai Coup   Putsch organised by Chiang K'ai-shek on April 12, 1927 to destroy Communist and Trade Union organisations and known also as the White Terror. Nationalist troops co-operated with Shanghai underworld societies such as the Green and Red Gangs (qv). Trade Union headquarters were attacked and officials taken out and shot on the spot, and a systematic massacre followed of trade unionists, Communists and people suspected of being either. The Nationalists were in a strong position by April 1927 as the success of the Northern Expedition had given China its first semblance of unity since 1911. Relations with the CCP had become very strained because of fundamentally opposite political ideas. Hundreds died in the days that followed and the coup effectively wiped out Communist activity in Shanghai and then spread to other cities. It was the end of the urban-based CCP. After a series of unsuccessful risings in Nanchang, Canton and elsewhere the CCP fled to the countryside where its new strategy of peasant war was developed.

Shanghai Tariff Conference (1858)   Negotiations between Lord Elgin and Chinese imperial officials in October 1858 over new customs tariffs which had been stipulated in the Treaty of Tientsin (qv) earlier that year. Full ratification of the treaty was not carried out till the Convention of Peking (qv) in 1860.

Shang-ti   A Chinese term for God, meaning the Supreme Ruler. Shang-ti was originally one of the great mythical early sovereigns who was worshipped during the Shang dynasty. The Chou dynasty which followed adopted the same chief deity but gave it the name of *T'ien* or heaven.

Shang-tu (Xanadu)   Summer residence of the Mongol Great Khans, known to Coleridge as Xanadu in his poem *Kubla Khan*. Shang-tu was in the eastern part of Mongolia to the north of the Great Wall. Marco Polo visited it in the 13th century.

Shanhaikuan   'Pass between the mountains and the sea', where the Great Wall comes down to the coast of the Gulf of Chihli. It was the only route of easy access between China and Manchuria and could be sealed quite easily. The Manchus were able to seize Peking and take control of China in 1644 because the Chinese commander at Shanhaikuan, Wu San-kuei, allowed them through to help him defeat the rebel Li Tzu-ch'eng.

Shansi Merchants   Merchants from Shansi and neighbouring Shensi who were active in north China from the Ming dynasty onwards and in Mongolia from the 18th century. Like their southern counterparts the Hsin-an merchants (qv) their rise to prominence dates from the salt exchange system (qv) which brought them large profits. These profits were used to capitalise many commercial undertakings, notably the Shansi banks which were probably the most important pre-modern financial institutions.

Shansi-Chahar-Hopei Base (Chin-Ch'a-Chi) One of the Communist-held areas during the anti-Japanese war. It was formally created on January 10, 1938 but had its origins in troop movements after the battle of P'inghsingkuan (qv) in September 1937. The provisional Administrative Committee which governed the base was led by Nieh Jung-chen (qv) then deputy commander of the 115th Division of the 8th Route Army: Lin Piao was the divisional commander. The base was reinforced by Nationalist troops who were won over to the CCP by part of Ho Lung's 120th Division which joined it in 1939. Regular Japanese clean-up campaigns led to administrative problems but their savage reprisals increased local support for the CCP.

Shansi-Hopei-Shantung-Honan Base (Chin-Chi-Lu-Yü) CCP-controlled area during the anti-Japanese war, formed on the borders of the provinces named. It was created in 1937 when Liu Po-ch'eng's troops retreated from the Japanese advance and was reinforced by a regiment of the 8th Route Army in February 1938 and then by other units. Much of the political organisation was carried out by Teng Hsiao-p'ing (qv). In spite of clashes with government troops as well as the Japanese the CCP position was consolidated and by 1941 they held a third of the seats in an elected provisional assembly. The base area was already famous as Liang-shan-po (qv) the site of the rebel activities of the Sung period.

Shansi-Suiyuan Base (Chin-Sui) Anti-Japanese war base that was built up around Ho Lung's 12th Division when it moved to north Shansi in October 1937. It was situated between the Yellow River and the Mongolian desert. CCP progress in the region was hindered by loyalties to the local governor Fu Tso-yi and by a campaign by members of the collaborationist Peking government. However CCP rent-reduction policies and the development of militia groups brought the region under CCP control by October 1942.

Shantung Base Anti-Japanese war base organised by the CCP in the area south of Tsinan in late 1937 before the arrival of Japanese troops. By 1943 almost half Shantung was under Communist control,

N

and the base became an important springboard for the reconquest of Manchuria after the Japanese defeat.

Shan-yüan, Treaty of   Agreement concluded in 1005 between the Sung emperor Chen-tsung (reigned 998–1023) and the ruler of the Khitan Liao dynasty, in which each acknowledged the other's right to the title of emperor. This was, as far as the Chinese were concerned, against all precedent as only the Chinese emperor could be the Son of Heaven, and it was hotly opposed and criticised in China. The policy of co-existence was carried further by recognition of the imperial title of the Hsi Hsia in 1403. The Liao later fell to the Chin dynasty which took over large areas of North China including the capital and paved the way for the Mongol conquest.

Sheng Hsuan-huai (1844–1916)   Official and assistant to Li Hung-chang. Sheng was involved with the China Merchants' Steam Navigation Company (qv) until his death and was the originator of the *kuan-tu shang-pan* (qv) concept of company organisation.

Sheng Shih-ts'ai (1895–   )   Sinkiang warlord from 1933 to 1942 when he was deposed after switching his allegiance to the Nationalists.

Sheng-wu-lien   Ultra-radical group that emerged during the Cultural Revolution. *Sheng-wu-lien* is the Chinese abbreviation for the Hunan Province Great Alliance Committee of Proletarian Revolutionaries. The organisation put forward a demand for a Shanghai Commune (qv) style administration in Hunan after a visit by Mao to the Hunan provincial capital, Ch'angsha, on September 17, 1967. They stated that China's 'red capitalists' under Chou En-lai were beginning to reverse the radical gains of the January Storm (qv) through the medium of revolutionary committees (qv) and called for the armed masses to rise against them, establish the Communes and build a new Maoist party. Sheng-wu-lien may well have been influenced by the ideas of Trotsky or by anarchism. Their numbers and influence are not known but the threat they posed was serious enough for the top people in the Cultural Revolution Group, Chiang Ch'ing, K'ang Sheng and Yao Wen-yuan, to denounce them vehemently. Their manifesto was unique, but their appearance in late 1967 was part of a wave of activities by ultra-radical groupings who feared that the gains they had made were going to be lost as the Cultural Revolution was brought gradually to an end.

Shen-Kan-Ning Base (Shensi-Kansu-Ninghsia)   Border territory controlled by the CCP from its Yenan headquarters during the anti-

Japanese war. The 'special border region' based on the original North Shensi Soviet Government set up after the Long March was the result of an agreement between the CCP and KMT in Nanking in September 1937 as part of the second, anti-Japanese, United Front. It was governed by an elected Border Region Assembly and the administrative structure included mass organisations representing women, youth and other groups, as well as the Communist Party. The main economic policies of the government were the reduction of land rent and interest on loans, the encouragement of trade and the creation of industrial co-operatives. Education and the press were organised mainly by the CCP. See also *Yenan*.

Shen-tsung, Sung Emperor (reigned 1067–1085) Emperor who appointed Wang An-shih as Chief Councillor in 1069. He succeeded his father Ying-tsung, who had reigned for only five years, at the age of eighteen, but was completely overshadowed by the sweeping reforms of his Chief Councillor. Shen-tsung died in 1085 aged only 36.

Shih Huang-ti The first emperor of the Ch'in dynasty and thus the first emperor of China. The title Shih Huang-ti, which means First Emperor, was adopted in 221 BC by the king of the State of Ch'in when all the other Warring States had come under his rule and China had been unified under the Ch'in dynasty. Much of the credit for the unification and the creation of a centralised government must go to the emperor's chief statesman Li Ssu (qv). Shih Huang-ti's rule was despotic and even cruel and the dynasty only survived his death in 210 BC by three years.

Shih Nai-an Traditionally, the author of *Water Margin* (qv), Shih lived near Hangchow in the years before 1400 and was responsible for the final form of the novel.

Shimonoseki, Treaty of (1895) Peace settlement that ended the Sino-Japanese war of 1894–95. It provided for the recognition of Korean independence, a 200-million-tael indemnity to be paid to Japan, Taiwan and Liatoung to be ceded to Japan, various ports to be opened to Japan for trade, and the right of Japanese nationals to engage in industry in China.

Shu Name of a semi-barbarian state in the Szechwan region during the later part of the Chou period in the 3rd century BC which was annexed by the Ch'in. The name Shu was also taken by two dynasties in the Five Dynasties period between the T'ang and Sung dynasties, the Earlier Shu (907–925 AD) and the Later Shu (934–965 AD), both of which had their capitals at Chengtu. Szechwan is known as Shu to this day.

Shu Han   One of the Three Kingdoms (qv), with the Wei and Wu, that ruled China after the collapse of the Han dynasty. Shu Han was based on Chengtu in Szechwan and founded by Liu Pei who traced his ancestry back to the Han royal line that began with Liu Pang. He called his dynasty Han but it has been known since as Shu Han after the ancient state of Shu.

Shun   see   *Three Sages*

Shun-chih, Ch'ing Emperor (reigned 1644–1661)   First emperor of the Manchu Ch'ing dynasty. Fu-lin, the five-year-old son of Abahai, succeeded in 1644 with Dorgon and Jirgalang as regents. His reign saw the consolidation of the Ch'ing rule and the elimination of Ming remnants. He took over the reins of government himself in 1651 and continued Dorgon's policy of enlisting the aid of Chinese administrators. He took an interest in religion and was in contact with the Jesuit Adam Schall von Bell between 1651 and 1657 although he was not converted to Christianity. From 1657 he became deeply involved with Ch'an Buddhism. The emperor died at 22 but by then had 14 children, the third of whom was designated as heir and became the K'ang-hsi emperor.

Sian Incident   The capture of Chiang K'ai-shek on December 12, 1936 by Chand Hsüeh-liang, the Young Marshal, at Sian. Chiang had gone to Sian to direct an offensive against the CCP although several groups within the KMT were already involved in negotiations with the Communists in Yenan. Chang Hsüeh-liang made eight conditions for the release of Chiang which broadly speaking called for national unity against Japan. Chou En-lai arrived in Sian to mediate and extracted from Chiang the promise of future collaboration against the invaders. Chang Hsüeh-liang released Chiang and was himself arrested and sentenced to ten years imprisonment, though this was later commuted to house arrest. The incident contributed towards the unification that led eventually to the second, short-lived United Front.

Silk   Knowledge of sericulture in China goes back well into prehistoric times, traditionally to about 2700 BC when Hsu Lung-she discovered the art of reeling and weaving silk. The art was widespread in Chou and Han China but did not spread to other countries till much later. Japanese silk production dates from the 8th century. The basic techniques involved were rearing the caterpillars on mulberry leaves in a high temperature, controlling the spinning of the cocoons, reeling the silk fibres, spinning and weaving, and these have been known for centuries. The Yangtze estuary in Chekiang and Kiangsu, the Pearl River delta in Kwangtung and Szechwan are the main silk producing areas. Although most of the production was done on a cottage-industry basis, during the Ming dynasty, Soochow, capital of Kiangsu, developed as a textile centre, specialising in silk weaving and dyeing. There was a government-controlled Imperial Silkworks in the Ming and Ch'ing periods which regulated quality and supplies of raw materials and put out contracts to private weavers. Silk was an important export from Han times onwards when it was traded with the Roman empire. Bolts of silk were also a medium of exchange before the common acceptance of coinage.

Silk Route   Route along which silk and other commodities travelled from China to the Roman empire and regions in the Middle East. The route led from north-west China through Jade Gate (Yumen) to the Tarim Basin, crossing the Pamirs at Kashgar into Afghanistan and Turkestan and from there to Persia and the Mediterranean. It stretched from Ch'ang-an, the Han capital, some 7,000 miles to Rome. The Silk Route was in reality a series of oases and separate caravan routes along which camels, yaks and pack mules transported luxury items — only small items of high value justified the expense of transport — such as silk to the West and gold, silver and precious stones to the East. Few Han merchants would have made the whole journey and indeed there is no record of such a journey till Marco Polo's time. Trade was carried on by stages and goods were passed on from merchant to merchant. The whole enterprise was risky as travellers were often set upon by bandits or armed raiders.

Silver Trade   Silver became important as a currency during the Sung dynasty. In the 11th century the increased use of money, replacing barter, had led to problems in the supply of copper coins, and silver ingots, supposedly of standard quality, were introduced. During the Ming dynasty, large amounts of silver, sometimes known as Mexican silver dollars, were imported by Spanish or Portuguese traders who brought it from silver mines in their new American colonies in the 16th century. Other silver came from Japan and the imports contributed to the increased use of currency in the Ming period. Taxes were levied in silver as it was easier to collect than taxes in kind. Towards the end of the Ch'ing dynasty the flow of silver was reversed as it was used to pay for imports from the European powers and by the mid-19th century the drain of silver was beginning to harm the economy. This outflow of silver was one of the underlying causes of the Opium War as opium was one of the imports paid for in silver.

Single-Whip System of Taxation   Reform introduced in the later part of the Ming dynasty, between about 1522 and 1619, which attempted to consolidate and simplify the existing system of tax levies. Land taxes were combined and levied at only one cash rate, the liability for labour service was consolidated into one levy and often commuted into a single cash payment, which effectively abolished the corvée system. The object of a single cash payment to cover all taxes was never achieved, partly because the reforms were not carried out to an overall plan but were introduced piecemeal, province by province. However the new system stimulated trade as the new cash payments encouraged the use of coinage and this eased the process of exchanging commodities.

Sino-Japanese War (1894–95)   War that broke out between China and Japan principally over the question of influence in Korea (qv). Korea was a tributary state of China although it enjoyed some autonomy, but from 1876 onwards Japan had been trying to open Korean ports to trade and later annexed the Ryukyu Islands. In spite of treaties with other powers to balance foreign influence in the area, Japanese influence increased and by 1884 Korea became effectively a joint protectorate of China and Japan. When Chinese troops put down an anti-government rising in Korea in 1894 Japanese troops intervened, negotiations failed to secure their withdrawal and war was declared on August 1, 1894. China suffered a humiliating defeat. Li Hung-chang's Huai Army was beaten badly at Pyongyang, the Peiyang fleet was defeated and the naval bases of Port Arthur and Dairen were captured. After Japan had captured the defences of Weihaiwei, China was forced to sign the Treaty of Shimonoseki (qv) recognising the independence of Korea and ceding land to Japan. The war showed the supremacy of the new Japanese naval and military forces and was the first stage in their expansion into Korea and later Manchuria and China. See also *Anti-Japanese War* (1937–45).

Sino-Soviet Dispute   Dispute that arose between the Communist Parties of the Soviet Union and China during the early 1960s and led to armed clashes on the border between the two countries. Relations between the Soviet Union and China were never easy. Stalin's support for the KMT even when it massacred Communists, and his insistence even after the Anti-Japanese war that the KMT would form the next government with CCP co-operation, led to basic differences in political approach. Even after 1949 there were strains in the relationship over the question of Soviet influence in Manchuria and Sinkiang. From 1949 to 1953 wrangling over these rights and over the degree of Soviet aid continued but after Stalin's death relations became more amicable and equal. Soviet aid was increased and China acknowledged the leadership of the USSR in the socialist camp. The beginnings of the later and more serious conflict can be traced back to Khrushchev's secret denunciation of Stalin at the Soviet 20th Party Congress in February 1956, an attack which was not accepted by the Chinese. The USSR strongly disapproved of the Great Leap Forward and commune policies and failed to support the Chinese in the Quemoy crisis of August 1958. In 1959 a nuclear sharing agreement was rescinded and by the Moscow Conference of 1960 the split had become public, all criticism previously having been indirect. In August 1960 the USSR withdrew all its technicians from China and terminated its aid programme. Throughout the 1960s the dispute worsened with the Chinese talking of the 'New Tsars' and Soviet 'Social Imperialism' and the Communist Party of the Soviet Union attacking the deviations from Leninism of the 'Maoist clique'. These denunciations became even more vitriolic during the Cultural Revolution. The border dispute (qv) between China and the USSR which had its roots in Tsarist foreign policy was renewed and fighting eventually broke out on Chen-pao or Damansky Island on the Ussuri River north of Vladivostok in March 1969. Negotiations since then have failed to solve the disagreements because of the basic ideological differences.

Sino-Soviet Treaty of Friendship, Alliance and Mutual Assistance Agreement signed on February 14, 1950 which presented a picture of a united China and Russia. The Chinese received a 300-million-dollar aid programme but in return had to accept the independence of the Mongolian People's Republic, which, as Outer Mongolia, had been part of the Chinese sphere of influence, joint Sino-Soviet exploitation of mineral resources in Sinkiang, joint administration of railways in Mongolia and joint use of Port Arthur (qv) and Dairen. The Soviet presence in Sinkiang, Manchuria and the ports ended in 1955.

Six Dynasties Period   Epoch that followed the fall of the Later Han dynasty, named after the six successive dynasties that had their capitals at Nanking between 222 and 589. The later part of the period (420–589) is also known as the period of the Northern and Southern Dynasties (qv) and the earlier part is known as the Three Kingdoms. This interregnum between the great empires of Han and Sui-T'ang was a time of great change. Chinese civilisation was confronted with profound challenges from Buddhism and the barbarian societies of the steppes, and succeeded in meeting the challenges by incorporating the new elements into a rich synthesis out of which grew a stronger, revitalised empire.

Six Ministries or Six Boards   see   *Ministries, Six*

Sixteen Kingdoms   Kingdoms that controlled north China during the Six Dynasties period from the fall of the Western Chin in 317 AD to the rise of the Northern Wei in 386. It was a confused time with many pretenders both Chinese and barbarian to the Han throne.

Sixteen Points   Document with sixteen clauses adopted by the Central Committee of the CCP on August 8, 1966 which laid down the guidelines for the Cultural Revolution. It provided outlines for radical mass action and the growth of Cultural Revolution groups and committees, methods for dealing with party and government officials, educational reform, attitudes to scientific and technical workers and the armed forces, and enshrined Mao Tse-tung Thought as the guide to action. However it was moderate compared with some activist groups and vague enough to encompass all kinds of activities. Its essential caution is seen from the clear instruction in Point 15 that the People's Liberation Army should only participate in the Cultural Revolution under the direction of the Military Commission of the Central Committee and the General Political Department of the Army.

Slaves   Contemporary Chinese historians often characterise China before the Warring States period as a slave society. Human sacrifices practised by the Shang dynasty and other evidence have led to the conclusion that part of the population then was enslaved and the same is true for the Chou period and the Warring States. Under the Han dynasty there was a small number of domestic slaves and there are records of revolts by slave labourers at the government iron works. Slaves were freed by the Later Han emperor Kuang-wu. Evidence on the sale and purchase of slaves before the Warring States period is very thin, but in Ch'in and Han times the relatives of convicted criminals were often forced into labour service for the government. It is difficult to assess the importance of slaves in the early Chinese economy, but official labour service duties for craftsmen and soldiers which were a legacy from slave-owning times were important in later centuries.

Small Sword Society   Offshoot of the Triad society which seized the walled Chinese city of Shanghai and held it for eighteen months in 1853–4. The Small Swords appealed to Hung Hsiu-ch'uan for aid from the Taipings but this was refused as Hung was trying to reduce secret society influence in his movement and the insurrection collapsed. Shanghai would have been an invaluable strategic base for the Taipings.

Sneevliet   see   *Maring*

Snow, Edgar   American journalist who produced the first report on the CCP-controlled area of Yenan. His *Red Star Over China* published in 1937 remains one of the most valuable single sources in the period. After 1949 he became very much *persona grata* in China and wrote many sympathetic accounts of the construction of the new China.

Social Imperialism   China's description of the policies of the USSR since the Sino-Soviet dispute (qv).

Socialist Education Movement   Mass movement in the period 1962–65 launched to propagate the Yenan model of society and particularly to stress the importance of class struggle in order to combat the dangers of a Khrushchev-type revisionism in China. Officials and intellectuals were sent to the countryside to learn from the masses and writers were urged to produce works reflecting the socialist transformation of Chinese society. It was during this movement that Chiang Ch'ing built up support for her new-style revolutionary operas and radical policies. Opposition to these operas and other radical ideas grew and the forces that were to oppose each other in the Cultural Revolution began to mobilise. In a sense the Cultural Revolution was necessary because the Socialist Education Movement failed to achieve its objects.

Socialist Youth League   Organisation founded by Ch'en Tu-hsiu in August 1920 which was an immediate precursor of the CCP.

Society for Literary Studies or Literary Research Society or Literary Association   One of the oldest and most influential of the hundreds of literary groups formed after the May 4th movement. It was formed in January 1921 to bring together all those writers who favoured the introduction of vernacular writing and language reform in general and played an important role in introducing world literature and contemporary ideas into China. Mao Tun was a member and Lu

Hsun a supporter of the society, and its members shaped much of China's modern literature.

Sogdiana   Former Greek kingdom corresponding to parts of present-day Uzbekistan and Turkmenistan in southern USSR. Its capital was Maracanda (Samarkand). Han armies were sent out to subdue Sogdiana in 42 BC.

Son of Heaven (*T'ien-tzu*)   Term for the emperors of China, first used by the Kings of Chou. This idea of the sovereign as the descendant of heaven combined the political and spiritual authority of the emperor and remained for centuries the central concept of sovereignty.

Soong Ch'ing-ling (1892–   )   Widow of Sun Yat-sen. Soong Ch'ing-ling was associated with the left wing of the KMT and as a member of the Revolutionary Committee of the KMT served as vice-chairman of the Central People's Government Council in 1949. She later served as vice-chairman of the People's Republic and vice-chairman of the National People's Congress. Her position derived from her relationship to Sun Yat-sen and from the wish of the CCP to link the People's Republic with Sun's revolutionary movement.

Soong Dynasty   Ironic term for the corporate influence of T. V. Soong and his sisters Soong Ch'ing-ling and Soong Mei-ling (qqv) on Nationalist politics in the 1920s and 1930s.

Soong Mei-ling or Mayling (1897–   )   Wife of Chiang K'ai-shek and sister of Soong Ch'ing-ling. Soong Mei-ling became a leader of various women's organisations in Nationalist China during the 1930s.

Soong, T. V. (1894–   )   Brother of Soong Ch'ing-ling and Soong Mei-ling and thus brother-in-law of Chiang K'ai-shek whom he served as Minister of Finance and later as Premier and Foreign Minister when he negotiated with the United States and the USSR in 1945. He was also governor of the Central Bank of China and was involved in private financial enterprises. After 1949 he took up residence in the United States.

South Manchurian Railway   Railway connecting the ports of Dairen and Port Arthur with the existing Chinese Eastern Railway (qv) which had extended the Trans-Siberian Railway to Vladivostok. Construction by the Russians who had extorted a concession to build the line began in 1898 but it was transferred to Japan after her defeat of Russia in 1905, and used by Japan to increase her influence in China. The South Manchurian Railway Company which ran the line acquired a great deal of power in the region, undertaking police, diplomatic and administrative functions and incidentally sponsoring much research on economic and social conditions in Manchuria and north China. After the Japanese surrender in 1945 the railway was not returned immediately to China. Under the Potsdam Treaty concluded between Britain, the United States and the USSR, Chiang K'ai-shek had to accept among other things that the railway be administered jointly by the USSR and China for thirty years, after which it would revert to China. The same condition was enforced on Mao Tse-tung when the new Communist government signed the Treaty of Friendship, Alliance and Mutual Assistance with the USSR in 1950. The railway was in fact returned to China in 1953.

Southern Sung   Sung Dynasty after the capture of Kaifeng by the Chin in 1126.

Soviet Technician Withdrawal   First clear indication of the Sino-Soviet split (qv). All Soviet technicians who had been working on aid programmes in China were suddenly withdrawn in August 1960. Many projects were left unfinished and severe harm was done to the Chinese economy.

Spheres of Influence   In the latter part of the 19th century and the early 20th century the Western powers who had been opening up China to trade came to mutual agreements about certain regions in which they exerted almost exclusive influence. Britain for example had special interests in Shanghai, the lower Yangtze and Hong Kong, France in South China near Vietnam, Germany in Shantung and Japan in the North-East.

Spring and Autumn Annals (*Ch'un ch'iu*)   Chronological record of major events, seen from the court of the state of Lu between 722 and 481 BC, which became one of the Five Classics of the Confucian literary canon. The annals are written in so terse and obscure a way that several explanatory commentaries have had to be appended to the book. Of these the best known is the *Tso chuan* (qv). Traditionally the Spring and Autumn Annals are thought to have been compiled and edited by Confucius and much of the commentaries is devoted to elucidating supposed hidden meanings in his words.

Spring and Autumn Period (722–481 BC)   Name for the period of the

Eastern Chou dynasty which preceded that known as the Warring States (qv). The name is taken from the *Spring and Autumn Annals* (qv) which chronicled the events of the time.

Srongtsan Ganpo   Ruler of Tibet 630–650. In 641 he married the Chinese princess Wen-ch'eng, a relative of the T'ang emperor T'ai-tsung, thus bringing Tibet into an alliance with China. Wen-ch'eng and Srongtsan Ganpo's other, Nepalese, wife helped to introduce Buddhism into Tibet.

Ssu-ma Ch'ien (died c90 BC)   Han historian and author of the *Records of the Grand Historian*. In 108 BC he inherited from his father Ssu-ma T'an the post of court astrologer which gave him access to the imperial library. The *Records* which he compiled were nothing less than a history of China from the earliest times to the Han dynasty. He claimed that he was merely completing a work that his father had begun but this may have been modesty or filial piety; it is usually accepted that Ssu-ma Ch'ien was the main author. In 99 BC he defended a prominent general who had surrendered to the Hsiung-nu and was ordered to be castrated for his disloyalty to the emperor. So great was his commitment to his historical work that instead of committing suicide as the aristocratic code and honour demanded, he retired, to live in disgrace and complete the work.

Ssu-ma Kuang (1019–1086)   Sung dynasty statesman and scholar who wrote the *Comprehensive Mirror for Aid in Government* (*Tzu-chih t'ung chien*), a chronological history from 403 BC to 959 AD and the first attempt to produce a single comprehensive history since Ssu-ma Ch'ien's *Records of the Grand Historian*. Ssu-ma Kuang retired from official life after a quarrel with Wang An-shih (qv) in 1070 but later returned to power and rescinded many of Wang's reforms.

Ssu-ma T'an   Father of the historian Ssu-ma Ch'ien. He preceded his son as court astrologer and is said to have begun the *Records of the Grand Historian*.

Standard Histories   see   *Dynastic Histories*

State Council   Highest administrative body in the People's Republic. The State Council co-ordinates the various ministries and includes the State Planning Commission, State Economic Commission and the Scientific and Technological Commission which are responsible for policy decisions in their particular fields. The State Council was formed in 1954 under the new Constitution accepted in that year and replaced the Government Administration Council. It was more effective than its predecessor in controlling military organisation and economic policy.

State Economic Commission   Organisation subordinate to the State Council which works out annual short-range plans and oversees current economic activity.

State Planning Commission   Commission of the State Council which is responsible for long-range economic planning.

Stilwell, General Joseph (Vinegar Joe)   Chiang K'ai-shek's American chief-of-staff, sent to Chungking in 1942 as Allied Commander-in-Chief of the China-Burma-India theatre of the Second World War. Stilwell was a West Point graduate, a First World War veteran and an old China hand who respected the people and spoke the language. He trained Chinese soldiers, believing in contrast to many Westerners that they could fight. His intention was to mount a joint campaign with the British army to open up the Burma road for supplies into Chungking, as the only supplies reaching the wartime capital were those brought in by the Hump Airlift over the Himalayas. Stilwell's irritation at the corruption and vacillation of the KMT bureaucracy through which he had to work brought him increasingly into conflict with them and with Chiang K'ai-shek. He was highly critical of Chiang's reluctance to fight the Japanese while saving his troops to use against the Communists and in 1944 was relieved of his command by President Roosevelt at Chiang K'ai-shek's request.

Stone Tablets   Standard texts of the works associated with Confucius which were engraved on stone tablets in the Han dynasty to provide a permanent authorised version of the classics. The project which began in 175 AD and took eight years, needed forty to fifty stones to take the 200,000 characters of the texts. Stone tablets were also common as monuments to the dead.

Story of the Stone   see   *Dream of the Red Chamber*

Straw Plaiters' Sect   Popular underground sect which joined the Taiping Rebellion (qv) in 1851.

Street Committees   Basic level of urban organisation in the People's Republic. The Committee is made up of representatives of residents in a street or area of a town or city, who have a say in the administration of the area, under the supervision of a street office, the lowest level of government in towns. The street committee also fulfils certain control and surveillance functions and because of this has been compared with the *pao-chia* (qv) system which operated in imperial China.

Stuart, John Leighton Last American ambassador to China. He was born in China in 1876, began missionary work there in 1905 and in 1919 became president of Yenching University. In 1946 he was appointed ambassador to China, but left in 1949 when United States mediation in the Civil War had failed and the CCP were on the point of victory. His departure was accompanied by a particularly vitriolic article by Mao Tse-tung, *Farewell Leighton Stuart*, in which he attacked both the ambassador and United States policy in general.

Su Tung-p'o (1036–1101) Also known as Su Shih. Sung dynasty lyric poet, prose stylist and calligrapher who was also a statesman and for a time governor of Hangchow.

Su-fan Movement Campaign to wipe out hidden counter-revolutionaries (*Su-ch'ing an-ts'ang fan-ko-ming*) which was launched in 1955. The campaign, one of many in the early years of the People's Republic, was connected with the campaign against the writer Hu Feng (qv), and its main object was the investigation of thousands of people, mainly cadres. Life histories were examined and some people were expelled from the CCP. During the Hundred Flowers movement of 1956 many people criticised the harshness of the *Su-fan* campaign.

Sui Dynasty (581–618) A short-lived dynasty which reunited China after the divisions of the post-Han era. It began when the leader of the Sui, Yang Chien, who may have been of Hsien-pei origin, conquered the Ch'en, the last of the Southern Dynasties. In spite of its short life it played a very important role in Chinese history, as its unification of China made possible the foundation of the T'ang, one of the greatest of Chinese dynasties. In this its part was similar to that played by the Ch'in dynasty which prepared the way for the Han. There were only two emperors, Yang Chien and Yang Ti, but the strong centralised government they established was able to carry out important tasks such as the reconstruction of the Great Wall and the digging of canals that later formed part of the Grand Canal system.

Summer Palace Imperial palace five miles north-west of Peking. Lord Macartney, the first English envoy to China, lodged there in

1793, and one of his successors, Lord Elgin, burned it down in 1860 as part of the British attempt to enforce the Conventions of Peking (qv). The costly reconstruction was carried out, partly with mis-appropriated naval funds, for the Empress Dowager Tz'u-hsi.

Summer Tax   One half of the Double Tax (qv) which operated during the Ming dynasty. It was a grain tax levied on crops such as winter wheat which were grown during the winter and harvested in early summer. It was a smaller collection than the other tax, the Autumn Grain.

Sun Yat-sen (1866–1925)   Leader and inspiration of the republican revolution in China. He is also known as Sun Wen, Wen being his personal name while Yat-sen was his style or secondary name, and in China always as Sun Chung-shan, Chung-shan being the Chinese pronunciation of the Japanese name Nakayama which he adopted when in exile in Japan. Sun was born into a peasant family in Hsiang-shan near Canton and because of their poverty he left in 1879 to join his elder brother who was building up a successful business in Honolulu. He was educated at various Anglican colleges and in 1886 enrolled in a medical college in Hong Kong. He practised medicine in Macao from 1892 but a year later moved to Canton. He was developing radical, anti-Manchu ideas, and founded the Revive China Society in 1894 and had to flee Canton after an attempt at an insurrection in the city. He went to Japan, the United States and finally to London where he stayed with a former teacher from Hong Kong, Dr James Cantlie. In London he was lured to the Chinese legation where he was kidnapped but later released after the inter-vention of Cantlie and the Foreign Office. He remained in Europe till 1897 when he moved back to Japan where he developed the ideas which were to form the basis of his *Three People's Principles* (qv) and continued to instigate revolutionary activities in China. The turning-point in his career was the organisation of the T'ung-meng hui (United League) with Huang Hsing and Sung Chiao-jen. Sun was in the United States when the 1911 Revolution broke out and hurried back to Shanghai. He was elected provisional president of the Republic of China on December 29 of that year but resigned in favour of Yuan Shih-k'ai (qv) on April 1, 1912 after the latter had successfully manoeuvred himself into power. In 1917 after Yuan Shih-k'ai's attempts to restore the monarchy and his subsequent death, Sun established a military government in Canton. His political base however was weak and he died in Canton in 1925 with his dream of a united, peaceful Chinese Republic still far off. Chiang K'ai-shek took over as leader of the Nationalists.

Sun Tzu Author of *The Art of War*, a classic of Chinese military history that was probably written in the 4th century BC. The book is a systematic guide to tactics and strategy aimed at assisting rulers and commanders in waging war intelligently and includes discussion of offensive and defensive strategy, manoeuvring and the effects of terrain. It has had a great influence on Chinese and Japanese military thought, notably on the guerrilla tactics of Mao Tse-tung. Sun Tzu, the author, was probably Sun Pin, the strategist of the Ch'i state who lived around 350 BC but the book was traditionally attributed to Sun Wu, a general of about 500 BC.

Sung Dynasty (960–1279) One of the most highly regarded dynasties in Chinese history, famed for its painting, poetry and ceramics and for unprecedented economic development. After the fall of the T'ang dynasty in 907 China was once again divided into numerous regional kingdoms and would-be dynasties, known as the Five Dynasties and Ten Kingdoms (qv). The reunification was carried out by Chao K'uang-yin, known posthumously as T'ai-tsu, a general who seized the throne in 960 when on a mission to prevent a Khitan invasion. In spite of pressure from border tribes, the Sung managed to establish a stable government with a more thoroughly centralised administration than ever before; the civil service examination system was perfected. Under the Sung, the Chinese economy developed to such an extent that the period is sometimes known as the Commercial Revolution. Private trade and industry developed apace with the aid of important technical advances such as the perfection of the traditional luxury goods industries, porcelain, silk, and lacquerware, and improved rice cropping. Commerce and an advanced money economy were also highly developed, the traditional aristocracy lost power to a new gentry class which did not depend so exclusively on agricultural wealth for its influence and there was a considerable increase in the number of people who lived in cities. In the arts, the Sung is noted for its sculptures, celadon and white porcelains, and the growing importance of landscape painting. Moveable type appeared in about 1030 stimulating the development of scholarship and literature, notably the works of Neo-Confucianism (qv). During the early part of the 12th century there were more and more raids on the northern borders by Jurched tribesmen. The border kingdom of Liao was destroyed in 1125 and by 1126 Kaifeng, the Sung capital, had been taken. The Jurched established a new dynasty, the Chin, which then ruled north China and the Sung emperor was forced to move to Hangchow, then called Lin-an, from where he ruled the south. The period up to the Chin conquest of Kaifeng is often called the Northern Sung and that after the conquest the Southern Sung. The south of China however was the economic centre of the country and Hangchow a grander capital than Kaifeng. The Southern Sung government was strong with none of the internal tensions that had caused the collapse of earlier dynasties. It was not destroyed till the Mongols, after overrunning the Chin dynasty in 1234, brought about the collapse of the Southern Sung in 1271 after a protracted campaign in the South.

Sung Chiang   Rebel and bandit who lived during the Sung period, about 1121 and was based in the Liang-shan-po region of West Shantung. Stories about his exploits were popularised by professional story-tellers in the late Sung period, incorporated into later Yüan dramas and finally woven into the *Water Margin* (qv) epic.

Sung Chiao-jen (1882–1913)   Early associate of Sun Yat-sen and founder member in 1905 of the T'ung-meng hui. In 1911 he was in charge of the organisation's Central China Bureau in Shanghai which was influential in the Wuchang rising and 1911 Revolution, and when the T'ung-meng hui absorbed other groups to become the KMT in 1912 he became the effective leader. He was assassinated by supporters of Yuan Shih-k'ai in 1913 during the conflict that became known as the Second Revolution (qv).

Sung Ying-hsing   Author of the *Creations of Nature and Man* (*T'ien-kung k'ai-wu*) (qv) the most important single work on Chinese historical technology. Sung Ying-hsing was probably born shortly before the end of the 16th century in Fenghsin, Kiangsi. In 1615 he passed the official examinations at the provincial level and then served in a number of official posts. The *Creations of Nature and Man* was written while he was Education Officer in Fen-i, Kiangsi province. He also wrote a work on phonology and a collection of critical essays which have only recently been rediscovered. When the Ming dynasty collapsed in 1644 Sung retired with his elder brother Ying-sheng and led a secluded life. He probably died in about 1660, not long after the suicide of his brother of whom he wrote a short biography.

T

Tachai Model agricultural unit which all others were supposed to emulate during the 1960s and 70s. Tachai is a production brigade and part of the commune of the same name, situated in the Taihang mountain area of Shansi province. The land available for cultivation was very poor, much of it being on ridges or slopes or in scattered mountain valleys. Agricultural development was very difficult and Tachai's special claim to fame is that it greatly increased cultivable land and crop yields without an injection of state aid by organising a co-operative in the early 1950s. The amount of land was increased by terracing the hillsides. Only manual labour was available and much of the credit for Tachai's success in organising the project has been given to Ch'en Yung-kuei, secretary of the local party branch and later a Politburo member. By 1964 crop yields had increased dramatically and Tachai was put forward as a model of self-reliance and the creative application of Mao Tse-tung Thought and much praised, particularly by the radical elements during the Cultural Revolution.

Taching Oilfield Industrial complement of Tachai and the radicals' model of self-reliance and improvisation to be aimed at by all industry. Taching is an oilfield in Heilungkiang province in China's North-East. Oil was first struck there in 1959, but with the withdrawal of Soviet aid in 1961, development had to rely on Chinese techniques and experience which were still fairly primitive. With very little equipment and in appalling climatic conditions the field was gradually opened, and today produces thousands of tons of crude oil.

T'ai-ch'ang, Ming emperor (reigned 1620) The T'ai-ch'ang emperor succeeded the Wan-li emperor but fell ill and died within a month of ascending the throne. He was succeeded in turn by the T'ien-ch'i emperor.

Taiping Rebellion (1850–64) Most important of the many rebellions that occurred during the last century of the Ch'ing dynasty, being roughly contemporary with the Nien rebellion and with the Moslem rebellions in Yunnan and the North-Western provinces. The decline of the dynasty was accompanied by great hardship for the peasants as individual landholdings became smaller. There were widespread natural disasters — droughts and severe floods — in the 1840s and

50s, and the political and military structures degenerated. The roots of the Taiping rebellion were in these conditions and in the partly Christianised Hakka (qv) population of South China. The leader of the rebellion, Hung Hsiu-ch'uan (qv) was a Hakka who had acquired a distorted version of Christianity and saw himself as the younger brother of Jesus. His followers, miners, charcoal-burners, boatmen and poor peasants, some of them secret society members, and many of them Hakkas, were first organised in the God Worshippers Association. When members of the Heaven and Earth Society rose in rebellion in Kwangsi during the great famine of 1849–50, the God Worshippers, although not active in the rebellion, were able to recruit thousands of followers and set up their headquarters in the village of Chin-t'ien in Kwangsi. On January 11, 1851 Hung Hsiu-ch'uan, who was then 37, proclaimed himself Heavenly King (*T'ien-wang*) of a new Heavenly Kingdom of Great Peace (*T'ai-p'ing t'ien-kuo*). Hung tried to retain the support of the secret societies while deploring their idolatry and managed to increase his following sufficiently to move north, taking several important cities including Wuhan. In 1853, the ancient capital of Nanking was captured by the Taipings and Hung was carried in as emperor. The rebellion lasted only until 1864. Its downfall was brought about partly by internal dissension when Hung's associates became dissatisfied with their secondary roles and partly because the Imperial government was prepared to allow Tseng Kuo-fan's Hunan Army, the Huai Army, and the Ever Victorious Army (qqv) sufficient freedom of action to defeat the Taipings. The rebellion ended in June 1864 when Hung Hsiu-ch'uan committed suicide in Nanking which was being besieged by the government armies. In spite of its short life, the Taiping Rebellion did leave a legacy of ideas which were taken up by later radicals. Their anti-Manchu stance — the Taipings were known as Long Hairs because of their rejection of the Manchu-imposed queue — and their proposals for land reform (qv) were taken up later by nationalist and communist revolutionaries. The failure of the rebellion can be blamed on faulty leadership, failure to control captured regions, conflicts inherent in their eclectic ideology, and inconsistencies between the egalitarian pronouncements and the luxurious life-styles of the leadership.

T'ai-tsung, T'ang Emperor (reigned 627–649)   The rule of Li Shih-min, known posthumously as **T'ai-tsung**, the son of Li Yuan the founder of the T'ang dynasty, is often considered to be the first high point of the T'ang era. He rebuilt the central government, constructed many palaces and other buildings, continued canal building and began the subjugation of the frontier tribes. In 630 the Eastern Turks were defeated by the Chinese, T'ai-tsung became known as their Heavenly Khan, and protectorates known as Pacify the East, West, North and South (qv) were set up to control all the border regions that were gradually brought into the T'ang empire. T'ai-tsung ordered the compilation of a great genealogy of the aristocratic families in 634 and also showered honours on the Buddhist pilgrim Hsüan-tsang (qv).

Taiwan or Formosa as it was known to the Portuguese. A large island off south-east China used by Dutch traders as a base for their activities in the early 17th century. Between 1661 and 1683 it was occupied by Koxinga (qv). Taiwan was ceded to Japan after the 1894–95 Sino-Japanese War and not returned till the Japanese surrender of 1945. Nationalist troops occupying the island provoked a popular rising in February 1947. Over ten thousand Taiwanese lost their lives in the rebellion which was suppressed by Ch'en Yi. After the victories of the CCP in the Civil War the Nationalist forces under Chiang K'ai-shek were compelled to retreat to Taiwan from the mainland. Since the proclamation of the People's Republic in 1949, the KMT have maintained a Republic of China administration on Taiwan.

Tamerlane or Timur or Tamburlaine (1336–1405) Mongol Khan of Chaghadai in Central Asia and conqueror of Persia, Mesopotamia and the Golden Horde in southern Russia. His empire was based on Samarkand and a vast military expedition which he had sent to conquer Ming China was halted when he died in 1405.

T'an Ssu-t'ung (1865–1898) Martyr of the 1898 Hundred Days (qv) Reform movement. T'an was born in Hunan and in his youth accompanied his father, an official, on journeys through much of China. He had had a traditional, classical education but was also interested in science, Buddhism and the less orthodox Confucian thinkers. He became a reformist and his ideas were put forward in a local provincial newspaper, the *New Hunan Study Journal*, and in a book, *A Study of Benevolence*. He attacked the conservatism of the ruling class and argued for a republican regime and ultimately for a frontierless egalitarian world. He and K'ang Yu-wei were particularly insistent on the prior need for political reform. During the heady Hundred Days T'an was appointed to the Grand Council, but when the Empress Dowager returned to take over the government and detained the emperor, T'an was executed with five other reformers.

Tanaka Memorial Document revealing Japanese plans to encroach on Manchuria and China. It was said to have been written by Baron Tanaka, the militarist Japanese Prime Minister and presented to the Japanese emperor in 1927. Although the authenticity of the document is questionable it does reflect the Pan-Asiatic, expansionist attitudes of the military clique in Japanese politics of the time. The memorial outlined detailed plans for the colonisation of East Asia and the development of a continental empire for Japan, using the South Manchurian Railway (qv) as a starting-point. It would be necessary for Manchuria and Mongolia to come under Japanese control before Tokyo's influence in China could be pressed successfully. This notorious document is interesting because a number of points in the plan were in fact put into effect during the Japanese invasion of Manchuria and China between 1931 and 1945.

T'ang Dynasty (618–907)   The T'ang dynasty, famed for its poetry, landscape painting and ceramics continued and consolidated the national unification begun by its predecessor the Sui. The new dynasty was founded by Li Yuan, who rose in revolt aided by his son Li Shih-min when the Sui collapsed, was proclaimed first emperor of the T'ang, and was known posthumously as Kao-tsu. However the first important reign for the reconstruction of the empire was that of T'ai-tsung (qv) as Li Shih-min was known after his death. In this and the later reign of the Hsüan-tsung (qv) emperor the frontiers of China expanded to include Tibet and large areas of Turkestan. The T'ang government revived the official examinations of Han times and rebuilt the civil service, in a way that was to serve as a model for the duration of the empire. Buddhism which had begun to reach China during the Northern Wei period continued to spread and despite much per-secution firmly established itself as part of the Chinese way of life. In many ways the T'ang dynasty was a watershed in Chinese history. The early T'ang, up to about the middle of the 8th century, was the end of the classical phase of Chinese history, whereas the later T'ang was nearer to the following Sung dynasty and can be considered part of the early modern period. The later T'ang was weakened by the rebellion of An Lu-shan (qv) and the decline of the taxation and militia systems which necessitated considerable reforms. When the T'ang finally collapsed in a series of popular risings the military Regional Commanders (qv) struggled for control and their power bases developed into what were effectively independent kingdoms. The chaos that followed before the reunification carried out by the Sung in 960 can be judged from the name given to the interregnum: the Five Dynasties and Ten Kingdoms (qv).

Tangshan Earthquake   Earthquake which devastated the industrial city of Tangshan about a hundred miles from Peking in July 1976. The catastrophe raised fears about a possible omen and when Mao Tse-tung died in September popular superstition was confirmed.

Tanguts Tibetan tribes who built up a powerful state in the Kansu and Inner Mongolia region in the 10th and 11th century and adopted the Chinese dynastic title of Hsia in 1038. They are known in Chinese as the Hsi Hsia (Western Hsia) (qv). Tangut speech was recorded in intricate Chinese-style characters which are still largely undeciphered.

T'ao Chu (1906–   ) Senior CCP and government member dismissed during the Cultural Revolution. T'ao was secretary of the important South China Sub-Bureau of the CCP in 1952–54 and governor of Kwangtung province from 1955. He subsequently became First Secretary of the Central Southern Bureau of the party, Vice-Premier of the State and a member of the standing committee of the Politburo. He lost all his posts in 1966–67 after being criticised by Cultural Revolution radicals.

Tao Te Ching Alternative title for the Taoist classic otherwise known as, and sometimes claimed to have been written by, Lao Tzu. *Tao Te Ching* means the classic (*ching*) of the way (*tao*) and virtue or power (*te*), and the title may simply have come about because *tao* and *te* are the first significant words in part one and part two respectively. The authorship is uncertain and the date of composition doubtful. The style of the writing is terse and cryptic and this has led to widely differing interpretations both in Chinese and in translation. In spite of, or possibly because of, its cryptic nature, it became the central text of Taoism with the works of Chuang Tzu (qv). The content of the *Tao Te Ching* ranges from the essentials of human nature to the practice of government and is much concerned with the relationship between human behaviour and the Way or *tao*, which is the essence and ultimate end of all things.

Taoism Next to Confucianism (qv), the most important and influential current in Chinese thought. The name derives from the *tao* or Way which is considered by Taoists to be the source of all being and the governor of all existence. The central principle is *wu-wei*, 'do nothing', that is nothing against the Way. Taoist writing tends to be mystical, paradoxical and very unworldly, in contrast with the staid, orderly thought of Confucianism. The main writings of Taoism can be found in the *Lao Tzu* or *Tao Te Ching* (qv) and the *Chuang Tzu* (qv) which dates from the 3rd century BC but draws on earlier thought. A revival in the study of these texts in the 3rd and 4th

century AD after the fall of the Han dynasty produced a loose amal-
gam of ideas which came to be known as Neo-Taoism, and in the
same period Taoism which had previously been just a set of philosophical ideas was taken up as a popular religion and absorbed by
rebel sects such as the Yellow Turbans and the Five Pecks of Rice
Band (qqv). Buddhism, which spread to China at this time, influenced
popular Taoist thought and the two currents practically merged in
the popular tradition. Throughout Chinese history, Taoism, as well
as providing an outlet for popular beliefs, also served as a counter-
balance to conformist Confucianism. In spite of the contradictory
natures of the philosophies people did not find them incompatible
and the scholar-official would be a responsible Confucian moralist
in his working life while at home he might well become a Taoist
mystic intent on blending with nature. Thus although Taoism had
little influence on practical matters of government, its ideas had a
profound effect on poetry and painting, the kind of activities practised
by the literati in their off-duty hours.

Tao-kuang, Ch'ing Emperor (reigned 1821–1850)   The first Ch'ing
emperor to take a serious interest in the suppression of the traffic
in opium. He issued a number of edicts prohibiting the smoking of
opium and his appointment in 1838 of Lin Tse-hsu (qv) as High
Commissioner charged with suppressing the trade precipitated the
Opium War (qv).

Tartars   Mongol tribes, known to the Chinese as Ta-tan, who lived
far north of the Great Wall in eastern Mongolia. In the early 15th
century the Ming emperor Yung-lo launched several campaigns
against the Tartars who had been raiding the borders. The term
Tartar or Tatar was subsequently extended and used loosely to mean
any Mongolian, or even Turkish nomads from Central Asia. See also
Oirats.

Tea   Tea was introduced into China from South-East Asia during
the Six Dynasties period and by the 6th century AD it had become
a common beverage, although it was valued at first as a medicine. By
the 8th century it had become so widespread that the T'ang government imposed a tax on it and was able to collect a great deal of
revenue. The demand led to the development of a widespread market
in tea and stimulated the manufacture of porcelain tea sets. During
the Ming dynasty it was exported by Portuguese and Dutch traders
and in the late 19th century it arrived in Europe in large quantities.
It was however superseded in Europe, and in England particularly,
by Indian and Ceylon teas which were more popular because of their

greater strength. Tea is grown throughout central China, many of the better known varieties coming from Anhwei, Chekiang and Kiangsi.

Temüjin see *Chinggis Khan*

Temür (reigned 1294–1307) Grandson of Khubilai Khan whom he succeeded as Great Khan in 1294. He maintained a firm central administration but was the last of the strong Yuan emperors. After his death in 1307 the dynasty gradually declined.

Ten Kingdoms (907–960) The statelets of south China during the interregnum between the T'ang and the Sung dynasties. North China at this time was ruled by the Five Dynasties (qv).

Teng Hsiao-p'ing (1904–   ) Senior CCP and government official and vice-chairman of the CCP under the post-Mao administration of Hua Kuo-feng. During the period before 1949 he was military commander and political commissar of the Second Field Army. After Liberation he held important military and administrative positions with particular responsibility for south-west China. In 1953 he became Minister of Finance and in 1954 he was vice-premier of the State Council. From 1956 he occupied the vitally important administrative post of General Secretary to the Central Committee of the CCP and was also a member of the Politburo. During the Cultural Revolution he was associated with the 'moderates' and denounced as the 'Number Two Person in Authority Taking the Capitalist Road' (Liu Shao-ch'i was number one). In 1973 he was reinstated as vice-premier and re-elected to the Central Committee and became vice-chairman of the CCP and chief-of-staff of the People's Liberation Army. However in early 1976 he was dismissed from all his official positions in the period when, it is said, the Gang of Four (qv) was in control. After the downfall of the Gang, Teng rose to power once again to become vice-chairman of the CCP under Hua Kuo-feng and a member of the crucial Standing Committee of the Politburo. Teng Hsiao-p'ing, who was a close associate of Chou En-lai, is known as a forthright man with an irrepressible sense of humour.

Teng T'o (c1911–   ) Journalist who edited various CCP newspapers in the 1930s and 1940s. From 1950–57 he was deputy managing director and editor-in-chief of *People's Daily*, and from 1957 managing director. In 1961–62 he wrote a series of articles under the heading *Evening Talks at Yenshan* (qv), many of them obliquely critical of Mao and the Great Leap Forward. He was denounced in the early stages of the Cultural Revolution.

Thirteen Classics One classification of traditional Confucian writings. The Thirteen include the *Book of Songs, Book of Documents* and *Book of Changes,* the *Record of Rituals* and the *Spring and Autumn Annals* (qqv), also known as the Five Classics (qv), but the *Spring and Autumn Annals* are counted as three of the thirteen, because of the three commentaries (*Tradition of Kung-yang, Tradition of Ku-liang* and the *Tso chuan — Tradition of Tso*) that accompany the main text. The other six are the *Rituals of Chou* (qv) (*Chou Li*), the *Ceremonies and Rituals* (*I Li*), the *Analects* (qv) the *Mencius* (qv), the *Book of Filial Piety* and the *Erh Ya,* a listing of difficult expressions occurring in these early texts.

Thought Reform (*Ssu-hsiang kai-tsao*) Special form of group psychology widely used in the early 1950s. Many individuals, especially those belonging to leadership groups, have to participate in group sessions organised by the CCP in which their entire personal backgrounds are exposed, analysed, criticised and reconstructed in terms of the current ideology. Thought reform is used to intensify the consciousness of an individual and cut his emotional ties to former authority figures such as the father or the landlord, and then to reintegrate him into the new society. This emphasis on the psychological transformation of individuals is one of the reasons for the cohesion of the new leadership groups being trained by the CCP. When details of thought reform began to emerge from China at about the time of the Korean War, they were taken up in the West as horror stories about 'brainwashing', a term never used in China.

Three All (*San-kuang*) Burn All, Kill All, Loot All: a brutal campaign of suppression launched by the Japanese in 1941 against the Communist-controlled regions whose populations then fell dramatically.

Three-Anti Movement (*San-fan*) Campaign aimed primarily at corruption, waste and bureaucratism in 1951–52 which was used to increase production and mobilise urban workers in parallel with the Land Reform Movement in the countryside. The first targets of the campaign were cadres who had defrauded state or other enterprises and then academics who had not changed their style of work. The movement was then widened to include corrupt relationships between the state and private sectors of the economy. In the early part of 1952 concern for production levels led to a decrease in the amount of time devoted to the Three-Anti Movement.

Three Chiefs System (*San-chang*) System for mutual control and responsibility developed under the Northern Wei and an early fore-runner of the *pao-chia* system (qv). Five families formed a neighbour-hood, five neighbourhoods a village and five villages an association. Neighbourhoods, villages and associations were all under chiefs, hence the name.

Three Feudatories, Revolt of The Three Feudatories were large areas in Yunnan, Kwangtung and Fukien granted to three Ming princes, Wu San-kuei, Shang K'o-hsi and Keng Chi-mao by the Ch'ing dynasty in return for their assistance in the Manchu conquest of China. The K'ang-hsi emperor decided to abolish these fiefs to reduce the power of the princes and tried to make them leave their land and settle in Manchuria. Wu rose in rebellion in 1673 and the others followed suit. The war that followed was extremely costly in terms of life and economic disruption. Keng eventually surrendered in 1676 and Shang in 1677 but although Wu San-kuei died in 1678 his forces under members of his family and various officials continued to resist until 1681.

Three Kingdoms Period (220–265 AD) Interregnum after the col-lapse of the Han dynasty, being the earlier part of the Six Dynasties period. The three succession states or kingdoms perpetually at war with each other were Wei in the north, Wu in the south-east and Shu Han in the south-west. The period, which ended when one of Wei's generals Ssu-ma Yen usurped the throne and briefly unified China under the Western Chin (125–316), is thought of by Chinese as an exciting and romantic time. Semi-historical legends which grew up around figures like Ts'ao Ts'ao and Chu-ko Liang were later incorporated in the novel *Romance of the Three Kingdoms* (qv).

Three People's Principles (*San Min Chu I*) Theoretical basis of Sun Yat-sen's revolutionary policies which was developed near the end of the 19th century. The three principles were Nationalism, Democ-racy and People's Livelihood, the latter being a reformist economic policy which stressed the need for the control of capital and the redistribution of land. Nationalism was aimed at both Western imperialists and the Manchus and the main point of the Democracy policy was the establishment of a parliamentary system. The Prin-ciples were accepted as policy by the T'ung-meng hui (qv) and later incorporated into the political philosophy of the KMT both in government in China till 1949 and then in exile on Taiwan. The Communists also consider their policies to be the successors to the Three People's Principles.

Three Sages Yao, Shun and Yü, legendary emperors from pre-historic times. Yao and Shun were both model rulers (see *Five Emperors*). Yü was noted for his success in controlling flooding and is regarded as the first ruler of the Hsia dynasty.

Three Sovereigns Fu-hsi, Shen-nung and Huang-ti, culture heroes credited with the domestication of animals, agriculture and the birth of the Chinese nation, respectively. Huang-ti was also the first of the Five Emperors (qv).

Tibet Autonomous region in the south-west of the present-day People's Republic with a distinct history and culture of its own. Tibet was first unified in 607 when it came under the suzerainty of the T'ang rulers of China. The connection with China was further cemented in 641 when Srongtsan Ganpo (qv) married a Chinese princess, but the relationship was less close in the dynasties that followed and from the 7th to the 9th century Tibet remained a small, independent power capable of harassing both China and India. Lama Buddhism (qv) linked Tibet with the Mongol rulers of Yuan China and in the Ming period regular tribute missions from Tibet were recorded in Peking. The incorporation of Tibet into the Chinese empire did not begin till the 17th century when the Ch'ing established a protectorate over it and eventually confirmed the Dalai Lama as the main temporal as well as spiritual power under the protection of the Manchu court. Tibet remained part of the empire until its collapse in 1911. It was formally re-incorporated into China by the CCP in 1949 and when a revolt in 1959 threatened secession the incorporation was made more permanent by firmer military control. Tibet is clearly distinctive in language, culture and nationality and considerable controversy has raged over China's policy there, and whether Tibet should be an independent state or whether its position parallels that of the other national minorities within China.

T'ien-an men Square Riots Serious disturbance which took place in the T'ien-an men (Gate of Heavenly Peace) Square, the main square in Peking, on April 4 and 5, 1976. The disturbances took place during the Ch'ing Ming festival (qv) when demonstrations of affection for the late premier Chou En-lai were held at the Revolutionary Martyrs' Memorial. Numerous wreaths and placards, with slogans and poems praising Chou, and by implication his protégé Teng Hsiao-p'ing, and attacking Chiang Ch'ing, were placed on the memorial and the disturbances began when these were removed. Over a hundred militiamen were injured, some seriously, and buildings and vehicles destroyed. The 'counter-revolutionary political incident', as it came to be known, revealed the latent support for Teng Hsiao-p'ing and he was dismissed from all state and party posts immediately afterwards. Similar disturbances took place in Chenchow, Kunming and elsewhere.

T'ien-ch'i, Ming Emperor (reigned 1621–1627) T'ien-ch'i came to the throne after his grandfather the Wan-li emperor and his father the T'ai-ch'ang emperor had died in rapid succession. He was more interested in carpentry than in ruling, and the government soon came under the control of the eunuch Wei Chung-hsien. See also *Eunuchs*.

T'ien-kung k'ai-wu see *Creations of Nature and Man*

T'ien Li Sect Branch of the White Lotus society (qv), also known as the Eight Trigrams.

T'ien-shun, Ming Emperor (1457–1464) see *Cheng-t'ung, Ming Emperor*

Tientsin Massacre (1870) Murder of ten nuns, two priests, two French officials and three Russian merchants in Tientsin. It was sparked off by a shot fired by the French consul which killed a Chinese servant of the district magistrate. The deeper causes of the mob violence which then erupted can be traced to the large number of foreign troops stationed in Tientsin and the anti-foreign feeling that had grown and crystallised around suspicions about an orphanage run by the nuns. Both Tseng Kuo-fan and Li Hung-chang were involved in the negotiations for the settlement demanded by the foreign community and a large compensation and an apology were agreed on.

Tientsin Military Academy Officer-training establishment set up in 1885 by Li Hung-chang as part of the Self-Strengthening Movement (qv).

Tientsin, Treaty of (1858) Treaty, or more precisely series of treaties concluded between China and her Western opposite numbers Britain, France, Russia and the United States in June 1858 in settlement of the Second Opium War or Arrow War. The main gains for the Western powers were the right to a resident minister in Peking, the opening of ten new ports, mainly along the Yangtze, to trade, freer conditions of travel in the interior for traders and missionaries and a huge indemnity. Full ratification of these conditions was not secured till the Conventions of Peking in 1860 (qv) as the Chinese tried to go back on what they had agreed under pressure in Tientsin at the Shanghai Tariff Conference in 1858.

Ting Ling (1907–   )   Pseudonym of Chiang Ping-chih, a writer from a Hunan landowning family who joined the League of Left-Wing Writers in 1930 and the CCP in 1931. Her unorthodox views on individualism and party authority earned her criticism in the Yenan period and in the 1950s she was accused of being a rightist, after which no more of her work was published.

Togh Temür (reigned 1320–1323)   Mongol emperor of China whose absorption in and sponsorship of Chinese poetry, calligraphy and painting indicate the degree to which the Mongol reign had become sinicised and moved far from the martial vigour of the early Khans.

Toghan Temür (reigned 1333–1368)   Last of the Mongol emperors of China. He continued the development of the arts begun by Togh Temür but his reign is most noted for the disunity of the Mongol leadership, famines, floods and a series of rebellions which eventually toppled the dynasty.

T'o-pa   Central Asian peoples from the Hsien-pei (qv) group who spoke a language related to Mongolian and founded the Northern Wei dynasty (386–534) in north China.

Treaty Ports   Ports in which the right of foreigners to trade and reside had been established by the unequal treaties (qv) after the Opium War. Previously only Canton had been open to trade, but the Treaty of Nanking and subsequent agreements obtained by force from the Chinese extended the privilege to Shanghai, Tientsin and other ports on the coast and along the Yangtze. Treaty ports became the bases for foreign economic intervention in China and many developed large European quarters where life became an extension of upper-class life in England or Germany. They also became the centres for great social and economic change. A large class of Chinese compradores (qv) developed to service Western commercial relations with China and in the early 20th century it was in the Treaty Ports that industrialisation began and the Chinese working class was created.

Triad Society (*San-ho hui* or *San-tien hui*)   Association of secret societies which traces its origins to the Ming loyalist movements that operated underground after the suppression of the anti-Manchu movement on Taiwan in 1683. The name Triad comes from the emphasis on the triple harmony of Heaven, Earth and Man, and the Triad group, which was very strong among south Chinese farmers and working people, included the Heaven and Earth Society, the Elder Brother Society and the Small Sword Society (qqv). They were active throughout the 19th century when they participated in the Taiping Rebellion, and also played an active part in the republican revolution of 1911. Later, because their radical and anti-Manchu policies became irrelevant the Triads, also known as the Red Band, degenerated into part of the criminal underworld and are now noted for their involvement in the international drugs trade.

Tribute System Traditional arrangement for foreign affairs, whereby subject peoples could acknowledge the authority of the Chinese emperor by presenting as tribute the rarest or most precious products of their land. Tribute missions from many distant lands are recorded throughout the dynastic histories. However the recording of missions was often simply a device to conceal the fact that state-sponsored trade was being carried on without damaging the reputation of the Chinese empire for self-sufficiency. Barter of tea and silk for Central Asian horses was described as the receipt of due tribute with presents returned graciously to the barbarians, and the first diplomatic missions from the West were only acceptable as tribute missions.

Ts'ai Yuan-p'ei (1876–1940) Prominent scholar who organised the Recovery Society to support revolutionary ideas at the beginning of the 20th century. Ts'ai had been successful in the imperial examinations and gained membership of the Hanlin Academy, and in 1907 went to Germany to study at the University of Leipzig. He returned home in 1911 and was appointed Minister of Education in Sun Yat-sen's government, but resigned when Yuan Shih-k'ai took over the presidency. He was in Germany again for a year from 1912 and then moved on to take charge of the Work-Study Programme (qv) for Chinese students in France. In 1916 he declined the governorship of his home province of Chekiang but was instead appointed Chancellor of Peking University. Under his guidance the university became an exciting and controversial institution of higher education. Ts'ai resigned his post in 1919 in protest at the arrest of patriotic students but later held a senior position in the Nationalist government of 1928.

Ts'ao Hsueh-ch'in (1715–1764) Author of the novel *Dream of the Red Chamber*. Ts'ao came of a wealthy family who had been directors of the Imperial Textile Works in Nanking. During his lifetime family fortunes declined and he taught in Peking, wrote a few poems and left his most famous work unfinished in 80 chapters, to be finished by Kao Ngo.

Ts'ao Ts'ao (155–220)   One of the greatest of the Han generals who unified and pacified north China after the break-up of the Han empire. He controlled what was later to be called the Wei dynasty, one of the Three Kingdoms (qv). He died in 220 AD to be succeeded by his son Ts'ao P'ei who named the state Wei, but his exploits live on in the *Romance of the Three Kingdoms*. He was also a poet, and a writer of letters. So famous was Ts'ao Ts'ao that he features in the Chinese equivalent of the English saying 'speak of the devil'.

Tseng Kuo-fan (1811–72)   Late Ch'ing scholar and military man. Tseng was born in Hunan and rose to high office in the civil service. In 1852 he was ordered by the government to form a militia to act against the Taiping rebels and raised the Hsiang Army (qv) of men from his own province. After clearing Hunan of bandits and completing the army's training he set out to attack the Taiping forces in Hupei in 1854 and eventually recaptured Wuchang. His army grew more powerful and, as governor-general of Liang-Kiang in 1860–65 he gained jurisdiction over the four key provinces of south-east China: Kiangsu, Anhwei, Kiangsi and Chekiang. It was on Tseng's recommendation that Li Hung-chang's Huai Army (qv) was formed and he also backed the Kiangnan Arsenal (qv). His role in the suppression of the Taiping and other rebellions was crucial and the regional power and influence that he acquired made him in some ways the precursor of the 20th century warlords.

Tsinghua University   One of the great universities of northern China which was built in Peking with American money. It was severely damaged during the Japanese occupation and was a centre of radical activity during the Cultural Revolution.

Tso Chuan (*Commentary of Tso*)   Commentary on the *Spring and Autumn Annals* written probably in the 4th century BC. It is a mixture of legend and fiction, reputedly written by Tso Ch'iu-ming and is far longer than the work to which it was later appended as a commentary. The *Tso chuan* contains much information on the history of the Spring and Autumn period.

Tso Tsung-t'ang (1812–1885)   Assistant of Tseng Kuo-fan. Tseng put him in charge of operations in Chekiang against the Taiping rebels. He became governor of Chekiang and then governor-general first of Chekiang and Fukien during 1863–66 and then of Shensi and

Kansu in 1867–80, where he helped Li Hung-chang defeat the Nien rising and recovered Sinkiang from the Moslem rebels in the 1870s. At his recommendation Sinkiang was made a province of China in 1884. He was a noted supporter of the Self-Strengthening Movement (qv) and was responsible for the establishment of the Foochow Dockyard in 1886 with machines brought from France.

Tsong-kha-pa (died 1419) Tibetan religious reformer and the founder of the Yellow Hat sect (qv) of Lama Buddhism which in the Ming and Ch'ing periods became the dominant sect in Tibet and Mongolia. Dalai Lamas (qv) are considered to be reincarnations of Tsong-kha-pa although the title was not used till his third successor in 1580.

Tsungli Yamen Office for General Management established in Peking in 1861 to consider the new status of foreign representatives and treaty obligations. Previously, China had had no foreign office as relations between states were not thought of as equal but were conducted through the tribute system (qv). The Tsungli Yamen was headed by Prince Kung, and the Imperial Maritime Customs and the interpreters' service were attached to it. It was only really effective until about 1870 when central authority declined and regional power became more important. In 1901 it was finally replaced by a modern Ministry of Foreign Affairs.

Tsunyi Conference Enlarged meeting of the CCP that was held during the Long March and was crucial for the later history of the CCP and for Mao's career in particular. At the beginning of the Long March the CCP was dominated by the Twenty-Eight Bolsheviks (qv) led by Po Ku and the Whampoa Faction led by Chou En-lai and Yeh Chien-ying. At the conference, which was held in January 1935 at Tsunyi in north Kweichow, Mao attacked the Twenty-Eight Bolsheviks for their failure to support the Fukien revolt and for the positional warfare strategy advocated by Otto Braun, which had failed. Mao won the day and from the Tsunyi Conference he became the unchallenged leader of the Long March and the CCP, a position which was consolidated in Yenan at the end of the March.

Tu Fu (712–770) One of China's two great national poets and almost always spoken of in the same breath as the other, his contemporary and friend Li Po. Tu Fu was a minor official under the T'ang dynasty and in contrast with the carefree Taoist Li Po his poems reflect the painful moralising of the serious Confucian. He was born near the capital, Ch'ang-an, into a family of the ruling elite, but not a wealthy one. In spite of his talent he surprised everyone by failing the imperial examinations and only managed to gain an official position by a 'special entry' route. The greatest influences on his life, apart from his friendship with Li Po which he acknowledged as vitally important, were his personal privations and his frustrated ambitions. Nevertheless his poems are particularly admired for their compassion and honesty.

T'u-fa Clan   see   *Hsien-pei*

T'ung-chih, Ch'ing Emperor (reigned 1862–1874)   Late Ch'ing ruler during whose reign the T'ung-chih Restoration stemmed, temporarily, the tide of dynastic degeneration. T'ung-chih was a minor during eleven years of his reign and a weakling for the other two with power firmly in the hands of his mother the Dowager Empress Tz'u-hsi (qv). The emperor was not an able leader but the accomplishments of his supporters permitted the restoration.

T'ung-chih Restoration   Series of reforms mainly during the reign of the T'ung-chih emperor which followed the rebellions and foreign invasions of the mid-19th century and temporarily restored the authority of the dynasty. After the suppression of the rebellions and the re-establishment of central control, local administrations were rebuilt and reinforced and the economy was refurbished with the revival of agriculture and handicrafts, but no attempt was made to modernise. Other constituent parts of the Restoration were the military reorganisation known as the Self-Strengthening Movement (qv) and a more modern system of foreign relations known as the Tsungli Yamen (qv). Attempts were made to modernise education and introduce the study of the West. The T'ung-chih Restoration is almost always compared with its near contemporary, the Meiji Restoration which took place in Japan in 1868, but whereas the Meiji Restoration provided Japan with a solid base for industrialisation, modernisation and eventually imperial expansion, the T'ung-chih restoration failed in the end because it was unable to provide new policies that could ward off internal and external threats while preserving the society and ideology of Confucianism which the leaders of the Restoration could not abandon. The most important figures associated with the restoration were Prince Kung, Tseng Kuo-fan, Li Hung-chang and Tso Tsung-t'ang (qqv).

Tung-lin Party   Group of scholars at the end of the Ming dynasty who attempted to reassert Confucian principles in the face of eunuch domination of the court, official opportunism and the gradual

collapse of state power. The Tung-lin (Eastern Forest) was originally
an academy formed during the Sung dynasty and was reformed in
1604 by a dozen scholars who had been dismissed from office during
factional disputes at court. They were attacked as a party or clique
(*tang*) in 1610 because of their denunciation of eunuchs and others
in the inner circle of the court. Their crusade reached a high point
in 1620–23 but in 1624 Yang Lien, one of the leaders of the Tung-lin
party, accused Wei Chung-hsien the chief eunuch of a number of
crimes including murder. Wei's response was to unleash a campaign
of torture and terror which wiped out the Tung-lin group by 1627.

T'ung-meng hui (United League)   Republican revolutionary organisation founded by Sun Yat-sen in Japan in 1905. Sun was chairman,
Huang Hsing (qv) his deputy and Sung Chiao-jen (qv) a member of
the judicial department. The philosophy of the league was based on
the Three People's Principles (qv) of Sun Yat-sen with the emphasis
on two of them - – Nationalism, principally the overthrow of the
Manchus, and Democracy, the establishment of a Republic. The
T'ung-meng hui was the first republican movement that went beyond
provincial and class boundaries and it brought Sun into the mainstream of Chinese nationalism. It provided the central organisation
necessary for a modern political party and in 1912 absorbed four
splinter parties to become the Kuomintang (qv).

Tung Pi-wu (1886–1975)   One of the elder statesmen of the Chinese
Revolution. Tung was a founder member of the CCP as a delegate
from Hupeh after a period of study in Japan. He took part in the
Long March and became a member of the Central Committee and
Politburo. During 1954–59 he was President of the Supreme People's
Court, from 1959 to his death Vice-Chairman of the People's
Republic of China, and from 1970 effectively acting Chairman,
fulfilling many of the functions formerly undertaken by Liu Shao-ch'i.

Tungus   Ancestors of the Manchus who lived in eastern Manchuria,
raising pigs, hunting and farming during the Liao empire (qv).

T'ung-wen kuan   Language school of the Tsungli Yamen (qv) which
was established in Peking in 1862 at the suggestion of Prince Kung
and known to foreigners as the Interpreters College or College of
Foreign Languages. It was originally intended as a school for joint
instruction in Western and Chinese languages (T'ung-wen means
Common Languages), but other subjects such as mathematics and
astronomy were later added. The importance of the school lay in its
work as a research institute for disseminating knowledge about and

from the West, particularly through a wide-ranging translation programme. A second school was established in Canton in 1864.

Tun-huang Central Asian oasis and trading-post during the Han dynasty. It was situated at the terminus of the Great Wall and was the beginning of the caravan routes to the West known as the silk road (qv). In about 1035 a Buddhist library in the Tun-huang cave temples was sealed shut to protect it from raiding Tibetans. Thousands of manuscripts in Chinese, Tibetan, Uighur and various other Central Asian languages remained there undisturbed until they were found in 1900 and have yielded a unique record of the period between the Han and the T'ang dynasties. The collection which is still being analysed is shedding light on many aspects of the history, language and literature of mediaeval China. It contains copies of Buddhist scriptures, 8th and 9th century vernacular prose, poetry and many other secular and religious documents.

Turfan Central Asian oasis which was the centre of an Uighur state in the 12th century and later. Many of the inhabitants were merchants and Nestorian Christianity was widely practised.

Twenty-Eight Bolsheviks Group of twenty-eight Chinese Communist students also known as the Returned Students Faction, who had studied at the Sun Yat-sen University in Moscow between 1926 and 1930 and subsequently returned to China. After the fall of Li Li-san in 1930 they came to dominate the CCP and the Politburo with the support of Pavel Mif and two of them, Wang Ming and Po Ku, were particularly influential. The Twenty-Eight were opposed to alliances across class barriers and against guerrilla war as they favoured more regular military operation, and came into conflict with Mao Tse-tung who was advocating building mass support among all peasants. The factional struggle between Mao and the Twenty-Eight continued throughout the life of the Kiangsi Soviet and the early stages of the Long March by which time it was clear that the positional warfare advocated by the Twenty-Eight and Otto Braun, their mentor, had failed. At the Tsunyi conference (qv) in 1935 the Twenty-Eight were finally ousted and Mao and his policies confirmed in the leadership of the CCP.

Twenty-One Demands Set of demands made on President Yuan Shih-k'ai by the Japanese in January 1915. The demands were in five groups, the first four of which called for Japanese control of Shantung, Manchuria, Inner Mongolia, China's south-east coast and the Yangtze valley. These four groups were accepted by Yuan

Shih-k'ai in a treaty he concluded without the consent of the legislature but he reserved judgement on the fifth group which required the employment of Japanese advisers in China's political, financial, military and police administrations and the purchase of at least 50% of China's munitions from Japan. Japan enforced acceptance of the first four groups, moved troops into Shantung and consolidated her control of key sectors of the Chinese economy. Yuan Shih-k'ai's failure to resist the demands led to the collapse of his credibility and ultimately to the nationalist May 4th movement in 1919 after the Versailles settlement had failed to repudiate Japan's territorial ambitions.

Two Chinas Policy Attempts made during the 1950s, principally by the United States, to solve the Taiwan problem by accepting that there were two sovereign states of China. The policy failed because of its total unacceptability to either side.

Two Lines Description of the divergent policies that appeared in the CCP during the 1960s. Broadly speaking, one line was that of the radicals and emphasised ideological correctness and continuing revolution, while the other, exemplified by Liu Shao-ch'i, emphasised technical expertise and more gradual progress. Much of the political upheaval of the 1960s has been interpreted by Peking as a struggle between these two lines although subsequent developments suggest that the demarcation lines between the two are by no means as clear as has been made out. See also *Red Versus Expert*.

Tz'u-hsi (1835–1908) Empress Hsiao-ch'in, born Yehonala, concubine to the Hsien-feng emperor and better known in the West as the Empress Dowager. When the Hsien-feng emperor died, their son, the heir apparent, became the T'ung-chih emperor at the age of five, and his mother and the senior concubine Tz'u-an grew very powerful as advisers to the regency. The two later overthrew the regency and formed a dual regency of their own in which Tz'u-hsi was the dominant partner. Even when the regency officially ended in 1873 the T'ung-chih emperor was controlled by his mother and on his death in 1875 she installed the three-year-old Kuang-hsu emperor, who was not in line of succession, so that she could control the court. In 1889 she relinquished control of state affairs and retired to the Summer Palace, north-west of Peking, but was frequently in conflict with the Kuang-hsu emperor and in 1898 intervened to prevent the success of the Hundred Days Reform (qv). Tz'u-hsi died on the day after the death of the Kuang-hsu emperor, but not before she had nominated P'u-i as the next, and in fact the last, successor to the Ch'ing throne.

U

Uighurs Turkish-speaking group, now a national minority of the People's Republic, living mainly in Sinkiang. The Uighurs founded an empire which lasted from 744–840 on the Orkhon river. After being forced out by the Kirghiz, they set up a second empire around Turfan in 840 and they have remained in the same region ever since. Uighurs had helped the T'ang emperor T'ai-tsung to seize the area around Turfan and became his allies when it was incorporated into the empire. The Uighurs remained within successive Chinese empires and today form one of the national minorities of the People's Republic. The Uighur script, derived from the Sogdian and thus ultimately the ancient Phoenician alphabet, was adapted by the Mongols to suit their language and later became the official Mongol script.

Unequal Treaties Treaties signed under pressure by the Chinese government in the second half of the 19th century, giving foreign access to the treaty ports (qv) and various commercial and diplomatic privileges. The most important were the Treaties of Nanking and Tientsin and the Convention of Peking (qqv). The treaties were rejected by the KMT who pledged themselves to abolish foreign privileges, but were not effectively abandoned till 1949.

United Front, First First period of co-operation between the KMT and the CCP which lasted from 1923 to 1927. The Comintern considered the KMT to be the mainstream of Chinese nationalism and urged individual communists to join it and use it to expand their influence. The alliance was approved in late 1922 after negotiations by Adolf Joffe (qv), and CCP members somewhat reluctantly entered the KMT in January 1923. During this collaboration the CCP remained intact but individual members worked in the KMT and achieved high office, promoted its peasant policies and supported the Northern Expedition (qv) while trying to retain independent bases of support among peasants and urban workers. Tensions increased as these aims became increasingly incompatible. When the Left KMT moved its government to Wuhan in 1926 it was supported by the CCP and this marked the beginning of the end of the United Front. The end came when the reorganised KMT right wing under Chiang K'ai-shek in Nanking launched a massive purge of Communists. This began with the Shanghai Coup (qv) of April 10, 1927 and spread to Nanking, Hangchow, Foochow, Canton and elsewhere. It ended with the retreat of the CCP into Chingkangshan (qv) and the rural soviets and the reunification of the KMT in the Nanking government (qv) of 1928–37.

United Front, Second Second period of CCP-KMT co-operation necessitated by the Japanese invasion of China in 1937. Chiang K'ai-shek had been reluctant to commit his KMT to the alliance, but after the Sian Incident (qv) of 1936 had very little choice. The co-operation was uneasy from the beginning. CCP forces were renamed as units of the Nationalist Army but retained *de facto* independence. The strategy of the Nationalists was not to resist the Japanese actively, particularly after the United States entered the war in 1941, but to preserve their forces for the inevitable conflict with the CCP after the war. For their part the CCP, who organised the most effective resistance, built up independent base areas. Tensions had mounted quickly when the German-Soviet non-aggression pact in 1939 removed the ideological basis for the United Front and it ceased to be a reality after the New Fourth Army Incident (qv) of 1941. Negotiations to maintain the United Front continued until 1943 but the disagreements between the CCP and the KMT were never resolved and erupted into civil war with the Japanese surrender of 1945.

Ussuri Incident see *Chen-pao Island*

V

Versailles, Treaty of (1919)   Although the Treaty of Versailles was intended to resolve questions of relations between European states after the First World War it had a profound effect on China. During the war Japan had been on the side of the Allies and had occupied the port of Kiaochow and large areas of Shantung province formerly leased by Germany. Japan's position was legitimised by Chinese acceptance of the Twenty-One Demands (qv) and agreements with Russia, Britain, France, and Italy ensured their support for her position. The warlord government in Peking conceded to Japan in return for a massive loan, but the Chinese delegation to Versailles fiercely contested the occupation. When the Conference accepted Japan's position, partly to ensure she joined the League of Nations, feelings in China ran high and the negotiations triggered off the wave of nationalism known as the May Fourth Movement (qv) which began with a mass demonstration by Peking students on May 4, 1919.

Veritable Records (*Shih-lu*)   Detailed chronicles of the activities of the Imperial court which were begun in the T'ang dynasty to provide materials for an accurate history of the dynasty. The Records of the Ming and Ch'ing were the basis for the Dynastic Histories (qv) of these periods.

Viceroy   see   *Governor-General*

Village Co-operativisation Movement   Early experiment in agricultural co-operation organised during the Yenan period (1937–45) which provided a basis for the collectivisation (qv) policies of the 1950s.

Voitinsky, Gregor   Comintern agent who arrived in China in 1920 and held talks with Li Ta-chao and Ch'en Tu-hsiu about the possibility of forming a Communist Party in China, discussions which led to the convening of the first Congress of the CCP in 1921.

W

Wade, Sir Thomas Francis Assistant of Lord Elgin who promoted Western culture and technology in China. He was British Minister in Peking during 1873–74 at the time of the Margary Affair, and was partly responsible for the Wade-Giles system of romanising Chinese.

Walking on Two Legs Communist policy of using both traditional and modern methods in medicine, science and other fields, which was enthusiastically promoted during and after the Great Leap Forward.

Wang An-shih Reforming Chief Councillor appointed by the Sung emperor Shen-tsung in 1069. His reforms were primarily concerned with finance and the army. He centralised financial control to an extent not seen for centuries by stabilising commodity exchange and prices, instituting low-interest loans to peasants, reassessing land taxes and commuting corvée services. He revived the collective guarantee system of the Six Dynasties period under the name of *pao-chia* (qv) and built up a cavalry militia. These reforms, later to be both attacked and praised as a primitive form of socialism, met with the opposition of vested interests, notably large land owners and officialdom. Because of mismanagement and obstruction the reforms never achieved the success hoped for, and Wang was forced to resign in 1076. After the death of Shen-tsung in 1085 the whole programme was rescinded by traditionalists.

Wang Chen Palace eunuch who dominated the court of the Cheng-t'ung emperor (qv) during the latter's minority. He demoralised the court and the army and was only removed from power after he had taken the emperor into battle against the Oirats and the emperor had been captured. See also *Eunuchs*.

Wang Ching-wei Early contributor to the *People's Tribune* (*Min-pao*) of the T'ung-meng hui (qv) who became a member of the KMT Praesidium in 1924. He became associated with the left wing of the party and dominated the Left KMT government in Wuhan in 1927, at first in conjunction with the CCP. After the purge of the CCP by the right wing of the KMT in the Shanghai Coup (qv), Wang eventually followed suit and ended the participation of the CCP in his Left KMT government in August 1972. The Wuhan government then ceased to exist and Wang went abroad where he continued to oppose

Chiang K'ai-shek's Nanking government. He returned in 1930 to attempt to set up a rival administration and after the Japanese invasion of 1937 agreed to Japanese peace initiatives and started a peace movement on Japanese terms. After being expelled from the KMT he organised his own government and signed agreements with Japan recognising Manchukuo (qv) and Japan's right to station troops in China. He carried his collaboration further by setting up a puppet regime in Nanking in March 1940.

Wang Hung-wen (1941–   )   Former Shanghai cotton-mill worker who founded the Cultural Revolution mass organisation the Shanghai Workers' Revolutionary General Headquarters in 1967, and became vice-chairman of the Shanghai Revolutionary Committee in 1968. He rose rapidly to the post of secretary of the Shanghai party Central Committee in 1973 and vice-premier of the People's Republic in 1975. As a close associate of Chiang Ch'ing and the other Shanghai radicals, he was toppled as one of the Gang of Four in October 1976 after the death of Mao Tse-tung.

Wang Kuang-mei   Wife of Liu Shao-ch'i (qv). Wang Kuang-mei had worked in the Foreign Affairs section of the CCP Central Committee since 1946 and from 1957 had been active in the All China Women's Federation. In 1966 she was sent to Tsinghua University as part of the work-team (qv) charged with carrying out the Cultural Revolution there. She was later denounced by the radicals who claimed that she was sabotaging the revolution.

Wang Mang (reigned 8–23 AD)   Wang Mang was the nephew of an empress of the Han dynasty and a marquis, who had intrigued his way to the highest position in the bureaucracy by 8 BC. After a short eclipse he returned to power in 1 BC and in 8 AD usurped the throne and established his own dynasty which he named the Hsin (New). He took the throne at a time when central government and its revenues were in decline and large-scale revolts were threatening the empire. Once in power he attacked the major economic problems of the day, made a short-lived attempt to redistribute the land owned by the large estates, strengthened the bureaucracy and built up the government monopolies. Like Wang An-shih (qv) he has been both attacked and praised as a socialist although he saw himself as returning to the perfect Confucian state. Wang Mang's policies lost him the support of the rich and powerful families, and famines due to bad harvests and the breakdown of the water-control system precipitated rebellions such as that of the Red Eyebrows (qv). Wang died at the hands of rebels in 23 AD while the borders were being raided by nomads and was succeeded by Liu Hsin, a descendant of the earlier Han rulers, who became the founder of the Later or Eastern Han dynasty.

Wang Ming (Ch'en Shao-yü) (1904–1975)   Born into a prosperous Anhwei family, Wang joined the CCP in 1925 and after training in the USSR returned to China in 1930 as the leader of the Twenty-Eight Bolsheviks (qv). From 1931–32 he was acting General Secretary of the CCP and took over the leadership of the Kiangsi Soviet although he spent part of the time in Russia. In 1935 he lost power to Mao Tse-tung at the Tsunyi Conference (qv). In 1954 he was stripped of even the minor government posts he then held and returned to Moscow, from where he took part in the Sino-Soviet Dispute on the Soviet side.

Wang Tung-hsing   Captain of guards for the Government Administration Council in 1949 and vice-minister of public security in 1955–58. From 1958–60 he was vice-governor of Kiangsi. In 1969 he became an alternate member of the Politburo and a full member in 1973. After the fall of Chiang Ch'ing in which he was instrumental, he supported Hua Kuo-feng and became a member of the standing committee of the Politburo.

Wang Wei (699–761)   Poet, painter and musician of the mid-T'ang period. He was a successful civil servant and also a practising Buddhist and his poetry was more inward-looking and contemplative than either of his better-known contemporaries, Li Po and Tu Fu (qqv).

Wang Yang-ming (1472–1528)   Also known as Wang Shou-jen. Leading Confucian scholar of the Ming dynasty who was opposed to the neo-Confucian doctrines of Chu Hsi. He promoted a school of idealism which was close to Buddhism because it viewed heavenly principle and human desire as part of a single unity rather than as being opposed, as in the Chu Hsi scheme.

Wanghsia, Treaty of   One of the unequal treaties (qv). It was signed by China and the United States in 1884 and extended the provisions of the 1842 Treaty of Nanking to the United States and conceded additional privileges of extraterritoriality including naval patrols and permission to build churches and hospitals.

Wan-li, Ming Emperor (reigned 1572–1620)   Emperor who reigned longest in the Ming dynasty and whose reign gained a reputation for cultural brilliance. In his first, youthful decade he was very much under the influence of his able Grand Secretary Chang Chü-cheng, but after the latter's death in 1582 he became irresponsible and withdrew from affairs of state, avoiding even his most senior ministers for years on end. He became entirely dependent on the palace eunuchs for communication with his ministers and this weakened the civil service. Towards the end of his reign court extravagance and military commitments in Mongolia and Korea precipitated a serious financial crisis. Factional disputes among scholar-officials were worsened by the revival in 1604 of the Tung-lin academy (qv) and by the time of Wan-li's death in 1620 the Ming dynasty was at a low point from which it was unable to recover. Nevertheless his reign was an important one. The novels *Golden Lotus* and *Journey to the West* became popular, industrial and commercial developments indicate what some Chinese historians have designated the sprouts of capitalism (qv), and outside China, the Manchus (qv) were developing into the powerful state that would eventually replace the Ming dynasty.

War of Resistance Against Japan   see   *Anti-Japanese War*

Ward (*fang*)   Residential subdivision of a town, also known as a neighbourhood. Walled divisions into wards were a prominent feature of the T'ang capital of Ch'ang-an and entry to the wards was controlled by gateways. Although walled divisions eventually disappeared, the term ward persisted for administrative sub-divisions of towns.

Warlords   Regional military rulers in China between the 1911 Revolution and 1949. When the early republican revolutionaries were unable to install a strong centralised government, power in the provinces fell into the hands of strong men backed by regional military formations. Warlordism in China has a long pedigree. It can be traced back to the Warring States period and reappeared in various forms at times of disunity and dynastic breakdown. Among the better-known warlords of the 1920s and 1930s were Yen Hsi-shan, Feng Yü-hsiang and Chang Tso-lin (qqv). Shifting alliances such as the Peiyang clique negotiated with each other and with the Nationalist government in Canton and then later in Nanking. In 1928 the Nanking government (qv) theoretically controlled all of China but many of the warlords retained a great deal of local power.

Warring States (403–221 BC)   The Warring States or Military States developed from the divisions in the empire after the collapse of the

Eastern Chou and followed the Spring and Autumn period (qv). The main states of the period were Ch'i in North Shantung which under Kuan-tzu developed centralised military, political and economic organisations, Lu, the home of Confucius, Chin and Yen in the north, the 'barbarian' Ch'in in the west, Sung, and Wu and Yueh in the lower Yangtze and Chekiang respectively. Continual rivalry between the states was finally resolved by the state of Ch'in (qv) which gradually defeated all the other states and unified China in 221 BC. The Warring States period was a time of great innovation and change in society and the economy, and of great philosophical speculation that provided the beginnings of all the main trends in Chinese thought, such as Confucianism and Taoism (qqv).

Washington Conference (1921–22) International meeting called by the United States to resolve the unfinished business left by the Versailles treaty, principally naval disarmament and the Far Eastern Question. It was attended by Britain, the United States, France, Portugal, Italy, Japan, China, Belgium and the Netherlands. The conference fixed the ratio of capital ships between the powers, agreed to guarantee Chinese independence and the return of Kiaochow (qv) to China by Japan. However the agreements were not enforceable and Chinese nationalist opinion remained dissatisfied.

Water Control Large-scale conservancy projects in the control of the Yellow River and other large rivers and the irrigation of agricultural lands. It has been argued that the need for central control of these projects led to a specific kind of authoritarian rule known as Oriental Despotism (qv). Water control projects date back to the later part of the Chou dynasty and in the 3rd century BC the success of the Ch'in in canalising the Wei valley was an important factor in their unification of China. From Han times to the present day new techniques in water conservancy and irrigation have been important in China's unity and stability.

Water Margin (*Shui-hu chuan*) Novel also translated as *All Men Are Brothers*, which dates from the Ming dynasty and relates the exploits of a bandit group in the Liang-shan-po region of western Shantung. It is loosely based on the true story of Sung Chiang who lived in the Sung period about 1121. During the later part of the Sung dynasty tales about his exploits were told around the market places by professional story-tellers and Yuan playwrights used the same theme. *Water Margin* was apparently cast in its final form by Shih Nai-an, a retired scholar-official of the late Yuan in collaboration with a novelist-playwright Lo Kuan-chung. The most complete

version in 120 chapters appeared in about 1600, but the best known
edition is a 70-chapter version brought out in 1644. *Water Margin*
proved popular throughout the Ming and Ch'ing dynasties despite
official disapproval and continues in vogue today. Chinese Communists have adopted the rebellious Robin Hood spirit of *Water
Margin*, but what were described as Sung Chiang's capitulationist
policies were attacked in a mass campaign after the Cultural
Revolution.

Wedemeyer Mission (1947)   Lieutenant-General Albert C. Wedemeyer replaced General Stilwell as commanding general of United
States forces in China and Chief-of-Staff to Chiang K'ai-shek in 1944.
In contrast to Stilwell he was mild and conciliatory. In February 1946
after the initial success of the Marshall mission Wedemeyer headed
a thousand-strong United States military mission in China which
was designed to train a national army to include the Communists.
In 1947 when the KMT-CCP civil war was under way, Wedemeyer
was despatched on a fact-finding mission, failed to convince Chiang
of the need for reform and returned with a report calling for military
and economic aid for the Nationalists, but under strict American
supervision.

Wei   One of the Three Kingdoms (qv)

Wei Chung-hsien   see   *Eunuchs*

Weihaiwei   Port and naval base on the north coast of Shantung
province captured by the Japanese in 1895 during the Sino-Japanese
War. In the scramble for concessions that followed China's humiliating defeat, Britain secured a 25-year lease on Weihaiwei in 1898
which was not relinquished till 1930.

Wei-so System   Ming dynasty system for maintaining a standing
army inherited from the Yuan and developed by the Hung-wu
emperor. Guards units (*wei*) and their component battalions (*so*) were
stationed at key points on the inner Asian borders, the coast and the
Grand Canal and in the capital. Each garrison was allocated land to
support itself (see also *Military Colonies*) and large campaigns could
be mounted by combining separate garrison forces into temporary
tactical units. Desertion and the problem of self-sufficiency in the
border regions meant that the *wei-so* garrisons had to be supple-
mented by local militia and conscripts from the non-military
population.

Wellfield System (*Ching-t'ien*)   Later idealisation of a system of cultivation said to have been practised on the manors of the Chou period. Eight peasant families, each with its own field, were said to have cultivated a central field for the support of their lord. The pattern of fields was supposed to have been in the manner of the character 井 *ching* or 'well', and so the system became known as the 'well-field'. Alternatively the system may have been that eight families worked a plot that could theoretically provide for them and a ninth, their lord, with the 'well-field' picture simply being an attempt to represent the system diagramatically.

Wen, King (Wen Wang)   King of Chou under the last ruler of the Shang dynasty. The Shang ruler is traditionally considered to have been a tyrant and in contrast King Wen has been celebrated as the epitome of the wise and benevolent ruler. He conceived the plan of overthrowing the Shang, but it was left to his son and successor King Wu (qv) to revolt in about 1133 BC.

Wen I-to (1899–1946)   Modern Chinese poet and liberal politician. Wen I-to was born in Hopei and educated at Tsinghua College, Peking, and in the United States. His first book of poems, *Red Candle*, was published in 1923 and was followed by *Dead Water* in 1928. He held various posts in higher education in China and in 1932 joined the staff of Tsinghua University. He was evacuated to Kunming at the beginning of the Anti-Japanese War in 1937 and in 1943 joined the People's Democratic League which was a minority, mainly liberal, third party, seeking to provide an alternative to the KMT and CCP. After a speech denouncing the Nationalist government on July 15, 1946 he was shot and killed by KMT gunmen. In spite of an early classical education, he took an interest in writing poetry in the vernacular and his reforming approach to language and literature paralleled his radical political ideas.

Wen-ti, Han Emperor (reigned 179–157 BC)   A son of the Han emperor Kao-tsu (qv), Wen-ti acceded to the throne after the death of the Empress Lü (qv) and the massacre of her family.

Western Chin Dynasty (265–316)   Short-lived successor to the Three Kingdoms which temporarily unified China before the Sixteen Kingdoms period.

Western Hills Group   Right-wing faction of the KMT named after the place outside Peking where it met in August 1925. The group demanded the expulsion of the Communists from the KMT and the dismissal of Borodin as adviser but was opposed by the remaining left-wing group of the KMT in Canton. After the liquidation of the CCP members in the KMT in 1927 the Western Hills Group proposed a reconciliation between the two wings of the KMT. It remained as a right-wing faction within the reunited party.

White Lotus Rebellion (1796–1804)   The White Lotus (*Pai-lien chiao*) was a secret society based in north China whose origins can be traced back directly to the Buddhist sects of the early 12th century and indirectly to the 4th century. The rebellion which broke out on the Szechwan-Hopei-Shansi border in 1795–6 had anti-Ch'ing and Ming restorationist policies. Although the rising was suppressed in 1804 elements of the White Lotus remained and certain of the Boxer (qv) bands were associated with them towards the end of the 19th century.

White Terror   see   *Shanghai Coup*

William of Rubruck   Flemish Franciscan Friar who travelled in Asia as an ambassador of Louis IX of France and reached Karakorum in 1253. He had an audience with the Great Khan and provided Europe with information on China and the Chinese language. He was the chief informant of Roger Bacon.

Willow Palisade   Series of ditches and embankments planted with willows across southern Manchuria which marked the boundary in Ming and Ch'ing times between Chinese settlement and the tribal lands to the north. The Willow Palisade stretched from Shanhaikuan (qv) to Kirin and then south to where the Yalu river meets the sea.

Work-Study Programme   Programme of the Society for Frugal Study by Means of Labour, a group organised by Chinese students in France in 1915. It superseded the Society for Frugal Study in France which had been formed in 1912 by anarchists who wanted to encourage Chinese students to study in France. In 1921 it became the Chinese Socialist Youth League and this in turn became the French branch of the CCP in 1922.

Work Teams   *Ad hoc* teams of CCP members or unarmed soldiers which investigated and intervened in local disputes during the Cultural Revolution. These were revived versions of work teams organised as early as 1962 to carry out the Socialist Education Movement (qv) and at the beginning of the Cultural Revolution were used by the party authorities to stifle radical criticism. The role of the work teams was later criticised by the radicals.

Workers' Headquarters   Coalition of radical students and workers in Shanghai which struggled to seize power from the party establishment. The Shanghai Workers' Revolutionary Committee Rebel Headquarters, to give Workers' Headquarters its full name, had the support of Chang Ch'un-ch'iao and was the main radical Red Guard unit in the Shanghai January Storm (qv) and power seizure of 1966-67 when it was opposed by the Scarlet Guards.

Wu Ch'eng-en (1500–1582)   Poet and novelist from Kiangsu, best known for his novel *Journey to the West* (qv). Wu came from a merchant family and although at first unsuccessful in the imperial examinations later held an official post in Nanking.

Wu Ching-tzu (1701–1754)   Gifted but cynical author who repeatedly failed the highest examination in the imperial system but left to posterity *The Scholars* (qv), a satire on the imperial bureaucracy, its shallowness, greed and corruption. He lived in Nanking and probably wrote *The Scholars* between 1739 and 1750.

Wu, Empress   Successor of the T'ang emperor Kao-tsung. Kao-tsung made her his empress although she had originally been a concubine of his father, T'ai-tsung. She dominated Kao-tsung in his later years and after his death she ruled through two puppet emperors before assuming the title of Emperor in 690 and changing the dynastic name to Chou. Traditional historians have condemned her usurpation and she is often compared with the Empress Dowager Tz'u-hsi (qv), but she was a strong, capable ruler, a zealous patron of Buddhism and a supporter of the civil service bureaucracy against the aristocratic elite. She was forced to abdicate in 705 at the age of eighty.

Wu Han   Deputy mayor of Peking, member of the Democratic League and university teacher before the Cultural Revolution. Wu Han, who is a historian and the biographer of the first Ming emperor Hung-wu, came to the notice of the West when attacks on his play *Hai Jui Dismissed* (qv) precipitated the first stage of the Cultural Revolution. Between 1961 and 1964 he had collaborated with Teng T'o and Liao Mo-sha (qqv) on articles in the Peking journal *Frontline* critical of the CCP leadership. Wu Han was denounced for his humanism and lack of a class viewpoint, an attack which was a preliminary to criticisms of his immediate superior P'eng Chen (qv) the mayor of Peking. On December 30, 1965 Wu Han formally recanted.

Wu, King of Chou   Wu Wang, the son and successor of King Wen (qv) who rose against and overthrew the corrupt and tyrannical last emperor of the Shang dynasty. Wu came to power in about 1133 BC in the Chou principality and defeated the Shang emperor in 1122 BC. He founded the Chou empire and ruled with the aid of the Duke of Chou (qv), traditionally thought to be his brother.

Wu Kingdoms The name of Wu was adopted by several kingdoms or minor dynasties. In the Warring States period it was the name of the kingdom that ruled the lower Yangtze area around modern Shanghai and Nanking. Wu also was the name of one of the Three Kingdoms of the post-Han period and controlled the same area and lands as its earlier namesake, as far as the south China coast. After the collapse of the T'ang a Wu dynasty ruled from Yang-chou between 902 and 937. The name Wu persists as an alternative name for the modern Kiangsu province which occupies roughly the same region.

Wu Kuang see *Ch'en Sheng*

Wu San-kuei (1612–1678) Chinese general of the Ming dynasty, native of and military commander in Liaotung. In 1644 he preferred to surrender to the armies of the Manchu prince Dorgon rather than see Peking fall to the rebel Li Tzu-ch'eng. He followed this up by pursuing and routing the remnants of the Ming loyalist forces and in 1662 had the last of the Ming claimants strangled in Burma. In repayment for his support the Manchus allowed Wu San-kuei to build up a power-base in Yunnan and Kweichow. Two other nobles, Shang K'o-hsi and Keng Chi-mao, had similar privileges and when in 1673 the K'ang-hsi emperor tried to break their power Wu rose in rebellion and proclaimed a new dynasty, the Chou, and the other two also revolted. The rebellion, known as the Revolt of the Three Feudatories (qv), was only put down in 1681 after eight years of bitter fighting and the death of Wu San-kuei in October 1678.

Wuchang Rising Single most important rising in the 1911 Revolution (qv) when an engineering unit of the republican New Army took over the munitions depot in Wuchang on October 10 and finally captured the whole city. On learning of the success of the rising at Wuchang and the subsequent ones in Hanyang and Hankow, Sun Yat-sen returned to China from exile, the Manchu emperor abdicated and the Republic was born.

Wu-fan see *Five Anti*

Wuhan Government Administration of Wang Ching-wei and the Left Kuomintang (qqv) in 1927–28.

Wuhan Mutiny Revolt by units of the People's Liberation Army under Ch'en Tsai-tao in Wuhan in July 1967. Ch'en had been keeping down radical worker and student organisations in Wuhan and refused to allow them to operate in spite of the personal intervention of Chou En-lai. Ch'en was dismissed after an airborne division, the Fifteenth Army and five naval gunboats were sent to the Wuhan region by Peking to neutralise his forces.

Wu-ti, Han Emperor (reigned 141–87 BC) Wu-ti (Martial Emperor) was the ruler who expanded and consolidated the Han empire, governing directly through a palace secretariat. He instituted a programme of canal building using forced corvée labour, embarked on a series of foreign wars, notably against the central Asian Hsiung-nu and extended the empire far to the west and the south. Although he was a despotic and in practical terms a Legalist ruler, Confucian thought developed strongly during his reign in spite of his interest in Taoism. It was Wu-ti who ordered the castration of Ssu-ma Ch'ien (qv).

Wu-ti, Liang Emperor Hsiao-yen who founded the Six Dynasties state of Liang in 502. He was a great patron of Buddhism, demanded that all his court officials adopt the religion and enriched Buddhist monasteries. He ruled the most stable of the southern successors to Han rule but lost his capital to a barbarian general in 549.

X

Xanadu see *Shang-tu*

Y

Yakub Beg (1820–1877) Uighur prince who rebelled against the Chinese in 1862 and founded an independent state in Turkestan. There had been a number of Moslem secessionist movements in the region during the early 19th century and after Yakub Beg seceded he was supported by British interests who favoured a buffer state in Turkestan between Russia and China. In 1871 Russia occupied Ili to protect its frontiers and in 1877 Tso Tsung-t'ang (qv) suppressed Yakub Beg's rebellion. Turkestan lost its autonomy and in 1884 became a new province of China as Sinkiang (New Frontier).

Yalta Pact Agreement signed by the USSR, Britain and the United States at Yalta in the Crimea in the absence of Chiang K'ai-shek in February 1945. In return for a pledge that the USSR would join the Allies against Japan after Germany had been defeated, Stalin was granted concessions in Manchuria, notably railway and harbour facilities. China then had to sign a treaty with the USSR on the basis of this agreement, a treaty which paved the way for the Soviet occupation of Manchuria in 1945. Soviet troops withdrew from Manchuria in 1946 amid allegations by the Chinese that industrial and military installations had been looted.

Yamen Official establishments under the imperial government, a term most often applied to the offices of the local magistrates (qv). Some offices of central government staffed by eunuchs in the Ming period were also known as *yamen*.

Yang Kuei-fei Beautiful and notorious consort of the T'ang emperor Hsuan-tsung from 745 onwards who caused him to neglect his imperial duties. Both she and the emperor gave their support to the general An Lu-shan (qv) and Yang Kuei-fei even adopted him as her son. Their patronage brought him great power and he revolted against the emperor in 755. Hsuan-tsung, forced to flee to Szechwan, reluctantly agreed to Yang Kuei-fei's execution for her part in bringing An Lu-shan to power, and then abdicated in grief.

Yang-chou Prosperous imperial city now a town in modern Kiangsu province at the junction of the Yangtze river and the Grand Canal. It was an important commercial city depending largely for its wealth on the salt trade of which it was the main centre, and its salt merchants were famed from the T'ang and Sung periods onwards for their vast fortunes and lavish spending.

Yang-shao Culture   see   *Painted Pottery Culture*

Yangtze   The Yangtze is the single most important river in China, flowing nearly 3,500 miles from the Tibetan plateau into the sea near Shanghai. It was the main east-west line of communication for much of the imperial period. From about the 12th century onwards the Yangtze valley came to exert more and more influence on the Chinese economy and was one of the areas of densest urbanisation.

Yang-wu Movement   see   *Foreign Matters Movement*

Yao   see   *Three Sages*

Yao Wen-yuan   Radical Shanghai journalist and disgraced member of the Gang of Four. Yao was editor-in-chief of the Shanghai *Liberation Army Daily* when he sprang to prominence as the author of the criticism of Wu Han's play *Hai Jui Dismissed* (qv) on November 10, 1965. This was the first move in the Cultural Revolution during which Yao became increasingly important, with posts on the Central Committee and its Cultural Revolution group and Politburo while remaining Chang Ch'un-ch'iao's deputy secretary on the Shanghai Party Committee. His rise was due to his association with the other Shanghai radicals as was his fall from grace after Mao's death as one of the Gang of Four.

Yeh Ming-ch'en (1807–1859)   Governor of Kwangtung during the Arrow War and at the time of the Elgin (qv) mission. Yeh refused to negotiate British and United States demands made after the Arrow War and his office came under attack by British gunboats.

Yeh T'ing   One of the leaders of the 1927 Canton insurrection and later a commander of the New Fourth Army when it was organised in December 1937.

Yeh-lü A-pao-chi (872–926)   Chinese transcription of the name of the Khitan chieftain who declared himself emperor of the Khitan in 907 and founded the dynasty which in 947 became known as the Liao. The Khitan state survived tribal disputes and feuds between Yeh-lü A-pao-chi and his brothers, and his leadership, deployment of mounted archers and employment of Chinese advisers made it into a state that was strong enough to conquer north China twenty years after his death.

Yeh-lü Ch'u-ts'ai (1190–1244)   Descendant of the Khitan royal house who became the Mongols' expert on Chinese-style administration, taxation and industry and showed them how to use China's economy rather than destroy it. He became chief minister in the conquered parts of North China after 1230 and set up schools and examinations to recruit Chinese into the Yuan administration.

Yellow Book   Copy of the book of census figures for a particular area submitted to the imperial government in Nanking in 1381 after the Hung-wu emperor had decreed that all the population be registered. Copies were also deposited with the district, prefectural and provincial governments but the name derived from the Nanking copy which had a yellow cover. In the register, households were nearly all included in one of four categories: the general population, hereditary military families, artisans and saltern families.

Yellow Hat Sect   Reforming sect of Tibetan Lama Buddhism properly known as the Ge-lugs-pa or 'virtuous sect' but deriving its name from yellow costumes in contrast to the older Red Hat Sect. It was founded by Tsong-kha-pa in the early 15th century and in the later part of the Ming, the 16th century, spread widely in Mongolia. Tsong-kha-pa's third successor was given the title of Dalai Lama by the Mongol prince Altan Khan.

Yellow River (Hwang Ho)   Although the Yellow River is a smaller river than the Yangtze it played a more important role in early Chinese history. The loess plain created by the deposits of fine soil laid by the Yellow River was the cradle area of China's civilisation in the neolithic period. The easily-worked soil permitted the early development of agriculture and the first distinctively Chinese civilisation grew up in the region, notably the Painted and Black Pottery cultures and the Shang dynasty. As the economy developed, however, the agricultural centre moved south of the Yangtze. The North China plain suffered both from a short growing season and from the flooding of the Yellow River which earned the river the name China's Sorrow.

Yellow Turbans   Taoist-led rising led by Chang Chüeh that broke out in about 184 in eastern China. The rebels, who were known as Yellow Turbans because of the head-cloths they wore, were a military threat till the end of the dynasty. The rebellion contributed to the downfall of the Han and its adherents were still active as late as the 5th century.

Yen Fu (1853–1921) One of China's best translators of Western scientific and sociological works. He translated Adam Smith's *Wealth of Nations*, T. H. Huxley's *Evolution and Ethics* and Herbert Spencer's *Study of Sociology* among many works, into literary Chinese, and they exercised a great influence on Chinese thinking.

Yen Hsi-shan One of the warlords of the 1920s who, like Feng Yu-hsiang, belonged neither to the Northern Warlord cliques nor to the National Revolutionary Army of Chiang K'ai-shek although he was broadly sympathetic to the Nationalists. His base was in the Taiyuan area of Shansi province. After the dissolution of the Left KMT (qv) government in Wuhan he collaborated with Chiang in the defeat of the Northern Warlords (qv) and the recapture of Peking in 1928–29 in what became known as the Second Northern Expedition. Under the Nationalist Nanking government (qv) of 1928–37 Yen became known as one of the more-or-less progressive New Warlords who collaborated with the central government as long as they were able to maintain their regional power bases.

Yenan The CCP headquarters in north Shensi province after the Long March, and the capital of the Shen-Kan-Ning border region. The headquarters was moved to Yenan in December 1936 and the period 1937–45 is commonly referred to as the Yenan period in the history of the CCP. It was the formative influence on the modern CCP. The party was restructured and remoulded to incorporate the wide variety of people who joined during the Anti-Japanese War, important concepts such as the mass line (qv) were developed and the authoritative CCP positions on art and literature, nationalism and revolution, peasant power and many other questions were established through various campaigns. In the isolation and often desperate conditions of Yenan, Mao devoted much time to his philosophical work and the Yenan spirit evokes a revolutionary nostalgia in China, for its frugality, creativity and comradeship, notwithstanding some criticisms of elitism within the CCP which was already noticeable in the 1940s.

Yen-ching One of the old names for Peking deriving from the state of Yen in the Warring States period (Yen-ching means Capital of Yen). As Yen-ching it was the southern capital of the 11th century Liao dynasty, and in 1153 the Chin moved their capital there where it was destroyed by the Mongol campaign of 1211–15.

Yin Dynasty Alternative name for the later part of the Shang dynasty.

Young Pioneers   Junior branch of the Communist Youth League (qv).

Yu   see   *Three Sages*

Yuan Dynasty (1271–1368)   Mongol conquest dynasty that ruled China when it was incorporated into the Mongol empire. Khubilai (qv) adopted the dynastic title of Yuan in 1271, five years before the capture of Hangchow the Southern Sung capital. The new Mongol rulers had to cope with many new problems, including the administration for the first time of agricultural and densely populated settlements. With Chinese advisers such as Yeh-lü Ch'u-ts'ai (qv) they gradually built up a new administration based on the principles of the T'ang and Sung bureaucracies. However Mongol-Chinese relations were never easy after the brutality of the conquest, the Mongols relied heavily on foreigners such as Central Asian Moslems to govern, and the Mongol ruling class remained very much separate from the Chinese. Confucianism, Buddhism, Taoism and foreign religions such as Islam and Nestorian Christianity were all tolerated and even patronised by the court. Foreign trade flourished particularly through Central Asian Moslem merchants, internal commerce was aided by an increase in the amount of money circulated, and the Mongol unification of China made possible trade and cultural contacts between the south and the north which had been cut off from each other for a long time under the Liao and Chin dynasties. The Grand Canal was extended north to Peking in the 13th century to supply the court with grain and parts of the economy flourished in spite of heavy taxation.

  The Yuan dynasty witnessed the first direct contacts between China and the West, and many Europeans (of whom Marco Polo is only the best known) visited China. The Mongol disregard for Chinese classics gave new freedom to vernacular forms of literature and vigorous new forms of drama, stories and even early novels sprang up in the cities of the Yuan period. Important developments also took place in the arts and technology. The dynasty was at its height under Khubilai, and his grandson Temur (1294–1307) maintained a strong administration, but after Temur's death internal dissension weakened the Mongol court. Disunity, famine and floods were followed by peasant risings throughout China in the 1340s and 1350s and the Yuan dynasty finally collapsed after the rebellion of Chu Yuan-chang who became emperor Hung-wu of the Ming dynasty.

Yuan Shih-k'ai   Yuan Shih-k'ai was a military official who served in Korea as a Chinese adviser to the Korean army in the 1880s and joined one of the reformist societies in the years before the Hundred Days reform. However in 1898 he betrayed the reformers and supported the Dowager Empress Tz'u-hsi who he believed would win. His personal army fought in the Boxer Rebellion on the side of the court but towards the end of the Ch'ing dynasty he became involved in the movement for constitutional reform, forced the abdication of the Manchu regents and was declared Premier in 1911 in the attempt to stem the revolutionary tide. When the Chinese Republic was founded Yuan pledged his support and on April 12 he took over from Sun Yat-sen as President. In 1913 he suppressed the independence movements in the Yangtze area — the Second Revolution (qv) — and by 1915 was confident enough of his position to have himself declared emperor. His reign (Hung-hsien) lasted only a few months as he died in June 1916 and China, once again divided, lapsed into a period of warlord rule.

Yüeh State in the Warring States period in the region of modern Chekiang province. It was exterminated by Ch'u in 334 BC before Ch'u itself fell to the Ch'in conquerors.

Yüeh-chih Central Asian people possibly speaking an Indo-European language with whom the Han emperor Wu-ti's officer Chang Ch'ien attempted to ally against the Hsiung-nu in 139 BC. They had been driven out of Kansu by the Hsiung-nu and had displaced the Greek kingdom of Bactria in northern Afghanistan and subsequently set up the Kushan empire in northern India. In 73 AD Yüeh-chih forces were defeated by those of the Han general Pan Ch'ao but Chinese control soon collapsed and the Kushan ruler became independent and a powerful champion of Buddhism.

Yung-cheng Emperor (reigned 1723–1736) Ch'ing successor of the great K'ang-hsi. Yung-cheng ruthlessly suppressed family and palace opposition to his dubious succession but is best known for consolidating the administrative structure of the Ch'ing government. He set up the Grand Council above the Grand Secretariat as the highest policy-making body and thus gathered much power into his own hands. He was hard-working, conscientious and a great patron of scholarship.

Yün-kang Site of great Buddhist cave temples near the first capital of the Northern Wei dynasty in northern Shansi. Yün-kang contains some of the finest examples of Chinese Buddhist art, particularly sculpture.

Yung-lo, Ming Emperor (reigned 1403–1424)   Strong third emperor
of the Ming, who rebelled against the successor of Hung-wu and took
the throne for himself. He was a patron of scholarship, ordered
definitive editions of the classics to be printed, and sponsored the
Great Yung-lo Encyclopaedia (*Yung-lo ta-tien*). He expanded the
tribute (qv) system of Hung-wu and incorporated south and south-
east Asia into the system by means of a series of maritime expeditions
led by Cheng Ho (qv). In 1421 he moved his capital to Peking, a
reflection of the court's preoccupation with the Mongols. The town
was substantially rebuilt in his reign, and many expeditions were sent
north to keep down the Mongols from 1410 until Yung-lo's death
on one expedition in 1424.

Z

Zayton or Zaytun, Zaitun   Arab name (and the one used by Marco Polo) for the port of Ch'üan-chou in Fukien. Under the Southern Sung it replaced Canton as the leading port for overseas trade because of its proximity to the tea and porcelain producing areas of Fukien.

Zen Buddhism   see   *Ch'an Buddhism*

Zoroastrianism   Pre-Islamic religion of Iran which became very important in the T'ang dynasty capital of Ch'ang-an after reaching China in the 6th century. It survives in India as the Parsee religion.